Advance praise
God's Grace and the Homose...

One of the great movements in our time is that of the ex-homosexuals and ex-lesbians. These are broken people who have admitted their brokenness and found true happiness—not in the so-called "gay" lifestyle—but by living for Jesus Christ. One such man is Alan Chambers, currently president of the largest umbrella organization of ex-homosexuals, Exodus International. Alan Chambers' book provides believers with Christian and loving (but uncompromising) answers to this controversial issue.

D. James Kennedy, Ph.D., Senior Minister
Coral Ridge Presbyterian Church

I can't think of anyone more knowledgeable to lead someone out of sexual bondage than Alan Chambers. He is a man of integrity and compassion. His heart, life, and words are full of wisdom. He has personally touched my life with his kindness and love for God. It is friends like Alan I want everyone to get to know. In order to introduce you to this godsend to our nation, I highly recommend *God's Grace and the Homosexual Next Door.*

Dennis Jernigan, Composer, Author
Former Homosexual

If you're a believer who's touched by this issue—and these days, who isn't?—then you'll be as excited as I am about this book. It doesn't come a moment too soon.

Joe Dallas, author of *Desires in Conflict*
and *The Game Plan*

I'm so grateful this book is finally available. With wisdom, knowledge and grace, Alan offers those who struggle with their sexuality and those who love them a place to stand. It is with other broken people, welcomed into the life changing love of God. For those who long to understand the heart of God to the homosexual community and how to share that love, this book is a gift.

Sheila Walsh, Women of Faith Keynote Speaker

God's Grace and the Homosexual Next Door

ALAN CHAMBERS
AND THE Leadership Team
at Exodus International

HARVEST HOUSE PUBLISHERS

EUGENE, OREGON

Cover by Koechel Peterson & Associates, Inc., Minneapolis, Minnesota

Backcover author photo © Beverly Brosius

GOD'S GRACE AND THE HOMOSEXUAL NEXT DOOR

Copyright © 2006 by Alan Chambers and the Leadership Team of Exodus International
Published by Harvest House Publishers
Eugene, Oregon 97402
www.harvesthousepublishers.com

Library of Congress Cataloging-in-Publication Data
    God's grace and the homosexual next door / [edited by] Alan Chambers.
       p. cm.
    ISBN-13: 978-0-7369-1691-2
    ISBN-10: 0-7369-1691-1
    1. Church work with gays. 2. Homosexuality—Religious aspects—Christianity. I. Chambers, Alan, 1972-
    BV4437.5.G63 2006
    261.8'35766—dc22   2006011149

Printed in the United States of America

07 08 09 10 11 12 13 14 / V P - M S / 10 9 8 7 6 5 4 3 2

A Word from
Harvest House Publishers

More than a decade ago we published our first book on homosexuality, Joe Dallas' *Desires in Conflict*. That book, now in an updated edition, is still in print. Since then we've published several other excellent books to help those who struggle with same-sex attraction and the people who love them. These books have been well received, and we know many changed lives have resulted from their publication.

A couple of years ago, a large, well-known national ministry that had been using our books on this subject asked us if we would publish a book that "instructs the church on how to evangelize homosexuals." They noted that the books we'd done so far on this topic were geared primarily toward homosexuals and their families. This ministry suggested that "a broader book on what the church's response should be would be a valuable resource" for them and for individual Christians and churches everywhere. We agreed. And so we contacted Alan Chambers, the president of Exodus International, a ministry God has raised up to help with this crucial need. Alan graciously agreed to do the project, and he and several of his colleagues from Exodus have assembled the book you now hold in your hands.

We think you'll find this an excellent resource whether you're a Christian concerned about your homosexual friends or relatives...or if you're involved in the leadership of a church that's willing to reach out to the homosexuals in your city. In the following pages you'll find a host of varied information: chapters on developing a Christlike response to homosexuality, testimonies from several former homosexuals, and a final section where Alan responds to questions asked by those who have a heart for homosexuals.

It's our prayer that as a result of reading this book, you'll be equipped to minister God's grace to the homosexuals in your life.

This book is dedicated first to the ministry of Exodus International, now in its third decade of serving as the church's loving arms to millions of men, women, youth, and families affected by unwanted homosexuality.

Second, this book is dedicated to the worldwide church. Thank you for answering the call and for becoming a place where all people are welcomed, loved, and offered the restorative power of Jesus Christ.

About the Authors

 **Alan Chambers** is the president of Exodus International, headquartered in Orlando, Florida. Alan's own story as an adolescent who struggled with homosexuality uniquely positions him to address the problems surrounding this difficult issue. Alan is a frequent speaker at conferences, churches, and college campuses. He has debated on such campuses as the University of California at Berkeley, Pepperdine University, and Reformed Theological Seminary. He is a guest speaker for Focus on the Family's Love Won Out Conference, a seminar that travels to major cities each year addressing the roots and causes of homosexuality. Alan and his wife, Leslie, make their home in Florida and are the proud parents of a son and daughter.

 **Randy Thomas** is the membership director for Exodus International. He is responsible for managing more than 125 professional mental health and church-based member agencies across North America that make up the Exodus network and offer local support to individuals who want to leave homosexuality. Randy's story as a child raised in an abusive home who grew to struggle with homosexuality at an early age allows him to better communicate the hope of transformation to those struggling with unwanted same-sex attractions. Randy has been interviewed by numerous media outlets across North America and Europe. His story was the subject of an award-winning article in *The Dallas Morning News* and featured in the book *The Good Life*, by bestselling author Chuck Colson. Randy lives in Florida.

 **Mike Goeke** is the vice president of Operations for Exodus International. He is responsible for setting strategic vision and overseeing daily operations for Exodus International. Mike's own struggle with homosexuality almost destroyed him and his marriage. Ultimately God's healing and restoration birthed a desire to share the hope of transformation with others struggling with unwanted same-sex attraction. His goal is to equip the local church to address homosexuality with boldness and love. He is a frequent

speaker on many relational topics including homosexuality and sexual integrity. Mike obtained a bachelor's degree in finance from Baylor University and earned his law degree from the Texas Tech University School of Law. Mike and his wife, Stephanie, live in Florida with their three children.

 **Scott Davis** is the director of Exodus Youth, a division of Exodus International that helps young people struggling with same-sex attraction find life and healing in Christ. He educates and trains youth pastors and community leaders on this issue and currently oversees the Groundswell Conference—a nationwide training conference that equips community leaders with a powerful, redemptive response to the growing crisis of pro-gay initiatives in schools. Scott is a writer and frequent speaker at churches and conferences, including the Teen Mission Conference and Cornerstone Music Festival. He has been interviewed by many media outlets, including *Time* magazine and ABC's *The View*. Scott's goal is to encourage the evangelical church to reach out with radical grace and unswerving truthfulness to young people who struggle with homosexuality. Scott and his wife, Caryn, make their home in Florida.

 **Melissa Fryrear** serves as the gender issues analyst within the Government and Public Policy Division for Focus on the Family. As one of the nation's leading voices on gender issues, she is actively involved in speaking, writing, and educating the church and society on a wide range of subjects related to homosexuality. Her insights come from her own experience of having lived homosexually, as well as from the many years she has counseled thousands of individuals and families affected by same-sex attraction. A frequent media guest, she has appeared on dozens of radio and television programs. Melissa is also a keynote speaker at Focus on the Family's Love Won Out Conference. She is committed to proclaiming biblical truth with grace and compassion regarding homosexuality. Melissa holds a Master of Divinity from Asbury Theological Seminary. She lives in Colorado.

Contents

Foreword

Little did I know some ten years ago when I met Alan Chambers that he would influence me more than I him. He was only in his early twenties and looking for some mentoring—and now he mentors me in the cutting-edge challenge of reaching out to and ministering to homosexuals. Alan is fearless and tireless in his efforts to bring some spiritual sanity to this growing spiritual war. He finds himself attacked from two determined sides in the ministry: Christians who show no grace and radical homosexuals who have an agenda of retribution.

Alan's wisdom shines through as he walks through the minefield of angry people on both sides of the issue. He has acquired his knowledge at great personal cost and suffering. God's grace found him in his hour of need, and Alan gladly and joyfully passes it on to other hungry and desperate people. We assume that is the way all Christians feel, but sadly, in this instance, many do not. My compassion for people trapped in the demonic net of homosexuality has grown because God saw fit to bring Alan Chambers...and now others...into my life. I am so very glad they were tenacious enough to help me through my own prejudices and show me a vision of God's plan for this suffering group of people. I have hope now that things can change, and I have a renewed faith that people can change through the power of God and wise, compassionate ministry.

This book is good! Read it and absorb the hope that it will bring. Churches that engage in compassionate ministry to homosexuals can more effectively influence our culture.

Believe me—or better, believe Alan Chambers—that God cares deeply about redeeming *every* human being, including those whom a great deal of Christendom have written off as lost causes.

I have done my best as Alan's pastor to teach him about God's grace. He, in turn, has taught me to apply it across the spectrum of human need. Thanks, Alan, for your life-changing influence and model of Christ's power to change all of us human beings.

Clark Whitten, Senior Pastor
Grace Church
Longwood, Florida
www.graceorlando.com

*Do you not know that the wicked will not inherit the king-dom of God? Do not be deceived: Neither the sexually immoral nor idolaters nor adulterers nor male prostitutes nor homosex-ual offenders nor thieves nor the greedy nor drunkards nor slan-derers nor swindlers will inherit the kingdom of God. **And that is what some of you were. But you were washed, you were sanc-tified, you were justified in the name of the Lord Jesus Christ and by the Spirit of our God.***

1 Corinthians 6:9-11

Introduction

Alan Chambers

—ⵡ—

Sixteen years ago, as an 18-year-old young man desperately battling unwanted same-sex attractions, there wasn't much help available for me. But God knew what I needed, and He led me to the ministry of Exodus International. Since then many more resources have become available for men and women who struggle as I did. And yet there is still so much to be done.

Christians with "gay-identified" loved ones are eager to share the good news of Christ, but they wonder how they can do so without sounding judgmental. And can they actually promise those they love that change is possible—*is* change possible?

Churches too want to be involved with ministry to homosexuals, but they're unsure of how to proceed. Should active gays be invited to church?

Should the church start some sort of formal outreach…and what do they do when homosexuals *do* come to Christ? Are there effective ways to follow-up on new believers from a homosexual background?

As the president of Exodus International, I find the majority of the people I meet, regardless of their religious or political background, are anxious for answers to questions like these concerning homosexuality.

In fact, I recently had lunch with some friends, and the topic quickly turned to homosexuality. Feeling unequipped as Christians, they wanted answers to questions ranging from "Is it genetic?" to "Does the Bible *really* condemn homosexuality?" to "How can I love Christ and my gay neighbor without compromising what I believe?" Questions like these— and many others—are on the hearts and minds of Christians everywhere due to the increased awareness of homosexuality in our society. Fifty years ago a book like this could not have been published. Possibly not even twenty years ago. Being attracted to one's own gender was simply *not* a topic for meaningful discussion in most circles.

But all that has changed. And yet in the church we're lagging sadly behind in having a workable, scriptural response to the homosexuals who look to us for "good news." For many, the church seems like a place where certain sinners aren't welcome. With phrases like "turn or burn" and "get right or get left," Christians have made those inside and outside the church fearful of being honest about their very real struggles. Many Christians don't believe it's possible that their church has members who deal with same-sex attraction—and yet most churches do indeed have such strugglers…and that probably includes yours. For the most part, these men and women struggle quietly. To admit to homosexual temptations is too risky.

We in the church have also given some wrong signals to those who do come to faith in Christ. For example, we've taken verses such as 2 Corinthians 5:17, which says, "Therefore, if anyone is in Christ, he is a new creation; the old has gone, the new has come!" and mistranslated it to mean, "Come to Christ and get fixed immediately. And if you struggle after you come to Christ, there's something wrong with you." In reality, the reference to the "new" is related to *quality* and not to *time*. Transformation is a process. Many Christians struggle in their forward movement to maturity. God is gracious and more than able to love us in spite of our fallibility. And that's our task: to effectively communicate God's grace and power to change to a world that thinks to be a Christian one must either be perfect or a hypocrite.

But in order to effectively communicate God's love to the homosexual, one of the most important prerequisites for anyone—church or individual—is to be clear on your motivation and your message. *Why* do you want to reach gays? Do you truly love them as Christ loves them? And exactly *what* is your message for gay men and women? Here's a hint: If you think the Christian message for homosexuals is to "love the sinner, but hate the sin," then I really encourage you to read on. This book will change your way of thinking—and ministering.

Sixteen years ago, when I got honest about my struggles with same-sex attraction, my thought was: *I will go to counseling for six months, do everything I'm told, and be set free from my homosexuality, never to struggle again.* Of course, that wasn't how reality played out for me. I didn't get a lobotomy. I did, however, get a foundational education on who God really is, why He sent His Son, Jesus Christ, and how grace could be the single most healing factor in my life...if I grasped it. Today, I—like you—am still in the daily process of learning how to apply grace to my own life. And as I learn, I try to live out that message of grace and pass it along to those I'm called to minister to—men and women and youth who are dealing with unwanted attractions to their same sex.

God's Grace and the Homosexual Next Door is about redemption, mercy, compassion, love, and, of course, grace. The simple truth is that Christ died for all of us or He died for none of us. As we consider ministering to those whose lifestyle we don't understand, we must always remember to offer them the same grace, understanding, and love that Christ offered us.

There isn't a special antidote for ministering to those with same-sex attractions any more than there is one for ministering to those with an unhealthy love for money, food, heterosexual sin…or whatever. The same God who sent His Son for you, sent His Son for the homosexual.

It really is that simple.

After all, God wasn't after my homosexuality; He was after my heart. Once He had that, everything else began to change. I have watched that same wonderful scenario play out in the lives of thousands of men and women over the years as their eyes have been opened to the truth of God's grace, redemption, love, and healing.

At Exodus International, we work every day to get the message of God's grace out to as many as will listen. The combined experience of my colleagues at Exodus, who have pooled their vast wisdom on the following pages, should go a long way in answering your questions about reaching the homosexuals you know. I am convinced that as you read, you'll find the confidence to go out and share God's love and grace with your gay neighbor, or the one at work, or the close relative, or perhaps the one you've yet to meet.

God bless you as you go in His name.

Alan Chambers
President, Exodus International

Test Your Knowledge About Homosexuality

Before you move to chapter 1, where are you now in your knowledge of homosexuality? Take a few minutes and answer the multiple choice questions below. When you're finished, check your answers against the ones on pages 257–265. Or you can discover the correct answers as you read *God's Grace and the Homosexual Next Door*.

1. Most homosexuals first become aware of being "different" from their peers:
   a. as adults
   b. as teenagers
   c. as children
   d. they rarely express a feeling of being different

2. Homosexuality is
   a. always a choice
   b. always genetic
   c. always related to childhood sexual abuse
   d. none of the above

3. Approximately what percentage of the population is homosexually oriented?
   a. 15 to 16%
   b. 10 to 12%
   c. 5 to 8%
   d. 2 to 3%

4. HIV can be transmitted by
   a. casual contact
   b. breathing the same air as an infected person
   c. any exchange of bodily fluids with an infected person
   d. only through sexual contact

5. A child raised in a strong Christian home
   a. will not develop homosexually
   b. may only choose homosexual feelings when older and if he or she doesn't stay close to God
   c. can develop homosexually, just as a child from a non-Christian family
   d. must reject God in order to develop homosexually

6. When a homosexual becomes a Christian, he or she will
   a. always become heterosexual at the point of conversion
   b. always become heterosexual somewhere down the line
   c. always have to deal with their same-sex attractions
   d. still likely deal with their same-sex attractions for some time

7. The ideal response to homosexuality is to
   a. "love the sinner, but hate the sin"
   b. always preach repentance
   c. befriend them first, and allow God to bring up the matter of their homosexuality
   d. ignore them. They're too much in the news anyway.

8. Homosexuals are most often
   a. normal people like those you meet every day
   b. also pedophiles
   c. easily identifiable by their mannerisms
   d. actively engaged in promiscuous sexual activity

9. The only references to homosexuals in the Bible
   a. are full of condemnation
   b. offer acceptance of homosexuality
   c. are in the Old Testament
   d. none of the above

10. The leading pro-gay publication read by many homosexuals is
    a. *The Advocate*
    b. *Gay Life Magazine*
    c. *Act Up*
    d. *Get Over It*

11. Homosexuality...
    a. affects other aspects of a person's life than just sexual attractions
    b. has to do with only a person's sexual attractions
    c. has nothing to do with a need for intimacy and affirmation
    d. is rooted in the need for a connection with the opposite-sex parent

12. Which statement is the most true description of homosexuality?
    a. Homosexuality is an inability to relate properly to the opposite sex.
    b. Homosexuality is an inability to relate properly to the same sex.
    c. Homosexuality is an inability to perform sexually with an opposite sex partner.
    d. Homosexuality is an inability to love others without sexual contact.

13. There is a gay-affirming Christian denomination called:
    a. Open Door Church of God in Christ
    b. Friends Affirming Fellowship
    c. Christian Community International
    d. Metropolitan Community Church

14. Often homosexuals will accept Christ and turn from their gay lifestyles for a while, only to return to it later. Which of the following reasons is the *least* likely cause for this?

    a. They miss the support they found in the gay community.

    b. They face a lack of support for their struggle in the church.

    c. They were promised instant heterosexuality and when it didn't happen, they lost hope for true change.

    d. They missed the glitter and excitement of the gay culture.

15. Why is the term "ex-gay" not really a proper way to refer to homosexuals who have become Christians?

    a. It's not really true. They remain gay throughout life…only they hide or sublimate their attractions.

    b. It's a false identity because it defines them by their former attractions.

    c. It's become too politically incorrect.

    d. There is nothing wrong with the term "ex-gay." It properly identifies those who have left the gay lifestyle.

16. Which statement is most true about church leadership and homosexuality?

    a. Pastors should know the basics of counseling homosexuals.

    b. Pastors cannot grasp all that's involved in this issue and should have several places to which they can refer such people for professional help.

    c. Pastors should not attempt to counsel homosexuals until they're ready to accept Christ.

    d. Pastors should not attempt to counsel homosexuals without another person in the room.

17. The word that best describes how most gays view the Christian church is:

    a. hate

    b. distrust

    c. admiration

    d. humor

18. When talking to militant homosexuals, the most important thing to keep in mind is
    a. scriptural support for your arguments
    b. having boundaries for your conversation
    c. not conceding an inch of ground as you talk
    d. loving them as sinners, but hating their sin

19. Which statement is most true regarding lesbianism:
    a. Most homosexual women strongly desired to be like their mothers.
    b. Most homosexual women had a stronger attachment to their fathers than their mothers.
    c. The incidence of childhood sexual abuse among lesbian women is the same as among heterosexual women.
    d. Heterosexual Christian women cannot be of much help to a woman struggling with same-sex attraction.

20. The statement "Homosexuality is worse than any other sin"
    a. is true scripturally
    b. isn't true scripturally, but is true practically speaking
    c. shows a lack of understanding of one's own sin
    d. means that it is harder to overcome than other sins

Part 1
What Are We Missing About Homosexuality?

If you've ever shared the gospel with active homosexuals, you've probably wondered why they seem so hard to reach. What is it they don't understand or can't seem to comprehend about how great God's love is for them?

That's a fair question...but have you ever wondered just the opposite: What is it that we in the church aren't understanding about *them*? Is it possible that part of the resistance we find is because even though we may be well motivated, we just aren't effectively communicating the gospel to them in words they can hear and accept?

In the first three chapters of *God's Grace and the Homosexual Next Door*, we'll demystify homosexuality, answer the troubling question "Does God hate gays?" and explore the concept of change for the homosexual.

Learning the hows and whys of homosexuality and understanding God's perspective on same-sex attraction will go a long way in increasing our effectiveness in sharing the good news of Jesus Christ.

1

Demystifying Homosexuality

Alan Chambers

—⟋⟍—

To most heterosexual Christians, the idea of being attracted to your own sex is mystifying. Unimaginable. Not natural. *Why on earth would anyone...?* And then comes the day when you discover that a long-time friend or a close relative is homosexual. After your initial shock, you wonder how this could have happened. Did he (or she) wake up one morning and discover he was gay? Was he born that way? Can he change? *Surely* he's not happy being like *that.*

Your next reaction might be: What do I do now? Do I treat him (or her) as I've always treated him? Do I shun him? Do I accept him and his homosexuality? Do I urge him to repent or burn in hell forever?

Face it, if you're like most Christians, you're really puzzled by homosexuality…and yet you do care about that loved one, that coworker, that neighbor. You want to reach out in some way…but *how?*

The very first step is to become knowledgeable. So before we do anything else, let's clear up six key misconceptions most Christians have about homosexuality.

I became aware of some of these mistaken ideas and the resulting wrong attitudes shortly after I joined the pastoral staff of Calvary Assembly of God, a megachurch in Orlando, Florida, in 1999. When the church hired me, everyone thought it was a great thing. I was well respected at Calvary for my leadership and for my testimony of coming out of homosexuality. It was an obvious ministry opportunity for the church and for me. I can't be sure, but I believe that at the time there were some who were thinking, *Calvary has a wonderful ministry to gays, and now Alan will handle all of it in his office Monday through Friday, from nine to five.*

Neat and tidy. Yes, everyone was glad I was going to be addressing the issues of sexual brokenness in our community—but even happier that they weren't going to have to be the ones to do it.

That wasn't exactly my plan. I firmly believe that healing for homosexuals (in fact, for all who sin) comes from being open and transparent in a community of believers, otherwise known as the local church. I wasn't just going to offer underground counseling restricted to my office, and I certainly didn't intend to keep the ministry all to myself. Ministry often means getting your hands dirty, getting in the trenches, and helping hurting people in need. That's the job of the church—*all* of the church. We each come as we are, find healing in the community of believers, and then give back to those who are where we once were.

> What better place for a gay man or lesbian woman to be on a Sunday morning than in a Bible-believing, grace-living church.

And one reason this is so vital as it relates to ministry to homosexuals is that when we minister to gays and lesbians, we begin to notice one common trait many of them share: *Most people dealing with strong, same-sex attractions struggle with shame and a fear of being fully known.*

Healing comes when we adopt Christ's heart and attitude and learn to apply that to how we feel about ourselves. When I learned more about what God thought about me than what others thought, it was liberating. I found that I was able to walk into a room, fully transparent with my head held high. If someone rejected me because of my past—and some did—that hurt, but it no longer had the power to hinder me. My ministry at Calvary was to use that model for those seeking my help in being set free from homosexuality.

So when I started going on TV talk shows, writing articles, and being very public with my ministry at Calvary, *some* church people got nervous. I'll never forget the Sunday morning when one prominent church member stopped me in the aisle and said, "Alan, what do I tell Sister Helen when the gays you're ministering to start coming to church and sitting next to her in the pew?"

Flabbergasted, I took a deep breath and began to say something when our senior pastor tapped me on the shoulder and acknowledged that he would take that question for me. Directing some passion and rebuke toward this good member he said pointedly, "Aren't we called to minister to homosexuals too? What better place for a gay man or lesbian woman to be on a Sunday morning than in a Bible-believing, grace-living church."

With that answer, my pastor nodded his head in affirmation toward me and walked off. I turned to the church member, smiled rather proudly, and said, "I guess that's what you and Sister Helen can do when the homosexuals start coming."

Today, Calvary has a thriving and full-time Exodus ministry housed on church property. The members and staff have embraced it, and many in the Christian community have sought to duplicate that model in their respective churches.

The attitude of that dear church member is one of the first misconceptions we need to dispel: that homosexuals are somehow *worse* sinners than anyone else. To be truthful, the sins of a gay man and woman are really no worse in God's eyes than your sin. For some, that's hard to imagine. But when we understand that *any* sin is loathsome to God, then we see that he (or she) who has broken even the least of God's commandments is guilty of breaking all of them (James 2:10).

Myth 1: Homosexuality Is the Worst of All Sins

This then, is the first of the six key misconceptions anyone reaching out to gays must grasp: that there's some sort of hierarchy of sins from God's perspective. In the generally accepted hierarchy, at the bottom are sins that we personally have made peace with, such as lying, gluttony, cheating, and love of money. At the top we find the more unpalatable sexual sins like pedophilia, adultery, and, no surprise, homosexuality.

There is no biblical evidence to support this rating of sins. And even if there was a hierarchy to sin, the fact is that Jesus would have still had to die on the Cross to save us had there been one great sin or only one small one. Jesus said that to break even one of God's laws is to be guilty of breaking them all. Wow! That banishes any idea of castigating a homosexual because his or her sins are "worse" than ours, doesn't it?

We must stop trying to make ourselves look or feel better by presuming that someone else's sins are more disgusting than ours. All sin is disgusting in light of God's holiness. And the Bible says in Romans 3 that none of us is righteous. No not one.

When speaking publicly to Christians about the issues surrounding homosexuality, I always allow time for questions and answers. Inevitably, someone will try to point out that homosexuality isn't just a sin but an *abomination*. Translated, what they're really saying is, *Homosexuality is worse than anything else*. And further translation reveals yet another meaning: *Pat me on the back; your sin is worse than mine is*.

It's true that homosexuality is abominable to God. The Hebrew Bible uses the word *toeva* (abomination/hatred) to describe how God feels about homosexuality. However, that word is also used to describe how God feels about adultery. And in Proverbs 6:16-19, we see seven other vices that are also linked with the word *toeva* in the original text:

> There are six things the LORD hates,
> seven that are detestable to him:
> haughty eyes,
> a lying tongue,
> hands that shed innocent blood,
> a heart that devises wicked schemes,
> feet that are quick to rush into evil,
> a false witness who pours out lies
> and a man who stirs up dissension among brothers.

I don't know about you, but my guess is that the above list levels the sin playing field quite a bit. I can look at these verses and see more than one abomination that I've struggled with as a fallible human—apart from my (former) homosexuality. Thank You, God, for Your redeeming grace. Thank You, God for Your gift of Jesus. Thank You, God for forgiveness.

Too often I think we're so insecure about the work of grace in our own lives that we construct a false hierarchy of sin to assuage the guilt we feel over the daily sins we commit. The remedy to that guilt isn't comparing our sins with the sins of others. God never wants Christians to walk around with a defeatist attitude over sin. The weight of all our sins was lifted at the Cross and manifests in our lives at the point of salvation. Once we come into a lifesaving knowledge of Jesus Christ, we should no longer be walking around feeling guilty. When we grasp this, we will no longer think less of those whose sin we don't understand.

My homosexual sin wasn't measured against your respective sin. My homosexual sin was measured against the righteous, sinless life of Jesus. We all fall short through our particular sins because we fail to measure up to the real standard: Christ. So as you look at the issue of homosexuality in light of how sinful it is, realize that it's just as sinful as any sin you have committed, big or small. Sin is sin, and Jesus came to bear all of it.

Myth 2: Homosexuality Is a Choice

A second major mistake many Christians make is to assume that homosexuality is *just* a choice—that people wake up one day and decide to prefer their same sex in a physical way, thus making them homosexuals. Or perhaps they are "lured" into homosexuality by someone older and more entrenched.

I haven't ever met anyone who woke up one morning and simply decided, out of life's great big buffet, to be gay. I don't think such a choice has ever been made. When we make this false assumption, we invalidate the complexities of this issue and undermine an individual's struggle with it by assuming that same-sex attractions can be chosen like someone chooses to wear brown shoes rather than black ones. Such assertions are offensive and insulting.

Homosexuality is multicausal in that there are numerous factors and issues that over the course of years cause someone to develop same-sex attractions. These factors start most often before a child is old enough to walk or talk, long before he or she has any understanding about sex. This is why the "born that way" theory is so popular among the pro-gay crowd.

The truth is that people don't choose to feel gay any more than people choose to feel straight. Our sexuality happens without much input from us. Healthy developmental factors, such as being raised in a home with a mom and dad who love one another and are physically, emotionally, and spiritually involved with one another and with their children are foundational to a positive, heterosexual identity. But added to that is the fact that we live in a fallen world and so even the best families—even many Christian families—face struggles that can contribute to a child developing homosexual feelings.

I know that surprises many people. The idea that a child raised in a solid Christian home may have homosexual attractions is very hard for some parents to understand. Sadly, when this happens, these parents often spend too much energy blaming themselves and/or rejecting their child without going further to understand.

Also key to homosexual development is how growing children perceive themselves. What clues are they receiving about their identities from their home environment, their relationship with one or both parents, and with their peers? All this and more impacts a child's development toward (or away from) healthy sexual identity.

Personality plays a role, as well. In fact, when asked about an inherent link to homosexuality, I often cite personality. After all, God created us with a personality that's unique to each one of us...and yet sometimes our personality traits and strengths do have similarities with others. For instance, over the years I've found that many homosexuals have similar personalities and giftings. This falls in line with what I said about how a child perceives him- or herself.

In my case, for example, I was the youngest of six children, all with the same parents. Now, I don't want to rag on my folks, but they will be the first to tell you that we had our fair share of dysfunction. Yet none of my siblings responded to that dysfunction the way I did. They were affected, but their struggles manifested differently than mine did.

Labels also contribute to heterosexual struggles. If you call a kid gay who is already gender insecure (like most prepubescent kids) long enough, he (or she) will probably begin to question the reality of his sexuality. I was a very confused kid. I hated sports, my dad and I didn't connect relationally, and I honestly perceived myself as more of a girl than a boy. I was different than my brothers and far more interested in being with my sisters and mom. Kids picked up on that and quickly labeled me a mama's boy, a sissy, and ultimately, a fag.

I didn't know what a fag was at first. When I found out, it struck me to my core, confirming what I was becoming. By this time I had been molested by an older boy. I desperately longed for male attention. I daydreamed about being a girl and having a boyfriend to spend time with. Yes, everything was set in motion for me to assume a gay identity. In reality, what I needed was what God created me to need: an affirming, character modeling, loving relationship with my dad. In fact, that's what my homosexual journey was always about—finding a man to love me. Sex was just the means to an end.

Myth 3: Homosexuality Is All About Sex

What is the third important misconception about homosexuality that needs to be dispelled? The mistaken idea that homosexuality is primarily about sexual attraction and acting on those attractions. In reality, homosexuality has its roots in a wrong reaction to a legitimate need: the need to be loved and affirmed by the same-sex parent...and, ultimately, by God.

My friend Christine Sneeringer often says that even though sex is right in the middle of the word homosexuality, sex has little if nothing to do with the core of the issue. Truth be told, I wasn't in need of sex when I began struggling with homosexuality at the age of 11. And I certainly wasn't looking for sex.

I needed love. Affirmation. Acceptance. I wanted to be normal. I craved what God created me to crave: healthy, same-gender relationships, first with my dad and then with my peers. I needed these healthy relationships to grow and mature just as seedlings need water to grow into great oaks.

I learned about sex from an older teenage boy in my neighborhood who molested me when I was ten. Already confused about my masculinity, or lack thereof, this encounter reinforced my belief that I was different. It also introduced me to the most popular counterfeit to intimacy: sex.

Myth 4: Homosexuality Is Genetic

Listening to the way Hollywood portrays, and the media reports on homosexual issues, you'd think that it has been absolutely proven that being gay is completely genetic.

Wrong.

But let's consider for a moment that such an idea *is* true. Would that mean that genetic predispositions to behavior are the sole determinant of behavior? For instance, there is reportedly a genetic link to alcoholism. Yet people overcome that battle every day. I know *many* men and women who once were in bondage to alcohol and now live in freedom from that addiction. The same with drugs, lying, stealing, and you name it.

The truth is we are all fallen creatures: genetically, physically, emotionally, sexually, and in every other way imaginable. So even though there is currently no proof—despite numerous studies conducted over the past 50 years—that homosexuality is genetic, let's suppose that one day such proof is found. What then?

First Corinthians 6:11 is one of my all-time favorite verses, and one that I've clung to since I first read it 15 years ago. In reference to the homosexuality that had existed among the Corinthian Christians before they came to Christ, it says: "And that is what some of you *were.* But you were washed, you were sanctified, you were justified in the name of the Lord Jesus Christ and by the Spirit of our God."

I love this verse that gives evidence to the realization that for more than 2000 years God has been changing and freeing those who seek Him and are committed to a lifestyle of obedience and self-denial.

So what if a gay gene is eventually found?

I wrestled with this question during the early days of my healing and determined that if a gay gene was discovered, it would not alter my course—homosexuality is *still* not an option. The misery that homosexuality brings does not trump the happiness found in Christ—gay gene or no gay gene. Perhaps the discovery of a gay gene would simply help me understand more about myself and why I battled something so complex. Homosexuality is not simplistic and has no easy answers or quick fixes, no matter what its origin.

If it *is* genetic, that doesn't mean we must surrender to it. As my friend Dr. Neil Whitehead says in his book *My Genes Made Me Do It,*

"Our genes aren't meant to be a tyranny over us, determining everything that we do."

On a similar note, my wife, Leslie, and I have two adopted children. Having read more than a dozen books on the subject, nearly every author has stated related to behavior that it doesn't matter what the genetic or biological predispositions of the child are *because the environment the child is raised in plays a far more significant role in determining how the child will turn out.* Development can make or break genetic behavioral patterns.

Look, just because something is genetic doesn't make it healthy, optimal, desirable, or right. No group would ever advocate for the special rights of alcoholics. And who in their right mind would encourage others to become alcoholics or to celebrate their alcoholism? Genetics aren't meant to be used as justification for sin.

Genetics simply aren't as significant as we make them out to be. And apparently all of those who have overcome alcoholism, homosexuality, drug addiction, and other life-dominating struggles prove that point. My favorite example of this was a television commercial for Rogaine for Women—a treatment for female baldness. On the commercial, they made the statement that Rogaine for Women was *stronger than genetics to overcome baldness.* Hey, if Rogaine can overcome genetic baldness then certainly God can and will help people overcome homosexuality... should it ever be proven it's genetic.

Seriously, I think our answer to the question of genetics should be in the form of another question: "Who *cares* if it is genetic?" Science should never be used to try to trump God's Word.

Myth 5: 10 Percent of the Population Is Gay

The 10 percent figure began as a misinterpretation of studies done in the 1940s by sexologist/entomologist Alfred Kinsey and his associates. Scholars like Dr. Judith Reisman and Edward Eichel have challenged Kinsey's research methodology as flawed (he used an unspecified percentage of college student volunteers and convicted sex offenders) and therefore believe his statistics were faulty. A series of studies from 1989 through 2000 show different figures for the real proportion of exclusively homosexual individuals in America: about 2 to 3 percent.

This is not to diminish the problem. Every gay man or woman or youth—no matter what the actual number or percentage—represents a cherished person for whom Christ died. The important number to remember is that 100 percent of us are sinners.

Myth 6: Marriage or Dating Will Fix a Homosexual

If I had a dollar for every time I heard someone suggest that dating and/or marrying a member of the opposite sex can help someone overcome homosexuality, I would be a rich man. Like I said in Myth 3, homosexuality isn't about sex; *it's about unmet needs*. Homosexuality isn't an inability to relate to the opposite sex; it's an inability to relate properly and healthily to the same sex.

There are thousands of horror stories and testimonies of men and women who have gotten married in hopes that their same-sex attraction would go away, only to find that marriage compounded their problem. So many marriages have been devastated by this issue. The great news is that we have witnessed many such broken or damaged marriages restored.

Long ago I decided that before I could ever think about dating, let alone marriage, I needed two years of complete emotional and sexual sobriety under my belt; I needed more than behavior modification. *I needed real change.* That gave me the freedom to focus solely on my healing and my relationship with the Lord without any distractions.

It was just over two years after I found freedom from the remnants of my emotional struggles that I began dating Leslie. I have given this advice of waiting to others time and time again and witnessed its success firsthand. Never advise someone coming out of homosexuality to seek marriage right away. Encourage him or her to have a protracted time of healing before any thoughts of marriage are even discussed.

There is no rush to get married. In fact, many who come out of homosexuality may never get married. That doesn't make them less heterosexual, less masculine, or less feminine. I know so many godly single men and women who are incredible examples of healthy masculinity and femininity. Relating sexually to someone of the opposite gender is not a requirement—or a proof—of wholeness.

Grappling with and dispelling these six misconceptions go a long way toward understanding the needs of the men and women and youth you want to reach. But even having done so, reaching homosexuals with Christ's invitation to come to Him is still going to be difficult. After all, the gay community has its own misconceptions about Christ and Christians that they must deal with if they want to make an informed decision.

On your part, as one who would minister to this community, you'll face some challenges you may not have considered. You may find yourself paralyzed by fear of offending, fear of what others will think (you're wasting your time trying to reach *them*), fear of being labeled yourself (if I get too involved in this ministry, will my friends think *I'm* gay?), fear of the unknown (Lord, this desire to minister to homosexuals *can't* be from You).

You've taken the right first step by reading this book. And the goal for the rest of the book is to offer a brief-but-thorough understanding of what it will be like reaching gays for Christ. You will need to know exactly what Scripture teaches—and my colleague, Scott Davis, goes into that subject in the next chapter. This is very important because many gay activists who are encouraging Christians to accept homosexuality as normal have a better working knowledge of biblical arguments against homosexuality than most Christians. And these activists have their own answers against those arguments.

Some of these gay promoters may themselves have flirted with Christianity in the past and may even have made professions of faith, only to return to their fleshly desires when the going got tough. Or perhaps when they found no firm support in a local church or from Christian friends when they struggled, they gave up on Christianity.

Are You as Committed?

I believe that we, the church, need to take a page out of the pro-gay playbook. It's ironic, I know…but the gay community is organized, focused on their mission, and most of all passionately committed to making homosexuality acceptable at all costs. Can you say the same of your commitment? Are you as committed to winning the gay community for Christ as they are committed to changing your opinion about homosexuality? Hopefully the answer is yes. But if you're not quite ready to take that stand, please read on.

Part of our problem in the church is apathy—and not just regarding homosexuality. I think too often we pay attention to just what's in front of us, tending to our own affairs with an "if it ain't right in front of me causing extreme discomfort, I don't have time for it" mentality.

I've thought about this a lot. And I've prayed for some catalyst to *force* Christians to care and to take action. Sadly, one of the strongest motivations to get involved may be related to the way the homosexuality issue is being played out in the lives of our youth and children. Preschoolers are now taught that homosexuality is normal. And the effect is that polls show more support among younger adults for gay marriage than among older adults who have not been exposed to efforts to mainstream homosexual behavior.

The truth is we shouldn't need a crisis to get us interested in fulfilling the Great Commission to share the gospel of Jesus. Getting energized to fight homosexuality as an "issue" may seem worthy, but we shouldn't let that become more important than praying for the souls of the lost and hurting—and doing something positive to help homosexuals who want out of their captive lifestyles.

Along with becoming educated about homosexuality, we need to do some personal soul searching and reprioritizing of our goals. Our number one goal as Christians should always be to love souls. Everything we do must boil down to that primary, God-given desire.

2

Developing a Christlike Attitude Toward Homosexuals
(Does God *Really* Hate Gays?)

Scott Davis

—⁓—

In the first chapter Alan talked about some of the common misconceptions people have about homosexuality. One of those was the idea that homosexual sin is worse than other sins.

Alan also mentioned the first time he was called a "fag." Probably most gay men—at least openly gay men—have been called fag at one time or another, just as many lesbians may have been called by equally negative names. Name calling is something we often see on playgrounds—we hear it from kids, and we teach them not to use destructive language when talking about people who are noticeably different than they are. But what happens when those who call themselves Christians resort to such language…or promote a philosophy that God hates certain people? What happens when they *act* on the belief that homosexuality is unforgivable?

Maybe you remember the following news story.

On a crisp fall morning in Lynchburg, Virginia, two sets of protesters squared off in front of Thomas Road Baptist Church. A surprising meeting was about to take place between Jerry Falwell and a group of gay activists who had charged him with inciting violence against gays. In anticipation of this meeting, activists of all stripes descended on the town on October 23, 1999.

One group of protestors held up placards with colorful messages such as "God hates fags" and "Sodomites burn in hell," referring to the biblical destruction of the city of Sodom. These religious protestors considered Reverend Falwell a turncoat for agreeing to meet with gays. The leader of this anti-gay group told a reporter, "Falwell used to be a good preacher. He believed that God doesn't just hate the sin, he hates the sinner. In those days, he believed the truth—that fags could not repent."[1] This man and his colleagues clearly embraced a hatred for homosexuals that they claimed was shared by God. To get their message across, these adults screamed at the gays and lesbians who stood on the opposite side of the street. They taunted them with cries of "Sodomites! Queers! Fags!" One of the men wore a body sandwich board that proclaimed to the gays on the other side of the street: "You're going to burn in hell!"

Looking on from across the street were the other protestors—pro-gay supporters who proclaimed that homosexuality was acceptable to God. As the taunts aimed at the homosexuals continued, three of the lesbian protestors held hands and hugged, further infuriating the opposition.

At this point, one Christian pastor who had been watching the scene approached the lesbians and apologized for the abuse they were receiving from the religious zealots. That, of course, caused him to become a target of the anti-gay protesters: "Don't talk to her," they yelled. "It's too late for her. Stop interfering with the work of the Spirit!"

A local reporter covering the event walked up to one of the authors of this book and, turning off her camera, began openly weeping, asking, "Where is Jesus in all of this? *Where is Jesus?*"

Indeed. Where *is* Jesus in the debate over homosexuality between Christians and gays in America? Was Jesus standing on the side of the street with the pro-gay protestors, who were pushing for Christians to accept homosexual behavior as good and normal? Or was He standing on the side with those who claimed to speak for God, proclaiming His hatred for the "perverts" across the street? Or was He not in that debate at all?

Where would *you* have stood?

Is It Our Job to Hate?

Were those who called themselves Christians in this protest right? Does God really hate homosexuals? Are people who engage in homosexual acts truly condemned to hell with no hope of repentance? If you or your church desires to reach gays with the gospel, *what* is the message you have for these men, women, and youth? What does God think about homosexuals? In order to reach homosexuals, you must know how to share God's view of homosexuality—and homosexuals—accurately.

Some people claim homosexuals are hated by God, or at least they're so sinful that they cannot be redeemed. Is this true? And if they *can* be redeemed, on what basis can that happen?

For answers, let's take a brief but careful look at what Scripture has to say about homosexuality. Anyone who plans to reach out to gays *must* know what Scripture says about it. In searching the Bible, we may find that Scripture offers a third option besides hatred and sexual license.

One key verse adorning many protest banners against gays is Leviticus 18:22: "Do not lie with a man as one lies with a woman; that is detestable." Leviticus was written to guide the Israelites how to live in the way of holiness in the Promised Land. The previous nations who lived in the land that would become Israel had practiced all sorts of idol worship, violence, and sexual perversion. God's people, on the other hand, were to live pure and holy lives, lest they be cast out of the land themselves, as Moses had warned (Deuteronomy 29).

In recounting God's admonitions, Leviticus, chapter 18, contains a series of prohibitions against sexual relations outside of a legitimate husband–wife relationship:

- incest (verse 9)

- sex between other close relatives (verses 7-18)

- adultery (verse 20)

- sex between two men (verse 22)

- and sex with an animal (verse 23)

The current occupants of the Promised Land had defiled themselves and the land through these sexual practices, and now God was expelling them from the land for this reason and giving it to the Israelites (verses 24-25).

The language in verse 22 is straightforward: "Do not lie with a man as one lies with a woman; that is detestable." Based on this passage alone, it's been argued that homosexuals are detestable to God, and thus ought to be destroyed. However, the language is clear and precise—the *act* of a man lying with another man is detestable, but the pejorative applies to the *act* rather than to the *person*.

These prohibitions against sexual perversion are repeated in Leviticus, chapter 20. Incest, intrafamily relations, sex with animals, and sex between two men (verse 13) are again prohibited. The language of 20:13 is similar to 18:22: "If a man lies with a man as one lies with a woman, both of them have done what is detestable. They must be put to death; their blood will be on their own heads." Again the language is clear—the *act* of a man lying with another man is prohibited.

Occasionally it's claimed by pro-gay supporters that these verses aren't speaking of loving, monogamous, homosexual sex, but of male prostitution or some other form of perversion. These arguments are not convincing. The language is clear and is parallel to other sexual prohibitions in the passage: a man is not to lie with his father's wife, his daughter-in-law, another man, or an animal (20:11,12,13,15).

One of the other favorite passages used to condemn homosexuals is found in the New Testament, Romans 1:26-28:

> Because of this, God gave them over to shameful lusts. Even their women exchanged natural relations for unnatural ones. In the same way the men also abandoned natural relations with women and were inflamed with lust for one another. Men committed indecent acts with other men, and received in themselves the due penalty for their perversion.
>
> Furthermore, since they did not think it worthwhile to retain the knowledge of God, he gave them over to a depraved mind, to do what ought not to be done.

Anti-gay protestors offer these verses as proof that homosexuals have been given over by God to a "reprobate mind," and thus will not and cannot repent and be forgiven. But does the force of the apostle Paul's argument in the entire chapter fit this interpretation?

In the first two chapters of Romans, Paul sets up a discussion about the gospel and the distinction between Jews and Gentiles. In Romans 1:1-16, he warmly welcomes the church in Rome and tells them that he is about to discuss the gospel with them, and he is glad to do it although many of them are Gentiles:

> That is why I am so eager to preach the gospel also to you who are at Rome. I am not ashamed of the gospel, because it is the power of God for the salvation of everyone who believes: first for the Jew, then for the Gentile (verses 15-16).

What is this good news Paul wants to share with them? That God's holy people (the Jews) *and* the pagan sinners (the Gentiles) are welcomed into the kingdom family of God through His grace displayed in Christ

Jesus. To accomplish this end, Paul demonstrates that both Jews and Gentiles are sinners, with hope to be found only in the righteousness of Christ.

Paul begins with a disturbing recap of the history of man outside of God's covenant. From the very beginning, mankind refused to honor God despite His eternal power and divine nature being obvious from creation. As a result, man's thinking became foolish and futile (verses 18-21). Humanity turned away from God Himself and their hearts become darkened as a result. Paul's description calls to mind the Genesis narratives before the flood—a time when almost all of mankind rejected the worship of God. Violence (Cain, Lamech, etc.) and foolishness (the Tower of Babel) ruled the earth. Man delved further into sin by worshiping people and idols rather than God.

> Therefore God gave them over in the sinful desires of their hearts to sexual impurity for the degrading of their bodies with one another. They exchanged the truth of God for a lie, and worshiped and served created things rather than the Creator—who is forever praised. Amen (Romans 1:24-25).

Throughout its existence, the nation of Israel fought to remain pure from the idol worship of the surrounding nations. Those nations worshiped gods in the forms of men and animals, often with degrading sexual worship practices. The prophets and priests of Israel consistently called the people to separate themselves from the worship of idols and the sexual practices that went along with them.

But the Gentiles continued in their sin and wickedness. They exchanged truth for lies and served the flesh.

> Because of this, God gave them over to shameful lusts. Even their women exchanged natural relations for unnatural ones. In the same way the men also abandoned natural relations with women and were inflamed with lust for one another. Men committed indecent acts with other men, and received in themselves the due penalty for their perversion (Romans 1:26-27).

Paul describes the degradation of homosexuality as a further step on the path away from God and toward foolishness. His Jewish readers would have remembered the Old Testament narratives of attempted homosexual rape in Sodom (Genesis 19:5) and in Gibeah (Judges 19:22-25) and seen these as frightening reminders of how far man's wickedness can sometimes go. Paul's Gentile readers would have been familiar with the celebrated homosexual practices of some well-known Greek and Roman leaders. Paul saw all of this as evidence that man's rejection of God had snowballed into increasing depravity. Man rejected God and became foolish. People

- exchanged the worship of the eternal God for idols and became degraded.

- exchanged the truth of God for a lie and worshiped only self-gratification.

- exchanged God's ordering of sexuality for homosexual acts and suffered the penalty.

The description of homosexual behavior as an exchange of the natural for the unnatural ties well into the rest of the passage, as it demonstrates the progression away from the Creator and His ordering of society to the disordered worship of self. The biological ordering of sexual functions may be "understood from what has been made, so that men are without excuse" (Romans 1:20). God's ordering of nature, family, and sexuality is consistent throughout Scripture and can even be discovered through nature.

Jesus recalled God's ordering of sexuality when He answered the Pharisees' questions about divorce: "God 'made them male and female'... 'and the two will become one flesh'" (Mark 10:6-8). Based on His understanding of God's intentions behind the Old Testament law, Jesus not only upheld the divinely given sexual boundaries but significantly expanded them: "You have heard that it was said, 'Do not commit adultery.' But I tell you that anyone who looks at a woman lustfully has already committed adultery with her in his heart" (Matthew 5:27-28).

The Bible is clear throughout that we are designed to express our sexuality only within a marriage relationship between one man and one woman. Any other use of sex ignores our Creator's loving instructions and degrades our bodies.

In the apostle Paul's mind, this disastrous exchange of God for idols, foolishness, self, and sexual perversion brought mankind to the point where people could no longer distinguish truth from lies. But Paul's history of descent into wickedness doesn't end with homosexuality:

> Furthermore, since they did not think it worthwhile to retain the knowledge of God, he gave them over to a depraved mind, to do what ought not to be done. They have become filled with every kind of wickedness, evil, greed and depravity....They are gossips, slanderers, God-haters, insolent, arrogant and boastful; they invent ways of doing evil; they disobey their parents... they not only continue to do these very things but also approve of those who practice them (Romans 1:28-32).

This is Paul's description of the wickedness of the Gentiles—living outside of God's law and covenant. He seems caught up in an angry rant against those who do not know God and thus engage in all types of sin. One might think that a Jew or Christian could easily read this passage— or even shout it from a pulpit—or across the street toward gay activists, denouncing those wicked sinners, those slanderers, those haters of God, those *homosexuals*. But Paul has set a trap. And it's a trap for the religious person:

> You, therefore, have no excuse, you who pass judgment on someone else, for at whatever point you judge the other, you are condemning yourself, because you who pass judgment do the same things....Or do you show contempt for the riches of his kindness, tolerance and patience, not realizing that God's kindness leads you toward repentance? (Romans 2:1,4).

The deeply religious of Paul's day took pride in their religious heritage and separation from the ungodly society surrounding them. They saw the wretched sinners around them engaging in all types of sin, including homosexual acts, and self-righteously judged themselves to be better based on the purity of their religious fervor and laws. Paul's trap reveals their self-righteous attitudes to be boastful and empty, for they have sinned against God's laws as well.

This Romans 2 passage has been twisted to mean "don't make any moral judgments." But clearly Paul spent almost the entire previous chapter making moral judgments (and he's only getting started). The warning isn't that we should never make moral judgments, but to expose the danger of self-righteousness. *In denouncing evil, we must never leave behind the humility found by recalling our own struggles with sin.*

> Homosexual sin does not disqualify one from salvation any more than disobeying parents or gossiping.

Paul uses his letter to the Romans to level the playing field for all men and women. God does not show partiality between people (2:11). *No one* is righteous; "Jews and Gentiles alike are all under sin" (Romans 3:9). After revealing the wickedness of all mankind before God, Paul is finally ready to reveal the greatness of the good news of Christ:

> But now a righteousness from God, apart from law, has been made known, to which the Law and the Prophets testify. This righteousness from God comes through faith in Jesus Christ to all who believe. There is no difference, for all have sinned and fall short of the glory of God, and are justified freely by his grace through the redemption that came by Christ Jesus (Romans 3:21-24).

All have sinned and fall short of the glory of God. *All* are in need of God's unmerited favor and forgiveness. Paul's diatribe against the wickedness of the godless Gentiles in Romans 1 was an important setup for his trap in chapter 2, demonstrating that religious Jews show themselves to be no better than the Gentiles when they fail to fully follow the law—and all people fail. Paul uses the convenient example of homosexuality (prevalent in Roman society) as an example of the disorder of mankind's rejection of the Creator. But the force of Paul's argument is that *all* have sinned, including the children of the covenant. Apart from Christ, *all* people live as fools, darkened in their understanding, being given over to reprobate minds.

It must be concluded that in Paul's understanding, homosexuality is one sin among a multitude of sins. Homosexual sin does not disqualify one from salvation any more than disobeying parents or gossiping. To be more precise, we are all disqualified from eternal life apart from the gracious, unmerited favor of Christ. No one stands taller than another apart from Him.

Those who hate homosexuals—or even those who think homosexuals are in some way *worse* sinners than they themselves—have lost sight of their own unworthiness in God's sight. No one who has received the unmerited favor of God can afford to hate others for their sin.

Jesus told a parable of a man whose master forgave him of a great debt, yet the man refused to forgive the debts of a fellow servant. The master in the parable condemned the unforgiving man and laid back on him the debts that were originally due (Matthew 18). We must never forget Christ's warning; we must constantly remember God's forgiveness of our own great sin when we consider the sin of others.

If we remember Paul's warning, tread humbly, and flee from self-righteous judgments, must we then accept homosexual behavior and call it good? Scripture says otherwise. No matter how culturally incorrect it may become, we must never be lured into affirming what Scripture denies. Those who affirm homosexuality have "exchanged the truth of God for a lie" and are giving approval to those who practice sin (Romans 1:25).

We cannot affirm homosexuality without denying Scripture and God's authority to judge right from wrong. Besides, accepting sin and pretending God approves of it is not loving! No sane person would buy an alcoholic a drink out of love and rejoice at his or her resulting drunkenness an hour later. Would it be loving to encourage a person to accept his alcoholism and continue to enjoy drinking as long as his liver holds out? *No!* And neither is it loving to encourage practicing homosexuals to continue in their sexual sin.

So instead of on the one hand hating homosexuals or on the other affirming them, *Christians should apply the gospel of Christ to all people equally.* Both the haters and affirmers make the same error of excluding homosexuals from the gospel! Both are saying the same thing: that those who engage in homosexuality cannot be changed. They are gay, and they will always be gay. The opposing sides differ only in their conclusion of whether God hates or loves gay people for their homosexuality.

And That Is What Some of You Were

So do we indeed discover a third way of viewing homosexuality in Scripture…a way that is in opposition to both the pro-gay and anti-gay messages? *Yes.* Such a third way is found in 1 Corinthians 6:9-11. This key passage comes in the midst of the apostle Paul's disciplinary language against the Corinthian church, which was allowing blatant sin and division to spring up unchallenged. He reminds the Christians that they are sinners saved for a greater purpose, that they should be looking forward to the resurrection, and that they should be living in light of their union with God. Since they've been rescued from the penalty of sin, they should now live holy lives and flee from sexual immorality:

> Do you not know that the wicked will not inherit the kingdom of God? Do not be deceived: Neither the sexually immoral nor idolaters nor adulterers nor male prostitutes nor *homosexual offenders* nor thieves nor the greedy nor drunkards nor slanderers nor swindlers will inherit the kingdom of God. And that is what some of you were. But you were washed, you were sanctified, you were justified in the name of the Lord Jesus Christ and by the Spirit of our God (1 Corinthians 6:9-11).

There are three important points here. First, homosexual behavior is again condemned. The Greek word translated "homosexual offend-ers" is *arsenokoite*, which is derived from *arsane* (male) and *koite* (couch, often used to imply sexual relations like our modern word *coitus*). The word *arsenokoites* does not appear in Greek texts prior to Paul, so it seems that he may have coined this phrase to suit his specific purpose.[2] The comparison to Leviticus 20:13, which in the Greek translation uses the phrase *arsenos koiten* to refer to homosexuality is striking.[3] Paul is directly referring to the Levitical prohibition on homosexual acts. The connection shouldn't be surprising, as Paul would certainly have chap-ter 20 of Leviticus in mind—verse 11 of that chapter forbids sleeping with any of your father's wives, the precise problem Paul was address-ing in the Corinthian church.

Paul thus explicitly *renews* the Old Testament prohibition against homosexual behavior—a man lying with a man. If the ban on homosex-uality were merely cultural, this would have been the time to say it. The Corinthian culture didn't condemn homosexuality, and the church in Corinth was failing to condemn any kind of sexual sin. Yet Paul writes to them with Leviticus 18 in mind and says that homosexual actions are out of bounds for God's holy people. As Christians today, we should stand unashamed for the truth that God affirms marriage and does not condone any sexual activity out of marriage.

Second, some members of the Corinthian church had formerly engaged in homosexual relations. Paul writes, "And that is what some of you were," meaning that some of them had been sexually immoral, some had been idolaters, some had been drunkards, and some had been active homosexuals. It surprises some people to learn that the first-century church had former homosexuals among their members. *But* they had been transformed: washed, sanctified, and justified by the power of Christ! This is a triumphant vision of the church as it truly is—*full of radiantly redeemed former sinners of all stripes.* Homosexual sinners should be as welcome in our churches as any other kind of sinner, *for all have sinned.*

The third important point is that those who are washed by Christ must no longer engage in their old sins, including homosexual behavior. Much of this letter to the Corinthians is devoted to chastising the church for failing to judge sin among its members and taking a lax attitude toward sexual sin. Our renewed relationship with God in Christ isn't a license to sin, but a strong reason to resist temptation:

> Flee from sexual immorality. All other sins a man commits are outside his body, but he who sins sexually sins against his own body. Do you not know that your body is a temple of the Holy Spirit, who is in you, whom you have received from God? You are not your own; you were bought at a price. Therefore honor God with your body (1 Corinthians 6:18-20).

Flee, Paul writes. Run away! Sexual sin degrades our bodies, which are now meant to be holy places for God to indwell. Furthermore, we have been bought at the price of Christ's suffering and death. We do not have the right to use our bodies for impurity and lust. Homosexuals who are called to Christ must leave the old life of sin behind and devote their lives to holiness—as must *all* men and women and youth who come to Christ. Sexual immorality isn't an option for us; *we were meant to live for so much more.*

Again, the pro-gay and anti-gay paths are not that different from each other. The error of hatred and the error of acceptance boil down to the same mistaken belief—that the gospel doesn't apply to homosexuals. Both exclude homosexuals from the gospel by claiming that change is either not possible or not desirable. But the gospel isn't just the hope of eternal bliss; it's also living a transformed life as a citizen of God's kingdom. The Scriptures demand and promise the same of homosexuals as of every man, woman, and child: transformation.

To many people, this redemptive path may seem narrow, and difficult. It's not easy for most churches and many individuals to redemptively love homosexuals. There are complex issues that the remainder of this book will lay out.

It's not comfortable for a pastor to deal with a congregant who is slowly experiencing freedom from homosexual behavior, but who slips and falls from time to time. It's not comfortable balancing grace and compassion in calling the church to radical holiness. It's not comfortable dealing with issues of church discipline. It's not comfortable dealing with parishioners who don't want homosexuals around their children, or— on the other side of the spectrum—who can't understand why homosexuality is wrong. But isn't the friction of grace and truth exactly the tension the church always contends with?

For the individual involved, the redemptive path can sometimes be painful and difficult, but this is true for all, no matter their particular sins and temptations. We mustn't pretend that transformation is ever quick or easy. It's always much easier to live after the flesh than obey Christ. But living for the flesh leads to death. The path of redemption requires us to deny ourselves daily and take up our cross. The road is long and has ruts and many false paths and traps along the way. But that road leads to a beautiful life as God intended.[4]

A 21st-Century Parable

One day Jesus was strolling down a busy New York street with a prominent minister named Simon. Whenever they passed an adult bookstore or bar, Simon would detour to the other side of the street, staying as far as possible from the filth. As they walked, the minister told Jesus of the drug addicts and prostitutes who frequented the street corners. "God's judgment is about to fall on this disgusting city," he said. "Their sin is too much. I'm sure He won't stand for it much longer."

Suddenly a brightly dressed man, with a swish in his step and a lisp in his voice, cried out over the noise of the busy city street. "Jesus? Is that you!" Jesus turned and smiled in his direction. The man leapt from the curb and ran directly across the street, crossing four lanes of traffic, oblivious to the buses and cabs swerving to avoid him.

He ran straight to Jesus without breaking his stride and wrapped his arms around His neck. The shocked minister, who knew this man as Fredrick—the owner of a local gay bar—was even more appalled when Fredrick's smiling face dissolved into tears on Jesus' neck. He sobbed uncontrollably as Jesus tenderly wrapped His arms around him and held him for what seemed like 30 minutes to the growing crowd, but could not have been more than one. "I'm sorry," Fredrick said as he stepped back and looked into Jesus' eyes. "And thank You."

The previous week, Jesus had found Fredrick outside the bar and begun speaking to him about sin, God's love, and the coming kingdom. Fredrick had stopped attending church after high school—religious people weren't too happy seeing a person like him in their churches—but something was different about this preacher. Even though Jesus talked about sin and God's judgment, He wasn't condemning—He was actually warm and welcoming. Without thinking about it, Fredrick poured out his life story to this preacher. He told things he had never spoken aloud in his life, barely even allowed himself to think: the uncle who had molested him, the boys who had called him fag, his first boyfriend at 16, the long string of boyfriends since, his profound loneliness, his fear of AIDS. With each memory, with each confession, a weight lifted from his heart.

"Jesus, do You think...would You mind could a person like me follow You? Could I be a part of God's kingdom?"

"Of course! I came here to personally invite you," Jesus assured him. They talked a bit longer and then as Jesus turned to walk on, He glanced back at Fredrick and smiled to see him standing dumbstruck on the corner in front of his gay bar.

But Simon the minister knew none of this. He saw only a gay man draped across Jesus, sobbing. *What an embarrassment!* he thought. *How can Jesus let such a God-forsaken sinner touch Him, much less make such a display?*

Jesus uncannily answered the minister's thoughts. "Simon, I have something to ask you."

"Ask me, Teacher," he said.

"Two men owed money to a bank. One owed $100,000, and the other owed only $10,000. Neither of them had money to pay back their loans. The bank was about to take the first man's house and repossess the second man's car. But the vice president of the bank had compassion on them and canceled both debts. Now which of them will love him more?"

Simon replied, "I suppose the one who had the bigger debt canceled."

"You have judged correctly," Jesus said. Then He turned toward the gay man and said to the minister, "Do you see this man? I came to your church and was greeted cordially with a firm handshake. This man ran when he saw Me to wrap his arms around My neck. You did not buy Me anything to drink on this hot day, but he has poured out his tears on My shoulder. Therefore, I tell you, his many sins have been forgiven—for he loved much. But he who has been forgiven little loves little."

Then Jesus said, "Fredrick, your sins are forgiven."

The crowd around Him muttered to themselves, "Who is this who claims to forgive sins?"

But Jesus said to the man, "Your faith has saved you! Go in peace."

Jesus—Friend of Sinners

As is often pointed out, the gospels don't record how Jesus responded to homosexuals who might have come across His path. But His response to sinners of all types was consistent: He treated them with respect but never hesitated to point out sin. He commanded the rich young ruler to sell all his possessions. He told the Samaritan at the well "all she had ever done." He didn't condemn the woman caught in adultery, but told her to go and leave her life of sin. He invited himself to Zacchaeus' house for dinner, and Zacchaeus spontaneously repented of his theft and paid back those he had cheated.

Jesus had an electrifying effect on those He came across. Some, like the rich young ruler, were unwilling to turn from their sin. Others, like Zacchaeus, joyfully repented when given the opportunity. If Jesus came across a homosexual on the streets of Jerusalem, I can imagine Him offering that person the gift of life, saying "Come, leave your life of sin and follow Me."

Scripture records that Jesus was mocked as a friend of sinners. I picture Him wearing that label like a badge of honor. If we are to be like Jesus, if we are to reach out to the homosexuals we know or the gay men and women we don't know, we must not be afraid to be seen as friends of those whose lives have taken a wrong turn. The woman struggling with lesbianism needs God's grace just as much as the rest of us thieves, gossips, slanderers, and fornicators.

Who are we to throw stones?

If this is your attitude, you're ready to be a friend to homosexuals.

Notes

1. Natalie Davis, "My Dinner with Jerry," *Baltimore City Paper*.
2. Richard B. Hayes, *The Moral Vision of the New Testament: Contemporary Introduction to New Testament Ethics* (London: Continuum International Publishing Group, 1997), p. 382.
3. For a more complete discussion of the scriptural answers to the pro-gay theology, the reader is directed to Joe Dallas' *The Gay Gospel? How Pro-Gay Advocates Misread the Bible* (Harvest House Publishers).
4. Ibid.

3

Is Change Possible?

Mike Goeke

—ᗰᗰ—

I nherent in the message of the gospel is the idea that through Jesus we all become new creatures. The gospel is about changed lives. It should follow that, through Jesus, the homosexual can likewise experience change. However, the idea of change for the homosexual is controversial for everyone, including Christians and gay men and women. Is change possible for the homosexual? And if so, what does that change look like?

There's a wonderful and completely modern story of amazing change and healing in the ninth chapter of the Gospel of John. The characters in this story offer great insight into the way twenty-first-century Christians react to the idea that miraculous change is really possible. This account shows that then, as now, miraculous change often precedes intense skepticism.

At the center of the story is a man blind from birth. This man had never been able to see; his eyes had known only darkness. But it isn't the fact that the man was *born* blind or even that his issue was "blindness" that makes this story so compelling. He could have had any affliction from any source. What's interesting about his problem is that it was something that completely dominated his life and something that set him apart from everyone except those who shared his affliction.

As a blind man during the time of Jesus, this man was likely an outcast in his community and in the synagogue. Even the disciples, in observing his affliction, assumed his blindness was some form of punishment. The disciples asked Jesus, "Who sinned, this man or his parents, that he would be born blind?"* They saw only one possible reason for something as grievous as blindness. Notice that they weren't concerned with helping the man with his problem, nor did it occur to them to petition Jesus to heal the man. Instead they were all about assigning blame. But Jesus responded with a statement that surely shocked the minds and sensibilities of the disciples. He not only absolved the man and his parents of blame, but in fact gave a rather magnificent reason for the man's blindness. He said simply that the man was blind "so that the works of God might be displayed in him."

The disciples, in their limited human logic and cultural perception, saw only bad in the blindness of the man. In their obsession with the man's affliction, they were blind to seeing the power of God displayed before their very eyes. Jesus, however, chose to display the works of God in a dramatic way. Through clay and spit and a rinse of water from the pool of Siloam, He gave sight to the blind man.

Jesus *changed* this man.

This man, this blind outcast, this one who probably begged outside the city walls, suddenly had sight. As he told people of his miraculous change, the skepticism began. Almost immediately the man's healing was questioned by the Pharisees, the religious leaders of his day. The Pharisees questioned the fact that the man was healed on the Sabbath

---

* Scripture quotes in this chapter are from the NASB.

and highlighted the illegalities of such a healing. Thus they attempted to divert attention away from what had happened by discrediting the healer, Jesus, who broke with tradition to heal the blind man. The Pharisees then questioned whether or not the man was ever blind to begin with. In essence, the Pharisees shifted their concern from the technicalities of the miracle to simply denying that anything *really* happened in the first place. The Pharisees brought into question both the *healer* and the *healing*. They were determined to cast doubt on the reality that Jesus actually healed a man of an affliction that was believed to be unchangeable.

The Pharisees were clearly threatened by what might happen if Jesus was proven to have healed the blind man. Even the man's parents were intimidated by the Pharisees and refused to answer their questions for fear of being kicked out of the temple should they insinuate that Jesus had indeed changed their son. The Pharisees worked the crowd and exhausted their efforts to find a "hole" in the healing...but to no avail.

After the Pharisees had discussed and disputed all the pertinent issues among themselves and the friends and family of the healed man, they turned to confront the man himself with their issues and questions. The formerly blind man responded in a way that echoes the testimony of men and women touched by Jesus since the time He walked on earth. When the interrogators referred to the man's healer as a sinner, the ex-blind man simply said, "Whether He is a sinner, I do not know; one thing I do know, that though I was blind, now I see" (John 9:25). *The only person who felt no need to explain or to understand or to analyze or to figure out the healing was the man who was healed.* He simply knew he had been changed and that was all he needed to know.

Most contemporary Christians, if they're honest, must admit that they have, at times, when confronted with serious affliction and/or when confronted with claims of miraculous healing or change, have assumed the role of the disciples and the Pharisees in the story of the healing of the blind man. Every person, at some time, has been more concerned about the "why" of a seemingly desperate issue than expectant about the ability of God to work in the midst of such an issue. Or they've been

like the Pharisees, looking for loopholes and doubting the reality of the
change. The non-Christian world often acts like the Pharisees in this situation, afraid of what it might mean if Jesus is proven to be the Christ...
the great Healer and Changer of lives. It's no wonder they feel they must
do all they can to deny the change, defame the healer, or discredit the
person changed by Him.

So *is* miraculous change really possible in this day and age?

This question has drawn, perhaps, more ire and disagreement in the
area of homosexuality than in any other area. Within the church and
without, the reality of change for the homosexual is a topic that at best
causes division among Christians and, at worst, splits denominations
and church bodies. For that reason, change needs to be fully understood
by anyone who wishes to work with homosexuals.

Is Change Truly Possible for the Homosexual?

The short answer is most assuredly yes. It's probably safe to say that
many of the readers of this book may want to believe that, but they find
themselves facing some level of doubt as to its accuracy. Clearly, the
idea of change in the area of homosexuality often brings with it extreme
doubt or skepticism, even from Christians who claim to believe in an all-
powerful God. There could be many reasons for this skepticism, including deep, unspoken doubt that God is powerful enough to do something
as dramatic as to change someone who claims to be gay.

Or possibly it's not so much doubt that God can change someone, but
more doubt and lack of belief that He *will* change someone. Or maybe
it's the result of a narrow view of change, and when the expected and
desired change doesn't happen, there's a failure to see the change that
actually has happened. Maybe this is simply because so few people seem
to reflect the occurrence of lasting change. In reality, it's most likely a
composite of all of these things.

In order to overcome doubt, it's important to examine the roots.
Exposing the wrong thinking that precedes wrong beliefs is the first step
toward truth. Let's take a brief look at the many sources of confusion

about the reality of change and see how they have conspired to create an atmosphere of skepticism about the possibility of true change for the homosexual.

The Message of the Church

One clear cause for confusion is the mixed messages being generated by the mainstream church. The modern Christian church is clearly not unified on the issue of homosexuality. Understandably, this division causes great confusion among Christians who look to the church for guidance and direction on moral and cultural issues.

On the far side of the spectrum are the churches and denominations that clearly teach that "gay is okay" with God. These churches proclaim the normalcy of homosexuality and, therefore, that change is not only impossible, but unnecessary. Churches that take this stance usually do so by defining "homosexual" or "homosexuality" differently than the Bible does or by suggesting that biblical prohibitions against homosexuality are taken out of context.

Some denominations have enacted pro-gay policies that affirm the practice and lifestyle of homosexuality, allowing full membership privileges for practicing homosexuals, supporting the right of homosexuals to marry, and permitting the ordination of gay clergy. Others publicly declare that gay, lesbian, and bisexual people (or those of all "sexual orientations") are welcome in the "full life and ministry" (e.g. membership, leadership, employment) of the church. One such denominational website notes that, as a denomination, it believes "God's affirmation of the gifts of loving relationships and sexuality are not restricted to those who are heterosexual."

Other denominations are not necessarily affirming of homosexuality but are moving in the direction of accepting homosexuality as a legitimate, Christian lifestyle. Several of these mainline denominations are currently actively debating the issue of homosexuality. The United Methodist Church, the Presbyterian Church (USA), the Episcopal church, and the Evangelical Lutheran Church in America are each confronting the homosexual issue head-on and are facing standards that range from legitimizing and blessing same-sex unions to ordaining practicing gay clergy.

Further down the spectrum are churches and/or denominations that acknowledge homosexual behavior as sin, but view homosexuality as unchangeable. These churches focus on behavior and view the "solution" to homosexuality as a celibate life, rather than confronting the homosexual *identity*. For example, one denominational website has several pages of excellent and, for the most part, accurate information about homosexuality and homosexual behavior. The website states clearly that homosexual behavior is always a violation of "divine and natural law" and clearly and intricately explains its position. However, the answer to the homosexual dilemma for this denomination is chastity, or celibacy.

Within this call to chastity, there is an acknowledgement that God will meet homosexuals in their desires and bring them freedom. The website states that "homosexual persons are called to chastity. By the virtues of self-mastery that teach them inner freedom, at times by the support of disinterested friendship, by prayer and sacramental grace, they can and should gradually and resolutely approach Christian perfection." However, there is a clear implication that true change is not possible.

Some churches believe homosexuality has its roots in some sort of demonic possession. These churches believe homosexual behavior to be sinful, and believe that the people can be freed from the condition of homosexuality through intense prayer designed to "deliver" them from that demonic influence. One denominational position paper on homosexuality encouraged people to pray for "the deliverance of those enslaved by [the] satanic snare [of homosexuality]." Proof of change, in this culture, often centers on attractions and desires, and is often seen and described not only as a complete eradication of same-sex desires, but also a restoration of desire and attraction for the opposite sex.

Finally, there are churches that believe God's Word to be true regarding homosexuality. These churches see homosexual behavior as a sin like any other. Rather than affirming people in their gay identity, rather than limiting people to a gay identity and a life of celibacy, rather than promising people a one-time ticket to heterosexual desires, these churches simply view the possibility of change as being not unlike the possibility of change for every Christian who submits his or her sins, struggles, temptations, and false identities to the Lord. These churches view change as a process or journey of sanctification.

Off this spectrum completely, and as Scott mentioned in chapter 2, there are some churches who preach that anyone living homosexually, or even struggling homosexually, is doomed to hell and that there is not only no hope for change, but no hope for salvation.

Christians expect their church and pastors to help them understand how to deal with the clash of culture and Scripture. With so many different churches voicing different positions on homosexuality, can we be surprised that change for the homosexual is doubted among the Christian community? The message being sent by each of these types of churches clearly impacts the way Christians view change. Scripture is being devalued, God's power is being minimized, and self is being exalted over God. Messages are being sent that God no longer cares about sin or, if He does, that He can sustain the sinner but not change the sinner. These mixed messages are clearly confusing the Christian community.

Popular Culture and Media

The church isn't the only reason for current doubts about the reality of change. Popular culture and media have also played a large part. It's only natural that a person will grow to believe what he (or she) hears the most often. When only one viewpoint is expressed, and if the viewpoint is expressed often and effectively enough, it will eventually take root. This is true even in Christians who may have a "hitch" in their spirits the first time they hear something. Ultimately, even committed Christians can fall prey to what is repeatedly conveyed to them. With regard to the possibility of change for the homosexual, many Christians accept what they have heard most often: Homosexuality is inborn and unchangeable.

Secular media and entertainment love the gay issue. Secular media, as a whole, treat homosexuality as a simple alternative to heterosexuality—sometimes even a *desirable* alternative. In most cases, practicing homosexuals are portrayed in a sympathetic light, and even as "victims" of the traditional church. Often the portrayals of homosexuals center on their early feelings of being different, their quest and failure to be heterosexual, the hurt they endured as gay teens and adults, the rejection they faced in their churches, schools, workplaces, and the conflicts with their families. These stories often include almost inspirational testimonies of perseverance and the acceptance and freedom found in the homosexual lifestyle and community.

Added to these very personal (and often truly heartbreaking) details are statements from psychologists, therapists, and other mental health officials that affirm the pervasive worldview that homosexuality not only is unchangeable, but that it's harmful to attempt to do so. Scientific data or studies, often presented as facts, usually discuss the possibility of a genetic link to homosexuality. If an opposing viewpoint is shown at all, it is mentioned briefly and usually with some amount of disdain and ridicule.

In the entertainment realm, homosexuals coexist with heterosexuals. Many television producers and writers now feel the need to have at least a token gay character in their shows. These characters are often funny, interesting, and endearing. They tend to be the enlightened characters, the dynamic characters, the talented characters, or the kindhearted characters. *Never has anyone professing a belief that homosexuality is wrong or that it can be changed been portrayed in a positive light.* If the character's homosexuality is brought into issue, the plot ends with either affirmation of the gay character or the denigration of characters in opposition to the homosexuality.

Through the influence of media and popular entertainment, it's easy to see how—absent contrary information—even the best-intentioned Christians might be inclined to question the reality of change for the homosexual, even though they are well aware of the way homosexuality is addressed in Scripture. Christians are every bit as susceptible as the world at large, and maybe even more so, to this sort of deception.

The Low Volume of the Voice of Change

While denominational issues and the media have proactively added to this confusion, it may well be true that what is *not* heard may cause Christians to question change even more than what they do hear. The changed homosexual is a largely unheard voice. How many Christians have heard from the trusted pulpit of their home church the message that change is possible for the homosexual? How many Christians have heard from the trusted pulpit of their home church a testimony from someone who has been freed from the bondage of homosexuality? Unfortunately, it's still the rare Christian who has actually heard the testimony of a redeemed homosexual.

Some Christians might think homosexuality is a topic too controversial or risqué for the church. Some might think their church doesn't have any homosexuals, so maybe their congregation doesn't need to address the issue. Some might not want children or teenagers to hear about homosexuality in church. But the reality is that most people in the church, even if they aren't struggling themselves, have someone they know or love who is gay. And the reality is that the world is talking about homosexuality, and the world will not quit talking about it until it no longer bothers anyone—until everyone, including the church, no longer cares about homosexuality. Once homosexuality is no longer seen as a problem, it becomes normalized.

The voice of the practicing homosexual in our culture is heard repeatedly, though often subtly. The constant denominational debates concerning homosexuality, the news media's positive portrayal of the gay lifestyle, and the inclusion of gay characters in almost every form of media and entertainment works its way into the minds of even the most faithful of Christians.

When the mind is inundated with only one side of the story, it's unrealistic to expect it to be able to discern truth easily. The church must speak to this issue with truth, grace, *and a message of redemption.* No one will know that God is changing homosexuals if their stories aren't heard loudly, clearly, and repeatedly. The world is talking about homosexuality from its view of acceptance, and the church must likewise share the redemptive side of the story.

The Reality of Change in the Homosexual

As with the blind man who received his sight, homosexuals *are* changing all over the world. The confusing messages, the skepticism, and the attempts to discredit change do nothing to alter the reality that *change is possible through Jesus Christ,* and that many people are living, breathing testimonies to that change. But "change" may look differently than we would expect, and a paradigm shift is needed to truly see the change that is happening. Change is about much more than whether or not one is sexually excited by one gender or the other. True change goes much deeper.

With regard to homosexuality, change takes many forms. The first step for those struggling and for those of you who choose to walk alongside a struggler is to allow for the truth that God can work change *in whatever way He desires.* It's important to free one's mind to experience change beyond imagination and not to limit God based on a narrow human perspective. Unrealistic expectations easily breed and grow doubt.

Many active homosexuals *and* former homosexuals claim they prayed for years for God to "change" them, but change never happened so they gave up. When this happens, some of these men and women return to an active gay lifestyle, while others just dismiss the idea of change and muddle through their lives as best they can.

The problem is that often these people are making demands of God under the guise of surrender to Him. Prayer is offered laying out exactly what people think they want, rather than submitting their issue to God for Him to do as He desires. If God fails to meet their demands, they deem the prayer unanswered. With regard to the issue of homosexuality, as with any issue, God often works in ways different than what the average human expects. And almost always, God's perfect ways are beyond the imagination of the human mind.

As was stated earlier, there are many different viewpoints, even within the Christian community, as to what "change" in the homosexual looks like. Let's examine some of those views, realizing that even within the following categories, the exact reality of change may differ from person to person.

Types of Change

Some Christians believe that change is always evidenced by full deliverance from homosexuality, resulting in complete and immediate eradication of strong homosexual desires and the establishing of heterosexual desires and feelings. This form of healing and change is rare. Most organizations that educate people on homosexuality are careful to state clearly how seldom this type of healing occurs and don't encourage people to expect this sort of change in themselves or their loved ones.

Others view change as having not so much to do with eradicated or diminished homosexual desires, but instead with the ability to live a fulfilled but celibate life. Many people who lived formerly as homosexuals will not claim to have changed attractions immediately. However, as they live in obedience to God with regard to their sexual behavior, they will often claim a change in their identities. While their attractions may or may not change, their perceptions of themselves and of God do change.

For most homosexuals who accept Christ and the new life He offers, their true change isn't so much behavior focused, attractions focused, or demon focused. Instead, their true change is *heart* focused. It's a change of *identity* from the inside out. And that identity change will result in behavior change.

A Changed Identity

Many who want to leave homosexuality behind are unwilling to accept that their only option is to live a life of celibacy, simply managing unwanted attractions. What they really want is a change in identity. They no longer want the gay label attached to them.

To say that someone has had a change in his (or her) identity means, essentially, that he no longer identifies himself as gay. His identity is not based on his feelings, and certainly not on his sexual desires or his struggles with sin. His identity becomes what he knows to be true from the Word of God.

Instead of accepting the labels placed on them by the taunting playground children of their youth ("sissy," "pansy," "fag," "butch," "dyke," etc.), or by the message of the world that labels them based on sexual attractions ("you are sexually attracted to the same gender, therefore you are gay"), these changed people gladly accept the identity bestowed on them by their God—new creatures designed for the purpose of glorifying their God, fully male or female, and fully righteous based on the blood of Jesus shed for their sins.

> Changed behavior is not necessarily an indicator of the important inward change in the life of the believer.

Often well-meaning Christians want to focus on behavior and assume that once a person quits acting out homosexually, that the healing or change is complete. Nothing could be further from the truth. The path of homosexuality *ends,* not starts, with behavior. And even after homosexual behavior has ceased, there is much work to do in the process of assuming a new identity.

While curbing sinful behavior is certainly part of the process of change, walking away from an old, ingrained identity and into a new and sometimes hard-to-grasp identity can be much more challenging than simply stopping unwanted behavior. For the friend, family member, or pastor of someone leaving homosexuality, it's very important to understand this issue and not to look solely at changed behavior as an indicator of a transformed identity. Changed behavior is not necessarily an indicator of the important inward change in the life of the believer. Even a non-Christian can cease certain behaviors for awhile. Men and women may evidence changed outward behavior but be raging with desire in their hearts. Again, for the friend or family member of someone leaving homosexuality, it is important to not look solely at changed behavior as an indicator of transformed identity.

By the way, this search for identity in Christ alone isn't unique to people leaving homosexuality. All people, at some level, are on a quest for true identity. People search for identity in heterosexual promiscuity, drugs, alcohol, work, money, and relationships. Coming to grips with our legitimate identities as men and women in Christ is essentially the same process for all Christians.

However, for many people the source of their false identity is not clearly evident. With homosexuality, the false identity is clear. This false identity, many times, provided the infrastructure for how they formerly lived their lives. The fact that the false identity of a homosexual becomes so integral to who they think they are creates huge burdens as they attempt to turn away from the false identity to embrace a new identity. Once the false identity is accepted, it takes root and is difficult to extract.

For many people who struggle with same-sex attractions, and especially those brought up in Christian homes or within the church sphere, there may have initially been strong internal battles *against* assuming a homosexual identity. The internet and even mainstream bookstores both have a wealth of information labeling same-sex desires as proof that one is homosexual. Strugglers often read and research, trying to figure themselves out. They are bombarded with the lie that their attractions mean they *are* homosexual and that their homosexuality is unchangeable.

When so inundated, these people will often finally decide to embrace this identity that they have fought against for so long. Understandably, there is often an initial sense of great relief. Almost immediately the identity they originally fought forms the foundation of who they believe themselves to be. The gay identity becomes something around which they can build their lives. Further, in this day and age, they have an entire subculture devoted to reinforcing and strengthening that false identity. Almost every gay person will testify that within the gay community they experienced their first true sense of belonging. Gay men or women go to gay gatherings or clubs or churches and think: *These people are just like me. They know my struggles. I am one of them. I belong here. This is* my *community. This is* my *identity.* For the first time in their lives, they actually feel comfortable with who they are.

Because of this depth of identity associated with their feelings, gay-identified people do not distinguish between who they *are* and what they *do*. Thus, the much overused Christian phrase "love the sinner, but hate the sin" simply does not compute for homosexuals. All they hear is the word "hate," because they do not distinguish between what they *do* and who they *are*. Their behavior is indistinguishable from their identity. When a gay person makes the decision to come out of homosexuality, it can feel like he (or she) is losing his very essence.

As people leave homosexuality, they must lay their gay identity at the altar of Christ and accept the new identity He has for them. For many, this is an incredibly difficult struggle. In their wrongly accepted gay identity, they have found some sense of bearing, of direction. When asking homosexuals to come to Christ, in most cases you're asking them to abandon the one thing that finally gave them a sense of who they are. Further, they are well aware that a conversion to Christ will mean leaving a vast support system behind. They face being treated as traitors to the very people who loved and accepted and embraced them. And they're trading that for a completely foreign and unknown support system that they may or may not find in the Christian community.

That being the case, Christians committing to helping someone leave the gay lifestyle must assess the strength of the support system the Christian community is offering. Will the person's new identity take root and flourish in the community of believers...or will he (or she) feel both abandoned by his old friends in the gay world and rejected and misunderstood by the new brothers and sisters in Christ? The healthiness and openness of the person's new Christian community is an important factor of just how successful any "change" will be in the life of the man or woman submitting to the process of change.

Interestingly, just as the term "gay" or "homosexual" indicates a false identity, actually so does the term "ex-gay." The desired change in identity should pull the focus from the sin or struggle with sin and onto the true, fully righteous, fully holy identity bestowed on them via the Cross of Jesus Christ. This concept is *key* for the people leaving homosexuality because it forces them to accept that who they are is not changed or altered by feelings or even actions. They begin to find freedom from untrue definitions of who they are and to accept who God says they are. They discover who they really are in Christ, and they experience true freedom.

Instead of the "ex-gay" tag, which again defines them by their former attractions, they must fully accept that their new identity is not based on their sexuality but on their having been born into God's family.

Changes in Attractions

As the person leaving homosexuality begins to base his (or her) life on his true identity in Christ, and as he or she begins to be free from the untruths on which he based his former identity, he will usually start to see changes in his attractions. Many (but certainly not all) people who have left homosexuality testify to new and amazing desires for the opposite sex. Sometimes the desire is for simple connection and intimacy. Men and women will, for the first time, find themselves longing for a healthy, intimate relationship with the opposite sex in marriage. But again, this is a *result* of being rooted in a new identity, not a presumptuous and hasty choice one just makes. The road to failure in homosexual healing is paved with wrong expectations and presumptions.

For men and women who have *not* dealt with homosexual desires, sexual attraction may be the *first* thing that draws them into a relationship with someone else. But with those who have left homosexuality, the *relationship* itself often comes first. As the relationship grows, new feelings and desires will often grow, as well. At some point, they find themselves sexually attracted to members of the opposite sex for the first time. For people seeking to overcome same-sex attractions who are already married to someone of the opposite sex, the amazing intimacy of a sexual relationship with their spouses is realized for the first time.

As mentioned previously, many times those dealing with same-sex attraction will share that they spent much time praying for "change" as young teens or adults, but that nothing happened. Often these prayers were entirely focused on attractions. The desire of the people praying was not to submit their struggles to the Lord, or to be changed, as much as it was to "have sexual attraction for the opposite sex." Someone once rightly said that God will not replace one lust with another. He does not substitute one sin in exchange for an alternative sin. God changes hearts from the core. Sometimes the outcome is what was asked for, and sometimes it is not.

The first sign of changing attractions for most people dealing with homosexual desires is a decreased desire to interact sexually with the same sex. As the roots of the attractions are uncovered, and as the true relational need is exposed and met by healthy relationships with the same sex, men and women find themselves less desirous of sexual intimacy with the same sex. It's important to realize that lust or temptation can, and often will, still arise. Oftentimes the capacity to be tempted or to lust for the same sex will not completely disappear. However, such temptations no longer dominate the lives of people or control people's behavior. The temptations are dealt with for what they are: a sign of some other problem that must be addressed with the Lord. This reduction in the dominating effect of same-sex attraction is a huge part of the change process, and one that brings incredible freedom and fulfillment.

Sometimes, but not always, a reduction in desire to act out sexually with the same sex will be followed (or accompanied) by a newfound desire *to connect* sexually or intimately with the opposite sex. Often the lack of desire for sexual intimacy with the opposite sex is rooted in childhood trauma, or vows, or other similar experiences. These deep emotional wounds and roots must be uncovered and healed—and that takes time. As these roadblocks to heterosexual feelings are uncovered, feelings for the opposite sex often surface, much to the delight and surprise of many former homosexuals.

Sometimes people question the change in attraction because it doesn't seem to result in a passionate desire or a lust for the opposite sex. Because sexual desire for the opposite sex in those leaving homosexuality most often begins *after* a relationship is formed with someone of the opposite sex, the changes in attraction are not necessarily focused on *gender* as much as they are on the *person*. Married men and women who have left homosexuality often share that they have true, rich desire for sexual intimacy with their spouses, and that their desires arise purely out of their love for their mates, and their desire to connect sexually with the ones they love.

The Process of Sanctification for All Believers

In the big picture, homosexuality is no different than any struggle with sin. Whether the struggle is with gossip, greed, envy, worry, self-hatred, heterosexual lust, hopelessness, hatred, idolatry, or homosexual desires, all Christ followers are the same. As writer John Piper puts it, "In the courtroom of heaven, an ungodly sinner is declared righteous by faith alone!" The righteousness that frees us from the penalty of our sin happens instantly. *But for all Christians, the moral process of sanctification begins at that point.*

The Holy Spirit works change in the homosexual in the same way He works change in each of us. We begin to seek Him and align our hearts with His heart. We desire more and more to live life in accordance with His Word. As our hearts become aligned with His heart, we begin to desire what He desires. He changes us, and we are no longer what we were. We grow in the knowledge and satisfaction of who we *now* are, and no longer desire to live in the pit of a false identity. We become God focused, rather than self focused. We wait on the Lord, and He fulfills us.

There is no magic bullet to "cure" homosexuality. The story of a redeemed homosexual is simply one more version of the story of redeemed man.

The process of sanctification is the journey of living the life God has called us to live. It's the promise of the power of the Holy Spirit for living, and it's the process that grows us into Christ's likeness. John Piper calls it "becoming what you are." It's a fight—and a battle—to become what we are through Christ. For all Christians, the walk to moral purity will last a lifetime and is possible only through the same grace that saves us. Our lack of sin does nothing to justify us before God. For all Christ followers, the righteousness that we receive through Christ should compel us to live as righteous people. The battle against who we were is a tough one, but one worth the fight to win.

For the Christian accompanying someone as he or she walks out of homosexuality, understanding the similarities between your own Christian journey and your gay friend's Christian journey will be a great aid to the progress of your friend. Similarly, an overfocus on homosexual behavior or an air of moral superiority will make things much more difficult for your friend.

Once homosexuality is taken out of a "special" category and put in the company of all sins, the prospect for change doesn't seem as daunting. The reality is that all Christ followers are in the same place—the battle to become who they truly are. The goal for change shouldn't be focused on any particular sin. The goal for change should not be heterosexuality, it should be holiness or, better yet, Christlikeness. Being Christlike has nothing to do with sexual attraction. It means having the mind of Christ, and being focused on living for the Father, and bringing Him glory. For all Christ followers, no matter their affliction, change does happen. The blind are made to see. Lives are transformed.

Part 2

How Welcoming Are We to Homosexuals?

To effectively reach homosexuals for Christ, we must make sure our message comes across as relevant to them. Further, we must help them see the church as a place where sinners of all stripes can feel safe—safe to grow in Christ, safe to become who God meant them to be, and safe to fail. And should failure come, the church is the place where the struggler can be helped up, dusted off, and strengthened against future stumbles.

For that to happen, the church must change. *We must change.*

In the next five chapters, let's consider the "angry church" (as perceived by the gay community) and "angry" Christians. Let's also look at how we can invite those who have had enough of what the homosexual lifestyle offers into the freedom of the church. We'll also discuss putting "first things first" with Jesus as our model as we interact with the homosexual next door.

4

Sinners in the Hands of an Angry Church

Alan Chambers

—⟋⟍⟋—

One night when she was still co-hosting the "700 Club" with Pat Robertson, Sheila Walsh felt impressed to pray for homosexuals. Honoring this divine instinct, she shared Christ's love for them and that He desired a relationship with them. She invited all homosexual and lesbian viewers to pray with her for salvation. When Sheila was finished praying, she encouraged those who had prayed to go to a church in their area, tell the pastor they had accepted Christ into their hearts, and to say, "Sheila Walsh sent me."

Some time later, Sheila received a note from a gay man who had been listening to the broadcast that night. He had asked Jesus into his heart, gone to a local church, met with the pastor, shared that he was gay and about the broadcast he saw. The pastor responded, "We don't have room for fags in this church." In his letter to Sheila after this meeting, the homosexual man shared that he was grateful to her, but that being a part of "The Church" was just not possible.

I have told this story on dozens of occasions, and I still cringe when I think of that poor, honest, broken, searching man who poured out his heart only to get slapped in the face by a pastor with a reckless tongue and an un-Christlike heart. I wish I knew where to find that gay man so I could share with him that not all pastors and churches are like the one he visited. Most of all, I want him to know that God's attitude toward him is markedly different than that of the pastor he spoke with.

Beat Them with the Truth

Like the pastor in the story, we often think that what sinners (the obvious ones outside the church) need is a good verbal spanking from the pulpit. We find a Scripture to share to make it seem as though God Himself wrote it just for the situation at hand. And it's usually not a Scripture that promises redemption—it's one that, out of context, pronounces harsh judgment on the sinner.

In my earlier years I remember sitting silently in the pew listening with fear as the pastor proclaimed, "All homosexuals go to hell." I remember what it was like to hear that declaration backed up with selected portions of 1 Corinthians 6:9-10: "nor *homosexual* offenders... will inherit the kingdom of God." I remember how hopeless that made me feel because, if my thoughts were any indication of who I was becoming, I was one of "those homosexuals."

As a teenager, I struggled in silence with unwanted and, to a larger degree, unacted upon feelings. I felt condemned to hell by a pastor and church that never *once* shared that there was any hope for someone like me. The guilt, shame, and condemnation became so unbearable that I well remember the day I deliberately ignored the stop sign at a busy intersection and sped through it with my eyes closed, hoping that another car would crash into mine and end it all.

Later, as a college freshman, I vowed never to return to the church because it did not have a life-giving answer or alternative for me. All it promised was deeper guilt and no hope for a way out. It was very easy for me—and it's very easy for many gay men and women today—to run bloodied and bruised into the open arms of a gay community that was more than happy to have me, love me, and *save* me.

When you're hurting...do you run into the arms of those who are hurting you or do you run to those who have also been rejected and who promise to accept you as you are?

The Velvet Brick

The kind of judgment I experienced seems to be common to many homosexuals I've spoken to. The irony is that today, all these years later, I can sometimes get so secure in my redemption that even I begin to look at unredeemed people through a colored lens. We must always be careful to remember where we came from and, most importantly, to communicate the truth with the love of Christ.

My friend Dr. David Uth, senior pastor at First Baptist Church of Orlando, regularly talks about this type of imbalance. Dr. Uth uses the analogy of Christians being velvet bricks. The brick is the truth we carry as Christians; the velvet is the grace that the truth or brick is wrapped in. He says that so often we Christians, especially ministers, get so tired and calloused that our velvet starts wearing thin. We become out of balance, and our truth becomes a dangerous weapon. As a result, we hurt the very people we're called to help.

We often see this when Christians or pastors lash out at gay activists, those who have had abortions, or at political leaders with whom we strongly disagree. We attribute societal catastrophes to sinful behavior and speak in anger about our fallen culture. We fail to remember that God still loves His creation, whether or not people love Him back or follow His path for their lives.

As for love—the primary motivation for winning others to Christ—we reduce love to the tired little cliché "love the sinner, hate the sin." We've gotten "hating the sin" down pretty well, but how are we really doing at "loving the sinner"? Far too often I think we forget that "but for the grace of God" we would still be sinners ourselves.

True, at times our anger can be justified. I'm not saying that we shouldn't be concerned at the state of our culture. I'm not saying that getting angry over sin is wrong. On the contrary, if you can turn on the news at night without getting concerned or sit idly by while pro-gay propaganda is being taught to your children in public schools, then there's something wrong.

Anger can be justified. But many in the church take their anger and turn it into hostility. My friend Joe Dallas says it so well: "anger corrects and hostility destroys." Hostility from the church toward gays has done a lot of damage. I know for a fact that one reason for the lack of success in reaching gays for Christ is because the gay community has come to see the evangelical church as its enemy. And, to some degree, that's been sadly true.

In our ignorance we lashed out at homosexuals, ridiculed them, made up jokes about them (yes, I've heard anti-gay jokes from pastors and church leaders—to their shame), and forbade them to darken the door of our holy churches. During the early days of the AIDS epidemic, we proclaimed that dreaded disease was God's judgment for their sin. That's why, in part, many in the gay community hate us. If they want to see churches silenced on the gay issue because of how we've treated them, should we blame them?

Over the next few pages I want to tell the tale of two churches. The first is the church that decided to reach out with uncompromising truth and grace—the church that saved my life. The other church is the one that wants to make grace more important than truth, while the reality is that grace and truth are inseparable parts of the gospel.

Discovery Church

In 1992 I was seeking help to overcome homosexuality. It was a very difficult year. I was fully immersed in sexual sin at that time...but mad at the church for often hating the sin but not loving the sinner. Like so many active homosexuals who fled from the condemnation of the church into the welcoming arms of the gay community, I found out firsthand that the gay life only offered *more* loneliness, deeper desperation, and a slow death.

Thankfully, at about this time, my brother and his wife stepped in and introduced me to a godly church in Orlando that called sin "sin" and yet loved people who felt unlovely. People like me. Here's how it came about.

In May of that year, during a routine visit with my sister-in-law, our conversation turned very personal. Knowing generally that I was in counseling, she asked if I was attracted to the same sex. Completely flabbergasted that she knew, I sarcastically said, "Well, don't beat around the bush!" That brief conversation not only changed my life, it also saved it.

As I sat and shared my anger at the church over its lack of service to people like me, she listened carefully and compassionately. At the same time, she didn't wallow with me in self-pity. She asked if she could tell my brother what I had shared with her, and then she invited me to their church.

I visited the Wednesday evening service at Discovery Church in Orlando, Florida, the following day. I went back the following Sunday morning and again that night. Not only were the messages relevant to me, the people enveloped me. No stranger to those struggling with homosexuality, the people of Discovery immediately clued in that I was fighting for my life in regard to homosexuality. And that made them love me all the more.

Having only attended Discovery Church a few weeks, I remember two bold and loving church members walking into a gay bar on Easter Sunday 1992 to tell me that God had sent them to remind me that He loved me, they loved me, and that they were committed to walking with me on the journey out of homosexuality. Recommitted to obedience, I was restored by that church. *They taught me that change takes more than just pointing the way; change requires grabbing a person's hand and walking with him or her.*

I was a member of Discovery for just under four years. I credit the body of Christ there for saving my life. Literally, I would not be where I am today without them. I speak and write of them often, and even today, more than a dozen years later, the mere thought of how they loved me reduces me to a crying mess. For me, Discovery Church was part hospital and part medical school. I went there lonely, hurting, and desperate. I left commissioned to help spread the message of healing in Christ.

> I found out that God had always loved me as I was, but that He loved me too much to leave me that way.

What was so special about Discovery? From the senior pastor to the men and women who served as parking lot greeters, everyone who set foot on the church property *knew* they mattered to the Lord and to the other people at Discovery.

They weren't wishy-washy about sin either. Sin was called sin, and no one pretended they didn't struggle with it. My sin wasn't overlooked but rather talked about openly in conjunction with every other sin. I learned that I could walk into church with everything out in the open and hold my head up high. I learned that I wouldn't be rebuffed, but embraced. No one ever pointed a finger at me, but hundreds of times I had people take my hand and choose to walk with me on my journey toward wholeness.

I think the greatest thing I learned at Discovery was personal responsibility. I learned that healing and freedom were choices I had to make for myself. I learned that I had to reach out to people even if they didn't reach out to me. Healing depends on healthy relationships, and my healing was my responsibility. I learned to be open and honest with my church family. I discovered that God wasn't embarrassed or ashamed of me, my struggles, or my past—and that my friends at Discovery Church weren't either.

That taught me to never be ashamed of myself. For the first time in my life, I began to be who God created me to be and to love even the broken parts just as He does. I found out that God had always loved me as I was, but that He loved me too much to leave me that way.

I often say that good counterfeit money spends for years. For me, the gay community was an excellent counterfeit to the real life-giving relationships that the body of Christ is meant to model. So many people stay trapped in or go back to gay life because they never find anything better than the counterfeit. I didn't leave homosexuality because it was awful. I left homosexuality because I found something better: the body of Christ. Only in the light of God's best, though, can I truly look back and see how far off the mark homosexuality and the gay community were from the *real* thing!

Today, the most amazingly wonderful part of my ministry is helping churches become places like Discovery, places that reflect the true heart and outreach of Christ. Also I love meeting the pastors and visiting churches that are doing this type of transforming ministry for their communities.

In thinking back on my youth, I sometimes wonder: If my own church had ever offered some small sign that it was safe to admit my homosexuality and receive help, could I have avoided immersing myself in the gay culture at all? I think the answer is yes.

First Church of Sloppy Agape

Sloppy Agape is a growing and unfortunate trend in the mainstream church today. By "sloppy agape" I mean giving grace at the expense of standing on the truth. The Gospel of John is clear in its description of Jesus. He was 100 percent grace and 100 percent truth. He didn't err on one side or the other. He was both—equally. If we are to truly represent

Christ's heart and mind then we must be equally balanced in those two critical areas as well.

In 2004, the United Methodist Church's Pacific Northwest Conference tried and acquitted Reverend Karen Dammann, the pastor of a 200-member Methodist congregation in Washington State, for being an openly practicing lesbian. The 13 members on the jury that exonerated her stated that the Bible *is not clear on the issue of homosexuality,* an argument directly lifted from the rhetoric used by those pushing for homosexual rights. This argument is in stark contrast to official, biblically sound, United Methodist doctrine and to how the majority of Methodists stand on this issue.

Honestly, I'm tired of the phrases, "but Jesus didn't say anything about homosexuality" and "the Bible's prohibition of homosexuality was only meant for that time." I am especially tired of hearing these worldly arguments from those who are or claim to be followers of Christ. Jesus' words were written in the Bible under the supposition that those who read them already knew the difference between right and wrong, between truth and lie. The truths Jesus lived by and the laws He obeyed were reflective of both God's creative intent for humanity and the man-made laws of the time. Homosexuality was not only an abominable practice in God's eyes and an absolute misuse of His design for physical, emotional, and sexual expression, but it was also a crime punishable by death. Jesus did not need to mention this act specifically just as He did not mention incest, bestiality, or spousal abuse. These acts were detestable and well understood prohibitions.

Jesus did, however, make it abundantly clear what He was for. He said in Matthew 5:17 that He did not come to destroy the law but rather to fulfill it. He also affirmed God's best for sexual and relational intimacy in Matthew 19, when He spoke of marriage in the only form that has ever been acceptable to God: between one man and one woman for one lifetime. Jesus may not have literally spoken about the issue of homosexuality, but the Bible clearly does both in the Old and New Testaments. In 2 Timothy 3:16 it boldly states, "All Scripture is God-breathed." God is clear about what He is for and about what He is against, and it is clear that the Bible is His written Word to His creation. And God never changes His mind.

It's time for those who bear the name "church," regardless of denomination, to either remove that word from their name or start truly reflecting and representing Christ's definition of the word. Churches were not designed to be the liberal and passive social clubs that some of them are becoming. God will not be misrepresented, especially not to those who are dying and going to hell for lack of truth.

One of the goals of Exodus International is to equip the church. As an arm of the body of Christ, it's Exodus' goal to serve the rest of the body. At times that means holding up the arms of the body as it proclaims the good news of freedom. Other times it means we are used as a link to other parts of the body in order to work together as a whole. Still other times the Lord might use Exodus to admonish other parts of the body to be more proactive, more graceful, or like in the case with the *small portion* of the United Methodist Church just mentioned, to be more truth focused and representative of God's written Word.

A Burden for the Church

Today, I long for every church to be a living example of God's kindness and tolerance so that many homosexuals (and all kinds of sinners) will come to repentance (Romans 2:4). But I realize that in order for that longing to become reality, we, as the members of the body of Christ, need to continually be reminded of our own desperation prior to coming into a personal relationship with Christ.

We need to admit that we may be ignorant, either by choice or by an honest lack of knowledge, of the issues surrounding homosexuality, such as its roots and causes and what it is like for Christians who struggle with same-sex attraction and want to experience freedom in Christ.

As the body of Christ, we must also renounce our fear and insecurity in dealing with the issue of homosexuality. The existing reality is that homosexuality and those who deal with it exist in our cities, churches, and even some of our own homes. Homosexuality won't just go away. Those struggling *must* be given the opportunity to choose Christ and change if they desire to do so. We must not be afraid to offer the truth in love.

I hope this book stirs the hearts of many Christians and their churches. Perhaps you might be realizing that you have only offered condemnation to the homosexuals you've met or that you have acted out of ignorance, believing that the opposite of homosexuality is heterosexuality—when it actually is holiness.

Maybe you've chosen to ignore the issue completely out of fear of offending or the misguided belief that homosexuality doesn't affect you. *It does.*

Rhea County, Tennessee

In late 2004, I traveled to Rhea County, Tennessee, in response to the county commissioners passing a law that banned homosexuals from living in the county. The story gained national attention. I was invited by the wonderful pastoral association of Rhea County, who hoped I could train them to address this issue redemptively in the media. They also called a town meeting and asked me to share my story and how they, as a town of mostly Christians, should respond to the issue of homosexuality and to those involved in it.

I must say I was a bit nervous to go. I had heard very bad stories about how homosexuality was being handled by many in this area of the country. I knew there were many who absolutely *hated* homosexuals and probably wouldn't look too kindly on anyone who even admitted to having ever had a homosexual thought, let alone lived that way for a period of time. I knew I was walking into a potential mess.

I flew into Chattanooga and traveled about an hour to get to Rhea County. I was met by a number of wonderful pastors, who absolutely shared my heart for those affected by homosexuality. Later I spoke at a luncheon full of pastors, teachers, and local leaders. All the while, I had my eye on a hard-looking woman in the audience, not just because of her bright orange hat and coordinating outfit, but also because she was staring at me with such contempt. If looks could kill...

As soon as I took a breath and offered to take questions, she started in on me. She called me a heretic. She told me I was selling a false gospel. She accused me of being New Age. She condemned me to hell and also everyone else who had ever had a gay thought. "You can't be saved," she insisted.

In the most respectful of vehement rebukes I could muster, I unleashed some righteous anger on her. Thankfully the crowd backed me up. I told her that even from the gay community that truly hates my message, I'd never encountered such venom when I've spoken.

That evening this woman showed up for my town hall meeting. She was verbally quiet, but even in a room of more than 1,000 people her sighs and humphs could be clearly heard. Yes, this woman was an extreme case. But when it comes to the issue of homosexuality, I often see milder forms of this anger and hostility in the eyes, hearts, and words of even the most well-meaning Christians.

Why do people get so angry over this issue? Why do they feel so bitter toward those affected by homosexuality? Aside from the specifics of *their* particular sin, homosexuals are sinners just like everyone else. Have Christians forgotten so quickly what God saved *them* from?

In churches all over the world I've seen pastors and congregations reach out to one type of sinner and sidestep homosexual strugglers. The alcoholic can find understanding, while the homosexual is scorned at worst and heavily scrutinized at best. Overeaters have support groups that meet in the fellowship hall on Tuesday mornings, but God forbid we even think about allowing a group of sexual strugglers to defile the sacred building.

Ironically, we might even be inclined to support AIDS organizations, but we won't address the issues that lead to someone contracting the disease. What are we so afraid of? Fear, I believe is at the heart of our anger. The Bible says in 2 Timothy 1:7 (NKJV): "For God has not given us a spirit of fear, but of power and of love and of a sound mind." I think we want someone else's sin to be uglier than ours. If it is, then that exonerates us to some degree. If someone is worse, more sinful, then maybe that bodes well for us. But a person who believes this doesn't really understand the depth of his or her own sin...or the depth of God's mercy for *all* who have sinned.

Responding in Love Without Compromise

So you are well into this book and maybe by now you're asking yourself, Where is the homosexual next door? Well, maybe not *right* next door. But I would venture to say there is one in your neighborhood, or in the office where you work, or even in your church. And perhaps in your family...and he or she is afraid to let you know.

And even if you know of no homosexuals in any of these places, you surely *do* encounter homosexuals by virtue of your daily activities: that waiter in your favorite restaurant, the drycleaner, the saleslady at the mall, the paperboy....

The truth is that we encounter broken people every day. And when we do, we usually have one of three responses: 1) we don't notice at all; 2) we notice and begin to judge them; 3) we notice but with a shrug of our shoulders and the thought *"Oh well,"* we move on in reckless apathy. Which response fits you best?

Are you response #1—the one who doesn't notice? If so, ask yourself whether that's because you're...

a) too busy

b) detail challenged

c) a truly gracious person who doesn't have a judgmental bone in your body

Regardless of your answer, I challenge you to get up every morning and ask the Lord to give you an eye for people's hearts so you'll *notice* their situations.

I'm not asking you to pray for the gift—or curse—that Jim Carrey's character received in the hit movie *Bruce Almighty*. Bruce thought he could do God's job better than God, and so God gave him a taste by making Bruce the god of his local community. Bruce began hearing people's prayer requests in unison, and it nearly drove him mad.

I don't think you have the capacity to handle seeing/sensing everyone's pain, but you can ask for God to give you one person a day to pray for—whether it's your neighbor or the woman behind the counter at Starbucks.

For those of you who just don't clue in to those struggling around you—the detail challenged ones—I pray you choose to take a closer look. You have no idea how powerful a prayer for someone can be or the impact of a kind word spoken. Who knows, maybe you are the very person God has chosen to minister to the gay man you ride on the elevator with every morning! Don't miss the opportunity for the Lord to use you in the life of someone else. Not only will you miss the blessing of being a minister, but he or she might miss the blessing of eternity.

Or you might be the response #2 kind of person (like me)—one who notices everything and judges it accordingly. God help those of us with this trait. Some call us prophets, others call us plain old mean. It actually hurts me as I type this to think of all those people I've cursed with my judgmental attitude.

The truth is that those who often judge others harshly are actually using the gift of encouragement, discernment, and/or prophecy negatively. I know that when the Lord is in the center of my life and I'm seeking to serve others as Christ did, I have incredible discernment and use that to find people to encourage and pray for.

For instance, last year I was in the Reagan National Airport in Washington, D.C., waiting on a delayed flight to Winnipeg, Manitoba, where I was going to speak at a Focus on the Family Love Won Out conference. I was in the coffee kiosk line, and I noticed a girl in front of me who was very obviously a lesbian. (I'm not being judgmental here, she walked in holding hands with her partner.) And I've been there, so I can usually pick up on these things.

Anyway, I felt the Lord speak very clearly to me that I was to tell this young lady, "God thinks you're beautiful." Oh how I didn't want to do this! I don't always get recognized, but there are days when I run into gay folks who know me and have an incorrect view of me and my work. And I didn't want the girl to think, "So God told you to tell me that He thinks I am beautiful. Why? Because everyone else thinks I'm ugly?" After the inner dialogue with the Lord that went something like, *Okay, God. If she looks to the left and then scratches her head with her right hand, then I will tell her what You told me to say.* That exact scenario played out, so I decided to tell her.

By this time the girl is further away and I have to be more on purpose about walking up to her and tapping her on the shoulder. Argh. So, I finally get next to her, awkwardly look over at her and say, "I am a Christian, and I know this is going to sound bizarre, but God told me to tell you that He thinks you're beautiful. Have a great day." She said thanks with an odd look, and we went our separate ways.

The point is, I could and might have judged her if I'd been in a different mood. I might have thought, *Yep. She's a lesbian...and unless she straightens herself out, she's doomed to hell. Tsk tsk.* But prayer and the heart of God captured me, and instead I spoke a blessing over her. Who knows why God chose that message, but maybe she, like so many women affected by gender confusion, might have always thought of herself as ugly. Maybe her mom or dad or peers called her names as a kid. Whatever the wound, I believe God used fallible little ole me to plant a seed in that girl's life that if watered might grow into a mighty tree!

If you're prone to judgmentalism, I encourage you to pray every morning that the Lord will harness that trait and, instead, cause you to flow with discernment, encouragement, and blessings for others. Imagine the result if you operated that way 365 days a year with one person a day! And as one who knows the joy of speaking a blessing, your life will be radically enriched if you choose to live a lifestyle of building others up.

Okay, that leaves response #3—the apathetic ones. How judgmental did that sound? Sorry, I'm not trying to make one response sound better or worse than another. The broken people we have the chance to speak life to will not receive our message of life in Christ unless we open up to their needs.

So let's say you work out near the same gay man at your gym every morning. You might even acknowledge him with a hello or even a brief conversation. Maybe you spot one another on the free weights. But day in and day out you think to yourself, *He's gay. What am I going to do about it?* And you go about your routine.

Other people's choices aren't your responsibility. And I wouldn't ever encourage someone, outside of the Lord's very specific leading, to just start talking to someone you perceive or know to be gay about the sinfulness of homosexuality. But to think that you can't make a difference—or worse—not *wanting* to make a difference is contrary to our mission as Christians. We are to be the salt of the earth and to make disciples of all people. You must care for those people God puts in your sphere of influence or they will perish.

What can you do to help the struggling people you see only once or interact with often? The truth is you can make a difference simply by being willing and open.

You go to the gym one Monday morning, and you take the conversation one step further with that guy you think is gay. You ask, "How was your weekend?" And he says, "It was great." You might then ask what made it so great—or leave it there for the time being. The point is, you're showing some interest in him as a person of worth. Eventually, you have some rapport with the guy. He gets to know you. And you go from there. Chances are you'll find out that he has some needs, and you can respond by telling him you will pray for him. Better yet, invite him to church or to dinner with your family or to lunch during the week.

Notice I didn't say anything about addressing his sexuality. That's because deep issues are best addressed when you're in relationship with someone. Unless a stranger or acquaintance asks you point blank or invites feedback, I encourage you to wait for the appropriate time to discuss complex issues.

But just shrugging your shoulders and thinking you can't make a difference or purposing not to care because you don't want to or don't have the time is the incorrect response. Everyone needs Jesus, and you might be someone's only shot at finding Him.

Don't miss the opportunity. You won't regret it.

5

Out of the Closet
and into the Church

Randy Thomas

—ᴧᴧᴧ—

In 1991, if someone would have told me that not only would I become a Christian but also become one of those infamous "ex-gays," I would have either laughed in his face or needed immediate coronary care.

Today I can praise God that in His mysterious way, He used ordinary people—probably very much like you—to reveal a spectacular and loving God to me. These people who cared for me were deeply committed Christ followers who challenged my thinking and allowed me to learn for myself about the love of Christ for the homosexual (for me!) and in so doing, revealed the greatest love a human soul can know.

Everyone who knows the love of Christ—from the individual to the corporate church—can minister to homosexuals. That's what the love of God does: It propels the Christian into a hurting world with the healing salve of God's mercy and forgiveness. I can't think of a mission field more in need of experiencing God's grace than the gay community. And almost any Christian who knows the love of God is eligible to share that love by mentoring and reaching out to the struggling homosexual or to our gay- and lesbian-identified neighbors. But to do so effectively there are several very important needs your gay friend has…and these are needs you and your church *can* meet.

1. Unconditional Friendship

The homosexual struggle, at its heart, is a *relational* struggle. God created human beings for a relationship with Him *and* for relationships with others. Most homosexuals search for meaningful relationships and, given the often transitory and conditional friendships available in the gay community, the church is the one place where a gay person should be able to say, "I trust my Christian friends. I know they're concerned about my homosexuality, but I also know that hasn't stopped them from loving me."

This is very important because most homosexuals struggle with profound feelings of always having been "different" from their peers. On the playground in school, in their family, in church, they've always known there was something different about them. And often those differences spelled disaster when it came to relationships. And this began for many in the very early impressionable years when their "friends" at school began to call them names or taunted them for not being just like them. For many homosexuals, it was hard to engage in meaningful relationships…unless some sort of mask was worn.

Is there a person who acts a little "different" in your life? Has this person confessed his or her struggle with homosexuality to you? Are you the sort of person a homosexual can feel free to open up to without fear of rejection, judgment, or denial? Since homosexuality is a relational issue at its heart, the road to healing is a relational road. Caring Christians willing to simply be there for a gay friend are one of the most positive things any church can offer strugglers.

With a relationship established—and growing—some specific needs will soon rise to the surface. These needs may continually occur along the road as you walk with the gay person toward wholeness as he (or she) discovers their new identity in Christ.

2. Overcoming Shame

A second profound need for most homosexuals is the need to overcome shame. How often do you hear of people dealing with homosexuality talk about "coming out of the closet"? You hear it *often*, no doubt.

The problem with this symbol is that it reframes the debate over homosexuality as one of coming out of culturally imposed silence and into embracing the politically correct truth that they are "gay." The homosexual is told, wrongly, that "coming out" is somehow empowering to them. But as said earlier, homosexuality isn't ultimately about identifying with a subculture or naming oneself as gay; it first and foremost is a relational issue. If your loved one has been led to believe that by "coming out of the closet" his problems will lessen, he'll likely soon see how wrong that is. In or out of the closet, the issue is still about overcoming alienation and learning to enjoy stable relationships. And stable relationships in the gay community is practically an oxymoron.

What homosexuals find when they "come out of the closet" is that they were in the wrong house to begin with. The whole premise of "the closet" is one of shame and rejection. Shame and rejection are the true enemies of someone seeking to walk away from homosexuality. Confronting these two issues right off the bat and continuing to guard against them consistently is one of the most important strategies of walking with someone to help them overcome homosexuality.

The most effective way to battle shame and rejection is to look for opportunities to bless and embrace. When the Lord looks on His family, He does not look at them through the lens of where they need help. He looks on them with eyes of love. We must ask Him to allow us to have eyes to see and ears to hear our loved ones dealing with homosexuality. We can invite them to dinner. Ask them honest, open-ended questions on how they are doing each time we have some time with them. We can do little or large things to bless them. Take your friend to coffee or go for a run. Ask him or her to be a part of your life in whatever way the Lord opens the door to do so. You can think of the different ways you have been blessed by others and go out of your way to bless your friend who struggles with same-sex attraction.

3. Trust

Someone who confesses his (or her) struggle with homosexuality will also be in need of someone they can trust. He will want to trust in God and in His people, particularly individuals like you committed to helping him.

Unfortunately, often people dealing with homosexuality are a bit uncertain whom they can really trust. Many have had their trust abused in the past. Some will be skeptical that you're someone they can rely on. If they need accountability in their lives, and they probably do, they will need to know that you—the one to whom they're willing to become accountable—won't abuse that relationship.

4. Motivation

If a person has confessed his struggle with same-sex attraction to you, he is obviously showing motivation to find hope and help. Working with this initial motivation to maintain lasting momentum is key. As mentioned, sometimes a person can be rooted in shame, and this is a very dispiriting place to start.

We must pray for our loved one to be empowered by the Holy Spirit to be motivated by God's love through the atonement of Jesus Christ on the Cross. We must provide hope through God's creative intent for all of humanity and for our friend uniquely. Legalism should be triumphed by grace. Celebration of freedom in Christ will lead to the discovery of a greater love than one presently confined and defined by homosexuality.

Motivation for change must be identified, addressed, and stewarded toward Christ.

A big motivating factor is to celebrate life and relationships. What about God's creative intent makes it the best way to go? Our world is full of condemnation and warning, but God created life to be abundant with joy and peace. I guarantee that if you take a daily inventory of what you are grateful for, it will not only lift your countenance, joy will spill over into the lives around you. Those with same-sex attraction will see that life can be so much more than what being "gay" has to offer. An abundant life fully appreciated and shared will be a beacon of hope to those dealing with homosexuality.

On another level, when your friend receives life-giving friendship and love from you, it undercuts the forces that empower the homosexual struggle. By getting his (or her) relational needs met in holy and pure ways, the relationship deficits are filled and the desire for homosexuality diminishes. Now granted, his repentance is not dependent on your actions, but your relational investment will help him in his pursuit of healthy relationships.

The number one rule is to be consistent in building up and encouraging your friends who are more than "gay." You may not ever bring up the issue of homosexuality in all of your conversations, but by remembering that you are looking to bless and model healthy relationships, you, the body of Christ, and the Lord will work together to disempower your friend's desire to turn back toward homosexuality.

When your gay friend struggles or falls, that's all the more reason to love and to encourage. Of course be honest in all that you do, and do not be afraid to be transparent about your own walk. Think about how you would want to be treated and the grace you need to keep motivated to pursue Christ and wholeness. Exhibit those qualities to your gay friend or loved one.

5. Wise Counsel—*Locally*

I'm going to confess something. Do you know what one of the most frustrating moments is with regard to the phone calls we at Exodus get from pastors? It's when a pastor who has had someone in his (or her) congregation come seeking help and he tells us, "I don't understand homosexuality at all...who do I send them to?"

It's right after the question mark that I have to bite my tongue and assume the best. I mean, the pastor did call, so he must care about the person and at least he's humble enough to admit being ignorant about this issue.

Even so, before I refer them to an Exodus Member Ministry or counselor in his area, I'll take a minute to challenge the reluctant pastor to review his role in light of Christian church history in dealing with this issue.

Exodus has only been around for 30 years. That's a long time with regard to the social movement toward acceptance of gay identity, but in the light of history, it's just a blip. But the church has been made up of transformed homosexuals since the very earliest days. We find in 1 Corinthians 6:9-11 that there were homosexuals in the Corinthian church who had come to Christ. It specifically states that they *were* homosexuals but that they were washed (forgiven), justified (given right and equal standing among the saints before the Lord), and sanctified (ongoing discipleship and mentoring) by the blood of the Lamb (the atonement of Christ on behalf of our sin).

Nowhere does it indicate through a footnote or any other Scriptures that homosexuals were somehow singled out from other converts or sent to the first-century equivalent of an Exodus support group at seven o'clock every Thursday night for the next one to three years.

In other words, while it's wonderful that Exodus International exists today, the Holy Spirit has been using pastoral and Christian counseling for more than 2,000 years to set people free from homosexuality. Church leadership and mentors should not hesitate to counsel someone struggling with homosexuality. It's not a terminally unique sin. The causes and effects of sexual sin might be different, but the path out of it is the same for all sin, and Jesus knows the way. Homosexuality wasn't set apart for special attention back then, nor should it be now.

Yes, it's good to have resources like Exodus to help, but not as a substitute for pastoral and personal care from the local church. The person dealing with homosexuality, like everyone seeking freedom from any besetting sin, needs wise counsel. It will be important to establish this expression of support quickly to help maintain the momentum behind the homosexuals wanting healing and expressing repentance if necessary. If a person is denied counsel because the counselor is uncomfortable with homosexuality, the momentum for change may be hampered.

6. Peer Support Groups and Resources

Exodus International currently represents more than 125 member ministries and is growing all the time. Exodus is the largest network of Christian ministries helping men, women, and families deal with and overcome homosexuality. Today there are also quite a number of excellent books, DVDs, and tapes dealing with homosexuality from a redemptive perspective.

Every church can pray and ask on what level they, as the body of Christ, can provide support to those within their congregations who struggle with or have a loved one involved in homosexuality.

For large churches it may be a great move to develop a peer support group that deals with this issue. That peer-level empathy and accountability is very sharpening and encouraging. For other churches that may not be a possibility. But at a minimum, any church can make these resources available in the church's or pastor's library.

It would a great blessing to wake up some day and realize that Exodus is no longer needed because every church has the knowledge or resources to deal with homosexuals seeking freedom.

7. Equal Treatment and Opportunities to Serve

The local church can also help by encouraging outward service in those who are growing in their faith. In order to truly become a disciple of Christ and be transformed into His likeness, we have to serve. As an elder of the church that I got saved in once said, "If you know Jesus, you have something to give…right here, right now." Granted, at that early point, I wasn't yet encouraged to give my testimony, run a support group, or write a book. Instead I was given the simple task of washing the food that our church handed out to the poor. It was humbling, a little gross, but transformative. It helped me see that life was more than my seemingly overwhelming issues.

> The church is the place for people
> to discover how God sees them as individuals
> as well as how God's creative intent will
> bring them into wholeness.

In fact, when my issues became "overwhelming," it was great to be able to hand out food and get out of myself for a while. The church can help break open the pigeonhole people dealing with homosexuality tend to get stuck in by expecting and enacting equal treatment of those dealing with same-sex attraction and calling on them, along with everyone else, to serve their neighbors as Jesus would…selflessly.

The church has a wide variety of opportunities to work out relationships in a manner consistent with biblical precepts. The church is the place for people to discover how God sees them as individuals as well as how God's creative intent will bring them into wholeness through personal communion with Him and godly interaction with His community at large. Healing can be found in personal reflection, but it will never be fully understood or expressed without interaction with the church and its efforts in the world.

The Church Can Help

Men and women who struggle with the relational issue of homosexuality are struggling with how they see themselves, how they relate to the same sex, as well as their relationships with the opposite sex. This can even affect how they relate to God. The reason why God is so clear about sexual, relational sin is that it can alter the very foundation of how a person interacts with the world around him or her.

The church is a reflection of God's creative intent for relationship with Him and within itself. For our loved one struggling with homosexuality, the church should be a safe haven where he (or she) can learn and realign his identification and relational issues in accordance with the Lord's plan. The Lord speaks to all of us on a personal level, but He will also speak through a church in a way that is unique, empowering, and liberating.

Your Role

Many Christians simply don't realize the amazing impact that unconditional friendship can play in the life of a homosexual. In my own life I wasn't raised in the church and did not like the Christian community as a whole.

I had individual friendships with people who were or became Christians that eventually challenged my established belief system to consider a God that transcended my human feelings and reason. These friends offered unconditional love, a concept I had not ever considered until I met them. These friends were transparent, modeled humility, and extended a particular form of Christlike love—unconditional friendship. If you have a friend or loved one dealing with homosexuality, you don't have to be bewildered or despair. There are some very practical tenets to keep in mind as you continue on this journey with him or her.

Transparency. How many people do you know like it when other people point out their flaws, give helpful advice, and hold them accountable without ever revealing why and how they know all of these edicts and lessons? In other words, how many people do you know like being preached at instead of talked to like a friend? The issue is one of credibility. You may not have ever dealt specifically with homosexuality, but have you ever coveted a relationship that was out of bounds? Have you ever lusted? Envied? Had to confess sin? In other words, why did you need a Savior? What is the depth of your sin? It was the people who were in touch with how much they had been forgiven that could speak to my need for forgiveness, healing, and wholeness. Not only did they have practical advice and tools to share for the journey, they were humble and always talked *to* me instead of past me. One of the best answers that can be given sometimes is "I don't know, but I will find out."

Also, consider that people struggling with homosexuality might learn a thing or two from you but you may also learn a thing or three from them. Do not put it past the Lord to humble you with someone else's wisdom and insight. Never think yourself above the person dealing with homosexuality because the moment you do is the moment you are not useful to him or her.

Relational modeling. Another way you can minister to someone struggling with homosexuality is to model positive, healthy relationships. By modeling our relationships with the Lord and with other people, as appropriate, those struggling with homosexuality will see that they are not that much different in what they desire and hope for in relationships. They can see that relationships are not perfect, and yet when stewarded within the boundaries of God's creative intent and biblical instruction, relationships on varying levels can be extremely rewarding. You can model healthy boundaries with your struggling loved ones as well as share how you approach relationships with the same sex and opposite sex. It can also be very helpful to explain the benefits and appreciation you have for appropriate same-sex intimacy and opposite-sex complementarity.

One tendency with those who struggle with homosexuality that is also represented in all forms of sexual problems is to equate all forms of intimacy with sexuality. A godly Christian who can model effective relational boundaries and freedoms will expand that person's sexualized view of identity and intimacy to a view that is more comprehensively fulfilling. Like the lady at the well, we can model how the living water of

Christ will satiate the soul instead of leaving us relationally dehydrated because of sexual sin.

Unconditional friendship. One of the first things the Lord taught me when I left homosexuality was through the example of a couple of friends around me. He said, "In order to have consistent friends, you must first start being a consistent friend." There were two friends in my life that I knew would always be there whether I was gay, accepted Christ, or whatever. That no matter what, no one was going anywhere because we loved each other enough to fight it out, switch the subject, or just press on until something else happened. See, with these friends, life was much more than my being gay or not. We recognized the vast complexity of each other and connected on more than one level. It was their willingness to meet with me, laugh with me, argue with me that let me know that it was worth being around them. They had the freedom to challenge my thinking and compel me to Christ because they were transparent and modeled healthy boundaries with the obvious fruit of peace in spite of circumstance. These friends showed selfless sacrifice and service. Plus, and I will admit it, I was mean to them! I tested their faith and resolve in any way I could—and yet they didn't run away or preach at me. They loved me with unconditional friendship. They earned the right to challenge my thinking by modeling humility and the love of Christ.

Do not forget the family and friends of those struggling with homosexuality. Often all the attention goes to the person who is actually struggling with homosexuality. Consider that each person dealing with same-sex attraction has friends, family, coworkers, and neighbors. This issue affects a lot of people.

On a Person-to-Person Level, Avoid "Culture War" Issues

One word of caution: The Scriptures state that we should "accept him whose faith is weak, without passing judgment on disputable matters" (Romans 14:1). At Exodus International, we hear stories over and over again of how a loved one or friend confesses his or her struggle with homosexuality, and the person to whom this person confesses gets distracted by what the culture war is saying. Then the person on the listening end seeks to deal with those important but superfluous issues rather than keeping the focus on spiritual issues.

Please do not do this.

Even if the person struggling with homosexuality brings up these "culture war" topics or some current controversy related to homosexuality, we need to be honest but work to keep the focus on what is personally important to strugglers. They must remain focused on Christ's love for them, not on the external world of politics. We all must exercise our civil liberties by voting and speaking out on public policies, but those liberties do not have to be hashed out at the expense of presenting the gospel to our gay-identified loved ones face to face.

At the time of this writing I have been out of the gay life for almost 14 years. I have watched many people who started the process of overcoming homosexuality go back. What a tragedy.

I have seen many stall and sputter in their relationships with the Lord. And I have seen many who have succeeded to the point of living a content and set apart life as a single person (like myself) or to move on into marriage with the opposite sex. Those who continue to grow and heal all have at least several of the traits mentioned in this chapter working in their lives—things like solid friendships with supportive Christians, good local counseling, peer support, and opportunities to get outside of themselves to serve the greater good of the church and the world around them.

To the degree you can help provide these qualities of life to those who struggle with homosexuality, you will be successful in communicating God's grace to the homosexual next door.

6

First Things First

Mike Goeke

———\\\\———

So...how do we reach the gay community? What do we do? These two questions are beginning to be asked within the body of Christ, and that is exciting! More and more, Christians are expressing a desire to see their church minister to the gay community. Across the country, Christians are recognizing that the church cannot simply turn a blind eye toward the gay community and the issue of homosexuality. Believers in Jesus want to make a difference. They want to help people change. They want to see the Lord work and lives transformed.

However, the cultural emphasis on homosexuality and many years of labeling homosexuality as the worst of all sins have caused many

Christians to have a misplaced focus in their desires to reach the gay community. When Christians see homosexuals, they often want to first discuss how to help them "get rid" of the homosexuality.

The sexuality of the person becomes the focus of the outreach, rather than the person himself or herself. But gay people who don't know the Lord are simply lost people, just like anyone who does not know the Lord. The focus in reaching gay people must first be introducing them to Jesus. He will do the rest. He cares more about their souls than He does about their sexuality—and you should, too.

The church has done a marvelous job in evangelizing the unreached people groups of the world. While the gospel is the gospel, we have recognized that in order to reach people, we must understand their culture. We must understand how they think and how they look at life. We must understand cultural and individual roadblocks to their receiving the gospel. Just as we prepare for mission trips to foreign countries, we must prepare for our foray into the gay community.

A couple of things should be noted before we look into the issue of how to share Christ with our gay friends and neighbors. First, the church must realize that, by and large, the gay community does not trust the church and, in fact, may hold serious disdain for the church. Some of that mistrust is based on real-life experience. Historically, the church has not approached the gay community with love and compassion, and it has certainly not seen the gay community as an evangelical target. Church mission programs rarely target the gay community. There are no missions training programs that teach missionaries about the gay culture for evangelism purposes. Instead, as homosexuality has moved to the front burner of culture, the church has responded with more fear and hostility than grace and acceptance. For many gay people, their first exposure to Christianity included signs with slogans such as "God hates fags" or "Turn or burn." One former lesbian said that "if those people were going to heaven, then I wasn't sure I wanted to go." It's not surprising that gay people confronted with this picture of evangelism would see no allure to Jesus Christ or His bride, the church.

Other churches that may have been less vitriolic in their approach to homosexuality were also equally damaging. They weren't necessarily hostile toward homosexuals, but the message shared was only about sin... and never about love and mercy and hope for change. The irony is that many gay men and women were raised going to church—even evangelical churches—but at some point they decided the church didn't have anything to offer them. They were struggling with attractions for the same sex that they probably did not want, yet the church simply called out their sin and offered no viable alternative.

Most gay people can probably remember the first time they heard their pastor preach on the sin of homosexuality from Leviticus 18 or 20, 1 Corinthians 6, or Romans 1, and how they were left feeling that *they* were an abomination to the Lord. The church was correct in calling homosexual *behavior* sin, but as with all sin, God offers forgiveness, restoration, new life, and transformation. Unfortunately, that part of the message for homosexual strugglers was often never heard because pastors rarely followed up the sin of homosexual behavior with the hope for change. Consequently, the church became a place of pain and hurt for many homosexuals. As a result, the homosexual community may well represent the largest unreached people group in the world and possibly one of our largest domestic mission targets.

So back to the questions that began this chapter: What do we do? How do we reach them? Frankly, the church must approach the gay community as it approaches any missions opportunity. Christians must see past behavior that confuses or scares them. They must see past angry gay activists and an agenda that seems to have a life of its own. Christians must see beyond the exterior of homosexuals and look deeper to see the people inside. We must begin to see gay people as Jesus sees them, and we must follow His lead in our evangelism efforts. We must see lost souls for what they are—precious, hurting people in need of a Savior, and our hearts must *break* for their lostness. Our motive must be saved and healed souls, not the sanitizing of our world.

The Person of Jesus Christ

To reach the gay community, we must first introduce them to Jesus, the friend of sinners. He is the source of their hope. He is the answer to the life-dominating sin of homosexuality. We must show them the true and real Jesus—the Jesus who came to preach the gospel to the poor, to proclaim release to the captives, to help the blind recover sight, and to set free the oppressed. We must show them the Jesus who loves them too much to allow them to stay where they are and who promises them a life of *abundance*.

How Would Jesus Approach the Gay Community?

The gay community may well represent the modern-day embodiment of the lepers and tax collectors and prostitutes of Jesus' day. Even those with the smallest of biblical knowledge will remember that Jesus was scorned for spending time with what were considered the "worst" sinners and the most "unclean" people of His day. But Jesus was determined to focus on those who had the deepest need of Him. As He said, He was sent not for the healthy, but for the sick. He had little tolerance for those who failed to see their own need for a Savior (like the Pharisees)—or in our present-day vernacular, those who failed to see their own brokenness. *Jesus hung out with sinners.* He dined with prostitutes and tax collectors. He interacted with adulterers and harlots. He touched those who were ravaged by socially unacceptable disease. And He simply loved them. He listened as much or more than He talked, and His compassion for them and His understanding of their hurt was clear.

If we are to reach the gay community with Jesus, we must do the same thing. A simple scanning of the gospels gives a good picture of several attitudes and actions that characterize Jesus' way of relating to those who did not know Him and who were lost in their sin.

Jesus routinely broke religious and cultural boundaries. Jesus healed people on the Sabbath, He entered the homes of undesirable people, and He spoke publicly to people the religious leaders ignored. He sacrificed tradition and reputation for the sake of the lives He sought to impact. He shocked the established church and became the object of great disdain and judgment. Jesus simply didn't suffer self-righteous people. Gay activists are correct when they note that Jesus spoke out most vehemently against the self-righteous. He calls out sin, but He stands up for the sinner and speaks out against the self-righteous and the judgmental. For the modern church to impact the lives of homosexuals, it too must see sin as sin and look inwardly even as it observes the sins of the world.

Jesus began His interaction with sinners by loving them first. He loved them and wanted to get to know them. He listened to them before He called out their sin. He met people at their point of need first, whether spiritual or physical, without regard for their state of repentance or purity. He thwarted the stoning of the adulterous woman even though she had clearly engaged in sinful behavior. He didn't assess first whether she had a repentant heart or whether or not she might commit adultery again before stepping in and rescuing her from the judgmental throng. Zacchaeus was desperately curious to see Jesus. Jesus didn't condition His time with Zacchaeus on whether or not Zacchaeus was repentant. He called him by name and invited Himself over for supper! While the religious people grumbled, Jesus fellowshipped with Zacchaeus, and the simple presence of Jesus caused Zacchaeus to repent and make restitution before Jesus even *has* to confront him! Jesus built relationships with sinners. Jesus, being Jesus, had quicker relational success than we might have, but His example in getting to know people and letting them see Him is vital for our evangelism efforts.

Jesus physically touched people. He wasn't afraid to get dirty. He touched lepers, blind people, bleeding women, and prostitutes. Physical touch was Jesus' physical manifestation of His love for people. In His day, it was considered unclean to even be in proximity with such people. His own disciples often tried to keep those people away from Him. But Jesus not only didn't avoid those people, He sought them out. And His touch healed them—physically and spiritually.

Jesus offered people something better than their sin. He pulled the attention away from their sin, actually, and focused them on what He could give. He told the woman at the well that He had living water, and then He offers her Himself, and she worships Him. After He saved the adulterous woman from being stoned, He offered her freedom from condemnation. After the harlot anointed His feet, He forgave her sin and saved her for eternity. While He healed many people of their physical ailments, He often indicated that the forgiveness of their sins was the true gift, even more so than the physical healing they so desired. He gave Zacchaeus His friendship, and Zacchaeus realized on his own that a relationship with Jesus was more valuable than the money he wrongly collected from people.

To reach the homosexual community, we must offer them something better than their sin.

How Do We Love Them Like Jesus?

Sometimes it is difficult to look at the life of Jesus without picturing the white robed, bearded, hands raised, glowing guy walking barefoot through dusty, ancient villages. When our view of Jesus is limited to Bible picture-book representations of Him, it can be hard to put His example to practice in our modern-day world. But Jesus' own examples provide us with several practical tools in reaching our gay and lesbian neighbors.

First, please understand that you have permission to love your gay friends or family members. You have *more* than permission, you have a mandate from the Lord. Many people have been so confused by the messages they've received from the church that they feel guilty for loving someone who is gay. True love is what will draw people to Jesus!

> If you're struggling with loving someone who is gay, the answer is to pray.

What does it mean to love them? It means that our souls must *break* for their hurt, for their pain, for their brokenness, and for the state of their souls. We must truly love them. If the Christian community simply goes through the motions, or acts out of a motive other than love, the homosexual community will not be fooled. Our motives must be pure. If we seek to "change" them for our benefit, we will fail. As Christians, we are called to love them and to show them Jesus. Jesus and the Holy Spirit do the work of cleansing.

And sometimes gay people are unlovable. In fact, sometimes Christians are unlovable. We are *all* unlovable at some time or another. God doesn't call us to love only those for whom it is easy for us to love. We're not called to share the gospel with those who are easy to love. We're called to sacrificial love, to love in the same way Christ loves us.

Jim Elliot, the martyred missionary to Equador, refused to defend himself with a gun when attacked (and ultimately murdered) by the very people to whom he was ministering. He said, "I am ready for heaven, but they are not." We must love with that sort of sacrifice. It's okay to admit you don't love in this way, but it's not okay to stop there. If you're struggling with loving someone you know who is gay, or if you are struggling with loving gay people in general, the answer is to pray. God *will* honor the honest and heartfelt prayer for love. Often He does so by showing us our own sense of unworthiness and by giving us glimpses of the magnitude of His own love for us. Sometimes He does so by showing us how much *He* loves gay people, and how our lack of love is painful for Him.

Building Relationships

Like Jesus, we must build relationships with gay people. We must earn the right to speak into someone's life. Christians are not in a place of positional leadership. We have not been placed in a position that requires our gay neighbor to listen to us and do what we say to do. We must *earn* that right.

Sit down and talk with your gay acquaintances. Ask them questions. Find out about their families and their desires and their likes and dislikes and hobbies and dreams. What was their childhood like? Do they have siblings? Do they have pets? Are they educated or creative or artistic or mechanical? What was high school like for them? Be ready to open up and share with them about yourself. Take risks and be vulnerable. The truth is that Christians have a reputation for being too surface oriented. Christians also have a reputation for putting on masks that hide their real selves. Share a struggle with them. Share a burden. Share your joys. Be their friend.

As Jesus did, invite them into your world. Yes, that means your home. Most gay people don't wear leather chaps, studded vests, or dress like drag queens. Most gay people are kind and thoughtful and caring, and most are perfectly sociable. You must protect the sanctity of your home, but the truth is that in many cases, gay people will be better houseguests or dinner guests than anyone else.

This is a way to touch them. If they know you're a Christian, they probably aren't expecting to be invited onto your turf. Invite them to family outings, or plays, or your kids' activities. Show them you're not afraid of them, nor are you disgusted by them. Invite them to your church. Walk into your sanctuary proudly with them, no matter what kind of church you go to. Church is to be a haven for the sick. If your church isn't "that kind of church," then do your part to make it one. Introduce your gay friends to your Christian friends. Let your gay friends see that you're glad you're with them.

Meet the needs of your gay friends or any gay person in need. Visit them at the hospital. Take them food when they are sick. Help them out financially if they need it. Offer to help them fix something at their house. Invite them to spend a holiday with your family.

Many gay people have been ostracized by their own families and are alone at the holidays. Don't let a gay friend spend a holiday alone under your watch. Be a caregiver at an AIDS clinic, or if you know someone with HIV/AIDS, aggressively pursue ways to minister to them in their illness. Rick Warren's wife, Kay, says that Jesus never asked a sick person why they were sick before He healed them—and neither should we.

Stand up for gay people. The church and conservative Christianity hasn't been a safe, welcoming place for homosexuals. Oftentimes pastors and youth leaders make insensitive remarks about homosexuality or gay people. These remarks can be devastating. When you're a witness to unkind words, or a judgmental attitude, or hate, stand up for gay people. Boldly and graciously confront injustice and hatred. Jesus always stood up for the sinner, and we should as well.

At some point, we must share our faith with our gay friends. We can love them, we can make them comfortable, we can stand up for them and meet their needs and let them into our world, but if we don't share Jesus with them, they will remain as lost as they ever were. Share your own story, and let them know the source of the love you have for them. Let them know your "before" story and the way the Lord changed you. Testify of the hope you have, and the reason for that hope.

Other Forms of Evangelism

There are many different ideas on how best to evangelize the lost. Evangelizing the gay community is no different. What works for you may not work for others. We are each wired for different forms of evangelism. As you pray for opportunities, pray for God to clearly show you who and where you should go in your efforts. Some churches and individuals have had success in their attempts to interact with homosexual people in predominantly gay settings, such as gay pride parades and gay bars. The conventional wisdom of those involved specifically in ministry within the realm of homosexuality is that such efforts are not overly effective. Most people leaving homosexuality express the impact of someone they had a relationship with, not the impact of large-scale evangelical outreach specifically to the gay community. Gay people will look with skepticism on most overt evangelical efforts. However, if God leads you that way, then you should obey the call. We may simply be called to plant the seed. And any purely goodwill extension of love to the gay community cannot hurt.

While Jesus socialized with sinners, there is no evidence that He frequented their dens of iniquity. Evangelizing in gay bars is probably a bad idea for most people. For someone who has dealt with same-sex attraction or has had issues with alcohol or drugs, a gay bar is absolutely not a safe place to be.

Other Issues

Sometimes Christians worry about getting too close to a homosexual out of fear that the gay person might become attracted to them. There is a chance of this happening, but the chance is small and is certainly no reason to avoid gay people. For the person building a relationship with a gay person, the key is to do your best to foster a healthy friendship. Look for signs of emotional dependency or codependency. If you see such signs, address them with your friend. Set appropriate boundaries. You may be the first heterosexual person to pay any attention to them, and it may mess with their emotions and attractions. Do not be afraid to ask questions and to clarify your relationship. They expect you to run away at some point. Prove them wrong.

Some people express concern that if they get too close to a homosexual person, the gay person's homosexuality might somehow rub off on them. Hopefully, this book has shown you that you cannot catch homosexuality, and that homosexuality cannot be forced on someone. Homosexuality is a deeply rooted issue. However, we may all be prone to emotional or relational enmeshments or attachments. Always be sensitive to these sorts of issues, and set appropriate boundaries.

Conclusion

While it may scare us, and while we may want a speedier fix, we must share Jesus if we are to truly offer homosexuals something better than their sin. The goal of the Christian community for homosexuals should not be heterosexuality. It should be changed lives through Jesus Christ. Jesus will deal with their homosexuality.

Homosexual feelings run deep. These people did not choose their attractions, and most gay people cannot fathom being different than they are or finding satisfaction in anything other than same-sex relationships. The power of the Cross is the only thing big enough to lure them away from what they know so intimately and have come to rely upon so deeply. Has your life been transformed and changed by Jesus? Make sure your gay friends know that. Tell them how they can experience the same transformation.

In all likelihood, Jesus would not have hesitated to be seen with gay friends. He reveled in building relationships with *all* sinners. As they probably were then, modern-day homosexuals are the outcasts of the religious establishment. They are often the objects of unjustified fear and loathing and miseducation. They are Jesus' kind of people.

The gay community is ripe for evangelism. The church has barely even planted seeds of salvation. The healing starts today—and it starts with you.

7

Understanding the Three Degrees of Homosexuality

Randy Thomas

—◊—

When I had been out of homosexuality for three years, I helped man a booth for a local Exodus ministry at a conference. At one point a very rough-looking but sweet-spirited man from a booth representing an inner-city ministry came over to our booth. I had heard him share his testimony several times to people who would stop by their booth. This man used to be a gangbanger and drug dealer and just about everything else that went with gang life.

I could tell that he didn't know how to read because he humbly refused the information I offered him and instead asked me to share

with him what our ministry was about. I read to him our mission statement, and his eyes got as big as saucers, "Jesus can do *what?*"

I said, "He can help us overcome homosexuality."

This hardened man's face literally shown with awe, and he asked,
"Were you set free from *that!*"

I said yes and this man stopped dead in his tracks, started weeping with joy, and exclaimed loudly, "Praise You, Jesus! Man, Jesus can
do anything!"

I just smiled and said in between his exultations, "Why yes...yes,
He can."

I marveled that here was an ex-gang member who had seen more
real-life violence than I could possibly imagine, and he thought it was
a miracle that *I* had been set free from homosexuality and that entire
ministries could exist to help others do the same.

Why is it so hard for some people to believe that people who struggle
with homosexuality can turn and walk away from that identity and
behavior through the power of Christ? Perhaps it's because people don't
understand that a loving God isn't afraid of the homosexual. Indeed, He
comes to us, invites us "home" with Him, and we follow...just like everyone else who has accepted Christ as Savior and Lord.

Even so, there are some interesting dynamics to consider. It's important, for example, to understand just where the person you're concerned
about is in his or her homosexual life. Joe Dallas, author of several excellent books on overcoming homosexuality, identifies three different
groups of homosexuals: repentant, moderate, and militant.

The following thoughts are based on Joe's excellent framework.
By teaming up with Joe in this manner, it's my hope you'll gain some
understanding of how the homosexual in your life feels about his or
her gayness.

Repentant

These homosexual people are really caught between a rock and a hard
place. On one hand, they have the gay community completely embracing

and condoning their sexuality as something they can't change. On the other hand, they must deal with the traditional message from the Western church that homosexuality is worse than other sins.

It's as if the world says, "You can't change, so embrace it" and some conservative circles say, "You are a pervert worthy of forceful opposition and in some cases even derision." Those homosexuals who consider their same-sex attractions as unwanted (and there are many such people) are left somewhat in the middle of these two opposing groups. Do they go for the solace of the actively gay community or do they shrink into the church woodwork and never reveal their struggle to a church that doesn't attempt to understand their struggle?

> I didn't become a Christian to not be gay.
> I became a Christian because Jesus made sense.

There is a wide variety of people who fall into this first category. We have people who were raised in church, backslid for a while, and then seek to come back. We have people who have struggled with their thought lives and private sin (such as pornography) and seek to throw off those shackles. Then we have people like myself whom the Lord went into the gay community and quite literally rescued. They had no idea who God truly was and yet He went to them anyway and brought them home and set up residence in their hearts.

To be honest, when I first began the journey out of homosexuality I didn't even like Christians, even though I had just become one. I didn't become a Christian to not be gay. I became a Christian because Jesus made sense. A few months after accepting Him as Lord, His Holy Spirit did a work in my heart, and I knew beyond a shadow of a doubt that I had heard from God and that I would never be gay again.

It took a while, but eventually I repented of my rebelliousness toward the church and received healing for some of the very real wounds inflicted by some of its members.

In the beginning it was very difficult. Church culture and the gay subculture were night and day from each other. I was the only one in my local Exodus ministry that I knew who had actively been a barfly and not raised in the church. I used to tell people all the time in those early years that the fact that I was studying Jonah and singing worship songs on Friday night instead of being high on XTC and dancing on top of a box in some dark bar proved that change was possible! As you will hear often in Exodus circles and maybe even more than once in this book… the opposite of homosexuality is not heterosexuality—it's holiness.

Holiness is something that the repentant homosexual will be hungering for. What I've seen and learned over the years is that if the goal for a repentant homosexual is heterosexuality, you might get some lasting behavioral change…but it will be accompanied by a lot of rules not empowered by grace.

If, however, the goal is to lay down the lesser love of homosexuality and embrace the greater love of Christ's atonement, His grace is what empowers every repentant homosexual to take the next right step in their journey toward Christlikeness. The goal is not to become "straight" or to glow like Moses after he had been in the presence of God. The goal is simply the journey itself…and that journey leads to falling deeper in love with Jesus every step of the way.

Some repentant homosexuals come to Christ with at least a basic understanding of God, His principles, and Christian culture. Other repentant homosexuals, like myself, don't even know the depth of what true "Lordship" means, even after asking Jesus into our hearts. The trick isn't to assume that since a homosexual wants to repent, he or she has a secure foundation in Christ to maintain that repentance. Each one must be treated with due respect and attention to where he or she truly is, mind, body, and soul.

One pitfall I see repeated far too often with repentant homosexuals is that they are often propped up to give their testimonies far too quickly. It's understandable why some churches do this. The people reaching out see the work of God in the lives of homosexuals. They watch people be transformed. They see miracles happening and want the saved people to begin sharing or showing others how to have a similar experience.

What's especially appealing is that we live in a culture fascinated with sensational news, shows, concerts, books, internet sites, and on and on. Homosexuality is one of the more sensational moral conflicts going on. This one issue grabs the attention of church-goers. So when a homosexual renounces the worldly messages regarding being gay and begins to embrace God's intent for his (or her) life, it can be a stark testimony to the power of God.

This is all well and good, but the problem is that if one combines this testimony with an overly zealous, eloquent, young-in-their-faith (and/ or repentance) speaker who hasn't resolved major inner issues they may not yet be aware of, they are a disaster waiting to happen.

The Bible warns us in 1 Timothy 3:6 that recent converts should not be raised up before others lest they become conceited and suffer in the same way as the devil. Repentant homosexuals are often neglected or shortchanged when it comes to mentoring or discipling for the long haul. Instead, the sensational aspect of their deliverance is seized upon and even exploited. Such rashness will ultimately add to their burden instead of liberating them to where they need to be.

People repenting of homosexuality should be treated with the same level of respect and compassion as anyone dealing with a lifelong, besetting sin. At the same time, they should be showered with grace and empathy in what it means to overcome sin. Homosexuality is very complex because human sexuality is very complex. If "Stop it!" therapy didn't work for you in your sin, you can see why it will not often work with homosexuality either.

> The truth of the matter is God doesn't see a bunch of walking, talking sexualities. He sees walking, talking sons and daughters.

Coming out of homosexuality doesn't mean coming out of temptation.

For many, those temptations remain to a varying degree. But temptation itself is not sin, and we often forget that temptation is as much an
opportunity for righteousness as it is for sin. In other words, same-sex
attractions are what we work through by taking every thought captive
to Christ (a daily choice and sometimes a moment-by-moment activity); actions of heart and/or body are what require repentance. That is
rarely easily evidenced in a newly repentant homosexual.

Praise God that people want to walk away from homosexuality, and
we Christians are ready to meet them wherever they are at. Repentant
homosexuals need daily contact with mature Christians who understand
walking through the fires of temptation and coming out unburned.

Clearly mature believers need only to know how to walk with people
through their struggles, and not necessarily have known the homosexual
struggle themselves. In the kingdom of God, the economy of who needs
help and wholeness is the same for everyone. The truth of the matter is
God doesn't see a bunch of walking, talking sexualities. He sees walking, talking sons and daughters. The ground at the foot of the Cross is
level—no one is superior or inferior in that humble place.

Fellowship and Prayer

As with all Christians, fellowship and prayer are crucial. Repentant
homosexuals don't need more or less prayer and fellowship than anyone
else. For the repentant homosexual, the joy of entering into prayer and
fellowship will satisfy them and you at a core relational level, provide
opportunities to test their wings with other believers, and short circuit
any negative fuel that would have pointed them toward homosexuality in the past.

You don't have to have a doctorate in sexual and identity issues to
invite a repentant homosexual to help weed your yard, feed the poor,
pray for a loved one in the hospital, or simply share the absolute worst
joke you have heard over coffee. People are people, and we all need
prayer and fellowship.

As ironic as it was to watch an ex-gangbanger drug dealer weep over my testimony, today I realize he and I are in no way different. We both were wrapped up in our own little worlds with our own little identities and communities. We both trusted in self-sufficiency, and we both were hostile to God's presence and people at one time.

Today we both love the Lord Jesus, and His Spirit, along with His people, met us exactly at our point of need without shame or condemnation. That was our "Big Bang" moment, the moment where our little self-sufficient worlds were cast aside to embrace a much greater universe of possibility.

Moderate

"Did you know I was a lesbian?" the late 20-something beautiful woman asked me. I had just told her that I had walked away from homosexuality a couple of years earlier. She was asking me the question about her being a lesbian because she thought that I had known and was revealing this about my own walk to maybe drag her along for the ride.

I assured her that I had no idea she was a lesbian, and I only shared what I shared because I talk too much. This young lady was not "Barbie" beautiful, but she was striking nonetheless. She sat next to me in a second-year, college-level English literature class. We would team up together to challenge our professor's crazy views and interpretations of literature. One day over lunch we spent a long time discussing Joseph Conrad's *Heart of Darkness*. We truly had a fascinating discussion over the symbolism and imagery found in the story and decided to do our class presentation on the book together.

It was during our time of preparation for this event that we disclosed our sexual orientations to each other. She never asked me about my life, never put me down, didn't cancel our agreement to do the presentation. We laughed, enjoyed each other's friendship, and talked and talked and talked about everything. Her partner invited me out with them to grab a beer, but I politely declined.

This couple was like many gays or lesbians you might meet. They may not necessarily agree with the morality or social issues that face them, but they pretty much adopt a "live and let live" approach. They considered themselves "married" even though the state didn't license them. They had their own "spiritual" journey, and they had a very secure financial setup.

Perhaps to your surprise, I can say that most people who identify as gay or lesbian are like these women. They understand, like most reasonable people, that in this day and age people can rant and rave about homosexual issues all they want, but chances are that if you're openly gay-identified you won't come to harm but find a great level of tolerance if not complete, outright acceptance. Most moderate homosexuals are grateful to live in the United States and will challenge the gay establishment's "groupthink" regarding gay activism. Many are also mortified by what the militant gay activist community proposes on behalf of everyone else in the gay community.

Indeed, many moderate homosexuals will agree that leaving homosexuality is possible but will say, "I just don't feel the need to do so." It's with this group that I get the most constructive feedback regarding the "ex-gay" message. Even when I say or do something that will get moderate homosexuals angry, they're usually civil and willing to not only share their views but honestly listen to my view as well.

Of course it goes without saying that I would love for them to see my point of view to the extent that they embrace Christ and turn away from the gay life. I also understand that they would love it if I would find a good man and go on a double date. These kinds of hopes are understood but not imposed. We understand that every human has worth to God and is deserving of dignity and that we should all live in peace with one another, laugh over coffee together, and shop in the same stores.

With moderate homosexuals I've found it most appropriate to meet them on common-ground issues. Like the lady I just mentioned. The moment I shared with her in the process of due time (not as a manufactured or pressured confession) that I was an "ex-gay Christian," she knew beyond a shadow of a doubt my beliefs on faith and sexuality. I didn't have to spell it out for her. I allowed her to test my tolerance when she began to share about her partner.

Essentially I felt no discomfort talking to this woman or her. I felt no pressure to make sure they believed like I believe. I truthfully told her that I didn't feel uncomfortable at all around her because of our differences and if she ever wanted to talk about my point of view, and vice versa, that I hoped we could do so respectfully. She agreed. I met her and she met me on the common ground of our school project. It was there that we enjoyed our friendship, and it never went beyond that. I must rest in the fact that my Lord is bigger than I, and He will watch over and guide her in His timing to His truth. I know the Holy Spirit… and His name is not Randy.

This is the key to working with moderate homosexuals. Love them, be as much a part of their lives as they'll allow you, and let them become as much a part of your life as you feel comfortable, without compromising the truth of the gospel.

Ask the Lord to reveal to you an honest, common-ground issue that you share with moderate homosexuals. Ask Him to reveal to you their giftings and areas that you can work together in honesty to accomplish goals that are mutually beneficial and sacrificially selfless on your part. If you notice, in this paragraph I have used the word *honest* two times. Honesty *is* the best policy. Do not manufacture open doors—that would be manipulation. However, if there is an open door for friendship and combined interests, don't be afraid to walk through. Remember, life is more than this one gender-related issue, and the moderate homosexual understands this.

Militant

At the Boston Love Won Out Conference, held in November 2005, there was a protest outside of the downtown church hosting the event. There were 15 to 30 protestors all day, but around noon things got a little scary.

At that time an anti-war march was scheduled to go right past the church. The organizers of the gay protest connected with the anti-war protest, and the throng of people (around 1,500 to 2,000) stopped their march to chant anti-ex-gay slogans. The leader would yell into a bullhorn "Intolerant churches!" and the crowd would respond "Shut it down!" "Focus on the Family and Dr. Dobson!" "Shut it down!" "Gay hatred!" "Shut it down!"

After about a half hour or so of this, the anti-war protest moved on, and the number of protestors dwindled to a mere handful by around four o'clock. My ex-gay friends and I have seen a lot of protests and vandalism. We have been the subjects of many a smear campaign and even received threats to our person, livelihood, and families. However, as I stood outside on the sidewalk with several other ex-gay leaders, my already broken heart was rent with bittersweet understanding. The Lord spoke to me in a profound way, and my hope is that I can convey what I sensed God showing me so that you don't become hardened and see "militant" homosexuals as anything other than real people with real lives and opinions. Each person is known to God by name.

If there truly is a "gay agenda," it's found in the very small, often affluent "militant gay activist" crowd. I say very small because, again, I think most who identify as gay or lesbian are more moderate and think the militant crowd is as unreasonable as the militant conservative activists.

Even so, this small militant crowd is very clever and powerful. They have moved beyond the days of simply wanting people to tolerate what they may not personally accept. They want to force acceptance of homosexuality and punish anyone who will not adopt their pro-homosexuality ideology.

It's very difficult to maintain civil conversation with this group of people and very tempting to fight back in like manner.

Very tempting.

Yet we don't fight as the world fights. And it *is* possible to make our points without getting dragged into a heated battle. Here are some tips.

Keep your yes a yes and no a no. If you're asked hard questions by someone who is volatile and full of emotion, you can simply say with a smile, "I don't know, but I'll find out." Don't be pressured to respond in kind or to come up with off-the-cuff answers that won't ring true to someone who might be more versed in the topic than you are.

If you *do* have a response, keep it simple. Most of the teachings of Christ are simple and direct, with a compelling point to think on long afterward. Jesus very rarely allowed the Pharisees to actually frame His response by the way they asked the question. You can do the same with the militant crowd.

Once you have given a response, it's likely that a preformulated, gay-activist talking point will be thrown right back at you. It's okay to simply restate your original answer and stick to that. Believe me, it turns into a quagmire quickly if you allow the militant homosexual to orchestrate the direction of the discussion.

Only veer into a new angle of the conversation if you feel the Lord is wanting you to witness to a particular subject the other person has brought up.

Sometimes it's okay to speak up…with strong conviction. There are times that in order to obtain credibility you have to say it like it is.

One young man in his early twenties emailed me after I lobbied for the defeat of a Hate Crimes bill that would add sexual orientation to the list of protected classes. After a lot of not very flattering speech, he basically said that since I had not "walked in their shoes" I should shut up about hate crimes statutes. I responded by saying that as a 37-year-old man I had lived life a little bit longer than he had. At his age I had been beaten mercilessly for being openly gay. The police came, took the word of my attackers, and never asked me a single question. They didn't file a report, and they even left snickering.

I also shared with the young man that I wasn't raised in the church, I was once very proud to be gay, and that I hadn't come to the conclusions I live by today through whim and fancy but through many tears, prayers, and critical review.

Walk in his shoes? I was walking, dancing, running in those shoes before he even knew he had a sexual orientation. I didn't hear back from the young man for a couple of months, but when I did he thanked me for my direct response because, as he put it, "It woke me up." He had been lapsed in his faith and emailed me to let me know that even though he wasn't quite sure I was right, he was going back to church.

And that is just fine with me ☺.

Back in my gay days, we used to say, "We're here! We're queer! Get used to it!" But now I've been known to say to gay activists, as gently as possible and with a genuine smile on my face, "I'm here, I'm not queer… anymore…whether you get used to it or not."

The thing to keep in mind isn't to speak out of unrighteous anger but out of a genuine spirit of humility to address the person where he or she is at. Being direct with relevant testimony isn't only appropriate, but it's often more honest than the pat answers we sometimes offer up, which gay activists count on us giving. I actually had a gay activist thank me for not playing around with Christianese lingo as I went toe to toe with her. I said, "Don't thank me. I'm still on a mission to change your mind and hope to make you smile at the same time."

Silence Is Also an Option

The Lord was silent for much of His trial before Pilate. As witness after witness bore false testimony against Him, He sat there silently. The Lord spoke when the Father told Him to speak. He said what He needed to say, no more no less.

Often conversations with militant gays quickly move past civil discourse into personal attacks. They'll either claim to be personally attacked by you or attack you and/or your thinking directly. It's at this point that I try to remember to keep my yes a yes and no a no, but also to set some strong boundaries on what I will allow and what I won't respond to.

At times my more public detractors will say outright lies on purpose in an effort to draw attention to themselves and try to draw me into a battle. I don't take the bait, and it is okay to not entertain these futile arguments. They are modern "stumbling" blocks for unbelievers, and while I can't stop others from creating them, I will not reinforce their efforts.

The important things to remember when dealing with militant homosexuals are to know your boundaries ahead of time, remember you can be completely human and not know everything (unless you are called to be an apologist or debator), and be humble enough to admit any potential mistakes and apologize if you feel the need to do so. Make sure you're not operating out of false guilt or unrighteous anger; that you're acting out of compassion and can actually see and listen to the people in front of you instead of arguing past them by reciting talking points.

Just like with anyone, a militant homosexual is more complex than one issue, and more often than not he (or she) will respect anyone who seeks to serve him in humility.

Now, back to the Boston situation. As the crowd assembled in front of the church, a very heavy burden, as if Christ Himself hovered over the street, impressed itself on my soul. I prayed, "Jesus, where are You?" and I noticed the snow that had been spitting started taking on the look of a genuine snowfall.

I looked to my friend Dawn and said, "I think the Lord is saying something through the snow..." and right then the crowd started its chant and the snow started drifting down heavily in a perfectly choreographed moment in time that my mind will never forget.

Amid all the chants of "Shut it down," obscene finger gestures, name calling, and pure hatred, I felt the love of the Lord so strongly I can only compare it to the different times in my life where He wanted to make sure I knew He was there. I felt immobilizing awe as He revealed to me His love for every soul on the street. The Scriptures state in Isaiah 1:18, "'Come now, let us reason together,' says the LORD. 'Though your sins are like scarlet, they shall be as white as snow; though they are red as crimson, they shall be like wool.'" This surprise Bostonian snowfall (the first of the season and one that literally covered the city from border to border) fell over a crowd of jeering protestors. It was as if the Lord was inviting them to reason with Him, and they were rejecting that opportunity.

God's people were before them, offering a well-reasoned testimony of change, and just like the mockers who stood at the foot of the Cross, the protestors jeered and cursed. With God's testimony right before them and His grace coming down around them, they were blinded by pride and deafened by their own mocking hatred.

Even so, God showers His love down on them, allows them the very breath they used to curse His people and His work in them. The love I felt from God to them that day was overpowering. Instead of being repelled by the ferocity of the militant gays, I can see my Lord running toward them with tears in His eyes, calling them to come home.

The Great Commission

Whether a homosexual is repentant, moderate, or militant, one great rule of thumb is to remember "The Great Commission" is not "The Great Gay Mission." Jesus didn't say go out into all the world and get to the gay community when you can. The best way to meet anyone dealing with homosexuality is to remember that the Cross of Christ isn't for the privileged few. God doesn't play favorites in saving people from sin.

You have been commissioned by God to love your gay- or lesbian-identified neighbor because the Lord has called you to be salt and light in the world and to preach the gospel to everyone. You are called to minister as effectively as Christ enables you to all three degrees of homosexuals. And in grace, mercy, and humility, you can do it.

8

Turn or Burn?
Five Things *Not* to Do

Randy Thomas

—⟳⟳—

In the culture wars of our time, Christians have been divided up into different camps. Some feel "called" to fight abortion, some to counter Hollywood, others to fight pornography, and still others to push back the "homosexual agenda." But in the midst of all these battles, many Christian friends have confessed to me privately that they've struggled with maintaining an attitude of humility. They confess to crossing over into belligerence or other counter-productive and un-Christlike attitudes.

On the other hand, other Christians see the culture wars happening, but because of the noise and turbulence, they back off from involvement. They don't want to take on the serious issues of the day or they feel ill-equipped to do so. They just don't have good answers to those on the other side of the battle.

The problem with both sets of Christians is precisely that their eyes are focused on the war…and not on the men and women who are the warriors on the other side—men and women who are often trying to pull together a life out of the devastation of sin. My goal in this chapter is to take us past just looking at the battle and consider the flesh-and-blood people who are engaged in it. When we come right down to it, what would it matter if we win the battle for the culture, but lose the war for souls?

Let's set aside our weapons for the culture and pick up the first-aid kits for the wounded. Ironically, that's the best way to bring out the renewal of our culture anyway—to reach the hearts of those who are perishing. A renewed culture can, in fact, only come about as a result of renewed hearts.

First, let me ask a question. Have you or your church ever thought about the gay-identified community as an unreached people group? If your church is like many, you have a "Missions Sunday," where different missions reaching across the world will come and talk to your Sunday school classes and take the pulpit for a Sunday. The goal is usually to bring honor to the Lord for His work, educate the congregation on where their missions support is being funneled, and serve as a fundraiser for those missions.

Mr. and Mrs. Joe Missionary will come in and share about the culture shock they experienced and how that was transcended through learning, humility, and service. Why even Mrs. Missionary has a new ear piercing at the top of her earlobe to signify to the rest of the tribe that she is married.

When it comes to foreign peoples or cultures, we understand the need to learn the language, customs, social norms, and cultural expectations. And where it doesn't compromise the gospel, we try to adapt and honor traditions.

But why is it that churches seldom help support a "missionary" to the gay culture? Why is there seldom a ministry reaching gays represented on missionary Sundays. And why are so few churches doing anything proactively to reach the homosexuals around them or help support those who *are* trying to have an impact?

I suppose it's because they don't see the gay-identified community as a true subculture like those based on race, economic status, location, ethnicity, or religion.

This is a notion I'd like to see changed. A subculture is defined as "a cultural subgroup differentiated by status, ethnic background, residence, religion, or other factors that functionally unify the group and act collectively on each member." It's the *other factors that functionally unify the group* that qualify the gay-identified community as an unreached people group.

Like it or not, we lived in a very homophobic world all the way up to the 1950s in Western civilization. The "sexual revolution" occurred in the 60s and 70s. Decadence, AIDS, and Christian antipathy/apathy led to pro-gay marketing and activism in the 80s. Hollywood, the mainstream media, and liberal churches bought into the marketing approach and are now teaching the young a wholly new set of social norms and expectations, including being "gay" as a valid and functional subgroup in our culture.

At the time of this writing I am 37 years old. At the age of 10, I suspected I was gay; at 13, I was absolutely positive. At that time, I assumed my future had "GAY" written all over it, and it was the only future I had. I wasn't raised in a church, so I certainly had no understanding from a Christian viewpoint that any other future could be mine. I was therefore left to assume the only identity that seemed available to me—and I embraced it wholeheartedly.

But now it's a different world with millions and millions of people right here, right *now,* living in a "gay" world with its own set of expectations, rules for normative behavior, language, and views of outside communities, relationships, and even God.

Some readers may have a problem with me claiming that the

gay-identified community is a valid, recognizable subculture. But I'm here to tell you as an expatriate, there *is* a gay-defined world in the hearts of millions of people who are attracted to their own sex. As a man or woman thinks, so he or she is. As millions of people think, so a "community" is born. This community...or subculture *exists* as surely as the Waodani tribe portrayed in the missionary movie *The End of the Spear* exists.

And in reaching out to any subculture, there are certain mistakes that can hinder effective evangelism. So let's take a look at five important hindrances to reaching homosexuals for Christ with the goal of helping *you* become Mr. or Mrs. or Ms. Missionary to the gay-identified community. But first I want to preface these points with an accurate view of how the gay subculture currently views the Christian community.

Ideally, we'd love to have the homosexual community see us as humble and loving followers of Jesus Christ, but the truth is that more often than not they see us as a group of people who are *against* them. They assume, correctly in many cases, that Christians do not see their gay or lesbian neighbors as peers, but rather as agents of a faceless agenda out to indoctrinate their children and compromise their churches.

Those in the gay subculture pick up on this really fast. As a result, they do *not* see us as humble and loving followers of Jesus Christ, but instead think that to be a Christian is to be a hypocrite.

Ouch! Yes, I know that sounds severe, but that's often exactly the way many gays see Christians. Sometimes that's a wrong generalization they may have picked up as a result of the media constantly portraying Christians in that light...*just as many Christians have a wrong generalization of most gays because of the way the media selectively portrays them.*

The first thing "not to do" is the current motto that seems to come up whenever Christians talk about homosexuality...and it's a phrase that causes gays to roll their eyes when they hear it. And that phrase is...

1. "Hate the sin, love the sinner."

Recently I saw the movie *Mars Attacks.* It's an awful movie that's sole purpose is to mock the campiness of B-rated, alien invasion films. Quite naturally I loved every minute of it! When the aliens first make face-to-face contact, everything seems to be going well when all of a sudden a hippie out in the stands releases a white dove. Conveniently the dove flies toward the alien, in slow-motion for effect, and the alien immediately whips out his ray gun and fries the poor bird in mid-air with a collision of a red squiggly laser beam and some sort of "squawk" of a sound effect. Then one of the bystanders states, "Maybe the aliens think that a dove means war?" That's when the aliens launch their initial attack on earth.

> To say that you hate homosexuality but love homosexuals doesn't make sense to those whose primary identity lies within their sexuality.

Of course there is nothing funny about the culture war over homosexuality, but as weird as it's going to sound, I'm going to compare Christians to the hippie with the dove. What *Mars Attacks* did was play off a stereotype of peace-loving hippies and shatter that with the reality that sometimes things don't live up to our catchphrases or symbols. We Christians tend to be satisfied with our own pat answers and don't realize that what we see as peaceful statements of love actually sound more like guided missiles closing in on a target.

This is certainly the case with the "hate the sin, love the sinner" cliché. Among our Christian brethren, we all know what this means because we know God doesn't view people by their actions but for who they are as souls. In other words, when we see a homosexual, we don't recognize him or her as the *inherent identity of someone struggling with same-sex attraction,* so it's easy for us to neatly conclude that we should "hate the sin, but love the sinner." But let's make this a bit more personal. What if your gay neighbor said, "Hate the Christ, but love the Christian"?

Now that I have your attention, remember, you are dealing with a subculture that identifies as "gay." *They are identifying themselves by homosexuality.* To say that you *hate* homosexuality but love homosexuals doesn't make sense to those whose primary identity lies within their sexuality.

At the very least you sound out of touch, as though you're speaking a completely different language. At the very worst, you sound out of touch, speaking a different language *and* being condescending. Either way it's confusing and ends up being a statement that only resonates among other Christians and has a negative effect in speaking to gay-identified homosexuals.

The underlying difference that "hate the sin, love the sinner" completely misses is that the Christian sees homosexuality as a condition to overcome whereas the gay-identified person sees homosexuality as an *innate identity* he or she has embraced.

2. Assuming the Gay Person *Knows* He or She Is Sinful

Many times after hearing me speak, a good-hearted, well-intentioned person will come up to me and say something along the lines of, "Randy, when you were living in that utterly dark place, didn't you just know in your soul that something was wrong? That something was terribly wrong with your homosexual lifestyle?"

Every time I'm asked this, I have to politely say, "No, actually I knew I was screwed up in a lot of ways, but being 'gay' seemed like my only anchor. Being gay was my first sense of identity and community. It was a *poor* anchor and failed to fulfill me, but at the time, identifying as gay and pursuing homosexual relationships were my only sense of peace."

At this point my questioner might ask me about the God-shaped void in the heart of those without the Lord, and I wholeheartedly agree with that idea. It was precisely that void that led me to Jesus—but the assumption that I thought there was something wrong with being gay at the time is simply not true. I didn't belong to Christ so I didn't have a belief system that challenged my gay identity, nor did I have "ears to hear" what the Holy Spirit was saying. Yes there was a void, but I didn't attribute that void to being gay until months after becoming a Christian.

Many Christians have an inner hostility toward gay- or lesbian-identified people. Even ex-gay Christians can harbor this same hostility if they've been raised in the church. This antagonism shows itself in a condescending attitude that acts on the assumption that the gay person "chooses" to act out his (or her) behavior and thus are willfully violating God's original intention for him.

While this may be true for the rarest of rare gay activists, this is *not* true for a vast majority of those who would identify as gay or struggle with same-sex attraction. Most gays have never known any other way of relating to the world and can't see what the Christian sees without the direct intervention of God in their lives.

Many Christians expect gay-identified people to live up to their own expectations, and until they do so, they deserve to be looked upon as a faceless "opponent" with a militant agenda. But when you consider it from the point of view of the person who simply doesn't know any different, it's unfair to expect the gay-identified to operate within our world system in a manner that suits our needs or doesn't offend us.

When you're talking to gay people, then, do *not* assume they see their own sinfulness and are just trying to make excuses or cover up for their lifestyle. The truth is, they do not see how their homosexuality is a problem that God would have a bad opinion about.

3. Just Say No to Manipulation and Bullying

When I was a senior in high school, several friends and I went to Daytona Beach for MTV's 1986 Springfest. We were there an entire week. Two of my friends were brothers who had a wealthy father. He bought us an old, short school bus. We sanded it down, painted it black, and painted "Party Barge" all over it. Even the little flip out stop sign at the front driver's side of the bus was remade into a party barge sign. We put a loud stereo system and mattresses in there and basically lived in that thing for a week. I slept on top of the bus the whole time. For a pagan senior in high school trying to get away from a terrible home environment, I had a blast.

One afternoon while my friends were wandering around somewhere on the beach, I decided to hang out at the bus and abuse some substances. In the haze, I looked out the window and could see two overweight women in long blue jean dresses, with really long straight hair, glasses, and flowery blouses. The two women were carrying signs and walking a lone two-person picket line on the section of beach in front of me. One sign was very scary looking with a black background and awful, hellish-looking flames. It said "Turn or Burn!" The other sign said "You are ALL going to HELL!" One of the ladies came up to the bus and well…to tell you the truth, I wasn't in the best of conditions to remember what she said, but I do remember laughing at her and offering her a beer, which she of course declined.

As you can guess, I didn't come to Jesus that day and really didn't come away with a favorable impression of His people. To me, it was humorous. I didn't feel at all convicted or inclined to repent from my sin because of their signs. Before and after that event, at different gay bars, pride parades, and events, I would often see other Christians hold up similar or worse signs. I never quite understood what those people were thinking. Did they really think the hate-filled, not grace-filled, signs would have a positive effect on the sinning masses in their midst? Didn't they stop to consider that instead they were a hindrance to sinners who needed to receive the love of God that leads to repentance?

Christians who approach ministry with a harsh, condemning message probably couldn't care less about truly reaching homosexuals with the love of Christ. I suppose they think they can spiritually bully people into the kingdom of God and trade in serving hearts for arm-twisting power plays.

It's been my prayer that those two ladies changed their ways by now. I'd love to think they might be reading this book. If so, I'm sorry for being mean to you that day, *but stop acting like that.*

Take the example of some other Christians I met on that same trip.

A couple of nights after meeting the picketing ladies, two of my friends and I went to the boardwalk. We decided to play a game called car surfing. We would be on the corner partying and invite ourselves into the cars cruising slowly by. Once we found a car that was game, we would jump in, share whatever substances we were abusing and then jump out of the car two or three blocks down the street. (I told you I was a mixed-up pagan.)

While we were waiting for a car to stop, this group of Christian guys came walking by and asked if we wanted to take a walk with them. They wanted to tell us about the "love of Jesus." They were our age, not a bit presumptuous, and even laughed at our jokes. I said "Sure…why the &*#! not?" Plus, I thought one of the guys was good looking.

Yes, I was a flaming homosexual pagan.

Even so, we went walking, and I remember laughing a lot *with* them not at them. I don't remember a lot of the conversation for obvious reasons, but I do remember this part:

> *Honest Christian dude:* "Do you know Jesus?"
>
> *Me:* "Oh yeah, yeah…"
>
> *Honest Christian dude:* "Do you really?"
>
> *Me:* "YES! Lord, Savior, Son of God…you know all that?"
>
> *Honest Christian dude:* "No, do you KNOW Him, do you know Him enough to fall in love with Him?"
>
> *Me:* "Fall in 'love' with Him?"
>
> *Honest Christian dude:* "Yes, Jesus blah blah blah…"

I was taken aback. How could you fall in love with Jesus? The honest Christian dude I'm sure told me the rest of the gospel, but I was off in my own little world in my buzzing head. To "know" Jesus, to "fall in love with" Jesus. The words rang in my ears.

I didn't come to Jesus that night, but the Scriptures say that the truth of God's Word never comes back void. The women on the beach weren't speaking truth. They were pronouncing a blanket judgment, seeking to bully all of us Springfesters into the kingdom. God knew better and sent someone who could speak to us where we were. What those women spoke to us were words of death and a hindrance to the gospel; what the honest Christian dude spoke were words of life that the Spirit of the Lord could actually use to shake up my spirit and implant seeds of faith that would eventually bear fruit six years later.

The young men didn't judge me from afar, but met me where I was at. They were honest about what they wanted to talk to me about. They were in unison with what the Spirit knew I needed to hear. They were not demanding.

They were ministering the love of God.

4. Don't Walk on Eggshells

For those seeking to reach their gay neighbors but are worried about the eggshells, you will be paralyzed for fear of offense. Don't worry about getting it down perfect before you say anything. Really, how many people do you know who live a completely perfect and inoffensive life?

No one.

Every single human, especially Christians aware of their need for a Savior, will make mistakes. *You have permission to be wrong, to say the wrong thing, to do the wrong thing, as long as it is not willful ignorance or purposeful offense.* In fact, I've found that the most common ground can often be found in the humble believers who admit they aren't perfect and will apologize and make restitution for mistakes made.

Sometimes the gay community indoctrinates its own by instilling certain assumptions and judgments of their own making. For instance, we get a lot of angry emails at Exodus. One time a lesbian woman emailed, "How dare YOU call ME depraved!" I emailed her back and said, "Where did I ever call you depraved? I don't see it anywhere on our website, my own blog, anything I have ever written...just where did you get that 'I' think you are depraved?" She responded with an apology but added "STILL that's what YOU think!" I responded, "Well as much fun as it is to have you think for me, I would rather think for myself. I don't see gay, ex-gay, lesbian, former lesbian, or straight. When I look at YOU, I see a daughter of the Most High God. A person He loved enough to die and be resurrected for. So I've never said you were depraved, what I have said is that I found a greater love than homosexuality and willingly gave up my gay life to pursue deeper holiness in Christ. If you are ever interested in that pursuit just let us know."

I was pretty direct with this lady and called her on her own judgments and assumptions. At the same time I didn't let a hyperbolic gay talking point determine how I viewed or responded to this lady. This was one time where not walking on eggshells gave me freedom to meet her on a peer level and, while the conversation served to only plant seeds with her, I believe it was successful because she had come to me with venom and left the conversation with at least a semblance of respect.

And then there have been plenty of times where I have completely stuck my foot in my mouth, said things out of anger, or was just downright snippy…okay, even mean. I'm a rare breed of male. I have a very high verbal quotient— meaning that I talk out my thoughts—and sometimes those thoughts should never see the light of day unless having been given to the Lord for refinement before verbalizing. In those times I must be humble enough to go back to the person and state the exact nature of my wrong—no blanket statements or generalizations, no public hullabaloo or false humility.

If I did something that was not Christlike, whether I initiated the response or not, I must take personal responsibility to make peace for my actions. It also doesn't matter whether they accept my repentance or not. My first responsibility is to honor the Lord by doing the right thing in His eyes. In all honesty, most of the times I have to eat my words is when I've temporarily forgotten from where the Lord has brought me or I've simply relied on my own self-sufficiency to respond to something that provokes me.

My basic point here is don't let fear of offense keep you from reaching out right now with what you know. You know the Lord…and that's a great place to start.

Jesus is the Lord of Romans 8:28: "And we know that in all things God works for the good of those who love him, who have been called according to his purpose." God can turn all things for good, not some things, not just holy things, not just clever answers, or amazingly creative outreach possibilities. He can turn *all* things for good. Keep trying, loving, praying, and serving your gay-identified neighbors, friends, and loved ones. Regardless of their response, you are living out God's heart.

5. Don't Forget Your Own Need for a Savior

One time I was in an ongoing conversation with a gay activist. He was complaining to me that he felt that ex-gays were the "velvet glove" over the brass knuckles used by the religious right for political purposes.

I explained that while some of us are concerned about public policy, our efforts are only to express our opinions on the subject and to also influence policy-makers toward what is truly appropriate for the social good as well as compassion and redemption.

The weird thing is that the very next day I was in a meeting with several prominent conservative leaders, and one of them actually said that a certain public policy matter was worth getting the "brass knuckles out for." I was astounded and immediately thought of King David.

Shimei Curses David

As King David approached Bahurim, a man from the same clan as Saul's family came out from there. His name was Shimei son of Gera, and he cursed as he came out. He pelted David and all the king's officials with stones, though all the troops and the special guard were on David's right and left. As he cursed, Shimei said, "Get out, get out, you man of blood, you scoundrel! The LORD has repaid you for all the blood you shed in the household of Saul, in whose place you have reigned. The LORD has handed the kingdom over to your son Absalom. You have come to ruin because you are a man of blood!"

Then Abishai son of Zeruiah said to the king, "Why should

this dead dog curse my lord the king? Let me go over and cut off his head."

But the king said, "What do you and I have in common, you sons of Zeruiah? If he is cursing because the LORD said to him, 'Curse David,' who can ask, 'Why do you do this?'"

David then said to Abishai and all his officials, "My son, who is of my own flesh, is trying to take my life. How much more, then, this Benjamite! Leave him alone; let him curse, for the LORD has told him to. It may be that the LORD will see my distress and repay me with good for the cursing I am receiving today."

So David and his men continued along the road while Shimei was going along the hillside opposite him, cursing as he went and throwing stones at him and showering him with dirt. The king and all the people with him arrived at their destination exhausted. And there he refreshed himself.

Now Shimei was wrong because Saul was not meant to be king once David had been appointed by God through the prophet Samuel. King Saul brought about his own destruction in many ways. Even so, David didn't take his attacker Shimei on stone for stone or order his demise. Why? *Because David was aware of his own weaknesses.* He had an accurate assessment of his situation. He had a journey to make and was going to continue on it regardless of the cursing. I can't help but think that David knew that while Shimei was incorrect in all of his vitriol and meanness, David knew he *had* been a man of blood. David knew that the Lord had said that the consequences of sin would visit his house. So while Shimei was out of line and wrong, his cursing caused David's reflective humility. And I believe in that humility he found a meek strength to continue his journey submitted to the Lord.

My activist friend doesn't shout from a hillside or literally throw stones. Indeed, he shouts via email and throws verbal stones at me and my friends. I don't see him like David's men saw Shimei, but I do see his actions as similar. My friend (notice the use of the word *friend*) is wrong in saying that my exercise of my civil liberties is the velvet glove over the religious right's brass knuckles. At the same time, he's right that there are some in those circles who don't mind thinking themselves righteous in pulling out their political fists.

When this U.S. political leader referred to brass knuckles, I cringed and knew immediately that the Lord had sent this activist to warn me and remind me of my own humility. David had committed many sins and I have committed many sins, and the Lord forgave us both. I accept the fact that as I press forward in truth with gay activists *and* the religious right, I have to be mindful that I do so as one who leads and is not blindly manipulated by others. I must do so with the humility of knowing that I serve the Lord as an empty vessel divested of the novocaine of self-importance.

Shimei talked of the Lord but did not know the mind of the Lord concerning David. Shimei talked of David's circumstance but did not know David's true state of affairs. This gay activist was doing the same thing. My friends and I are not pawns, but we are fully aware of what our situation looks like to others. We will continue to do what is right and allow the voice of criticism to be heard—but the reason for this is not to validate those voices but to allow those voices to keep us mindful of who we are and the Savior who guides our path.

I'm at the head of the line when it comes to struggling with being meek and humble. I can identify with wanting to go toe to toe, fighting as the world fights. It would be so easy to do so—and in our "infotainment"-driven culture, it would be lauded and soaked up for public consumption.

Even so, it would be nothing but a clanging gong, a noisy nothingness that has no eternal value. The leader who mentioned breaking out the "brass knuckles" is out of line. We do not fight as the world fights. We want to be straightforward, keeping our yes a yes and no a no. At the same time, we must be humble and meek. If we're confessing our sins to God and living a life of transparency before both Him and man, we will have no time or want to be anything other than lovingly straightforward with our convictions but willing to sacrifice our personal agendas to reach our gay neighbors.

In a literal sense, if anyone went after my gay neighbor with brass knuckles or threatened bodily harm, I would put myself in between them. Another story to illustrate the point comes from the situation Alan mentioned in chapter 4.

In 2004, Rhea County, Tennessee, passed a law that forbade homosexual couples from living there. The law was repealed within 24 hours, but the firestorm was ignited. News agencies around the world picked up the story and gay activists quickly responded by organizing huge protests in one of the local parks near the town center. It was a perfect flashpoint for the culture war over homosexuality.

Rhea County is not liberal…*at all*…by any stretch of the imagination. Even so, where the Spirit of the Lord is, there is compassion. Several concerned pastors contacted Exodus and invited Alan and me out to address the local area pastors and to speak at an evening Town Hall meeting at the local school. They wanted us to share our stories and how to redemptively respond to the issue at hand.

During our first presentation, as Alan mentioned, a lady stood up and accused us of preaching a false gospel. She stated that because we struggled with homosexuality, we were eternally damned and should be ashamed for giving false hope to those trapped by homosexuality.

This was not a good start to our time there.

Later, one man came up to me and with a half smirk on his face asked me to "take my Christian hat off" for a moment and then asked, "I've overheard that a lot of local good ol' boys are going to pile into three trucks and head down to the protest. They ain't goin' to shoot nobody but fire off their guns into the air. Do you think that will scare the gays off to the point they won't come back?"

I had to catch my breath and pick my jaw up off the floor. In two seconds I gained my composure and said, "First off, I don't wear a Christian 'hat.' I *am* a Christian. Second, you tell those good ol' boys that if they plan on doing this, I will be right up front with the gay activists staring them down. I will even help organize a protest in Rhea County for next year. The 'guns in the air' plan won't work, does *not* represent the Lord at all, is dangerous, and, if anything, makes the situation a hundred times worse."

Now admittedly, you may not be a public-policy activist wanting to figuratively break out the brass knuckles. You may not relate to the three truckloads of good ol' boys wanting to scare "the gays" right out of town. You may not be the lady who yells at ex-gay leaders that they are preaching a false gospel of "tolerance." But do you often pause to consider your own need for mercy and forgiveness? In that light, have you stood by and listened while someone degraded the homosexuals through jokes or hostile attitudes? Have you ever perpetrated those things yourself? If so, then I really think you might want to think back to how God had mercy on you, despite your past sins.

I guarantee that if a person spends any quality time with the Lord regarding their own sin and need for daily cleansing, he or she will be broken of any pride and self-sufficiency. When we sat at the pierced feet of Christ and allowed those wounded hands to take away our sin, how in the world can we look at others with anything other than empathy? *We cannot.*

If you can't see yourself as equally sinful as your gay neighbors, and that you need a Savior as much or perhaps more than they do, then you probably need to back off and let the Lord break you of false pride before you try to minister to the homosexual community.

You Have Permission to Love

Way back in 1995 I was part of a local Exodus Member Ministry in Dallas called Living Hope Ministries. That year we had a booth at the Promise Keepers rally in our area. It was amazing the amount of material we handed out to those godly men who, for the most part, were very open and honest in talking about homosexuality.

Many women were there as volunteers or to work in the ministry booths. I remember one dear Dallas socialite who was helping out. She was fantastic. She came up to the booth with her big blond hair, big bangle earrings, big bright-blue eyes, and she literally said right off the bat, "My hairdresser's gay, and he's such a sweetheart. I just love 'im to pieces. I do! I just love 'im to pieces. Is that wrong? Am I doing somethin' wrong by wanting to just love on him and continue to bring him my business and refer him to my friends?"

My response was, "Of course not!" And to my astonishment, she actually started to cry. "He's so nice and he has so many problems. He's so talented and kind to me. We have a real friendship. We both know what the other believes…and we get along anyway."

I then told her, "That's wonderful…and you know don't you, that you *do* have permission to love him?" She looked at me with tears in her eyes and a little confused. I said, "Jesus loves him, and it wouldn't be surprising to me at all if Jesus instilled a sense of that pastoral heart in you. Jesus sees your hairdresser as a unique and wonderful soul He came to save. If He looks on him with love, why wouldn't we?" The woman gave me a big hug. Thank goodness her mascara was waterproof.

Sometimes we think we have to set boundaries and be upfront and clear at every single turn of a conversation that this or that is right or wrong. Most of the time people just want to be listened to. They want to be cared for.

Jesus listens and cares.

The guy who cuts my hair also identifies as gay. I shared with him that I was an infamous "ex-gay," and his response was that he was an "infamous gay"! After assuring me that he was not going to butcher my hair, we laughed a little. On one of my recent visits, he shared about how his partner had given him an iPod Nano for Christmas. Instead of focusing on the fact that he mentioned his partner, we spent a good amount of time talking about how groovy iPods are. I go to him because he cuts my hair the way I like it and he's funny. I care for him in that limited client to hairstylist way.

In a similar way, I care for the lesbian couples who are always at the pool near my house. I care for my gay friends who attend 12-step meetings, for the ones still trapped in the bar scene. I pray for the lesbian city commissioner in my town. I also pray for the myriads of activists who read my blog. I care for them all and try to love them as Jesus does because spiritually, and in the final reality, there is not a single distinction between "them" and us. There is no gay, ex-gay or straight paradigm at the foot of the Cross. We have permission to love because Jesus first loved us. We are commanded to love even our enemies. Why then do we need special permission to unconditionally love our gay neighbors?

Bruce loved me. I met Bruce when I was 16 and working with him at a local grocery store. Bruce was a Christian, but everyone liked him. He was always helpful, kind of quiet, and stoic. He never complained and was always willing to help out with overtime and picking up extra shifts. When I was 19 or so, I was addicted to drugs and renting a couch for $40 a week (yes, I lived on a couch for 18 months).

The Lord told Bruce to find me at that time. I hadn't worked for the grocery store in a while, but he tracked down my mother and found out where I was through her. He invited me to a Bible study. I went with impure motives. I thought Bruce was a very handsome man. God was not offended by that, and He knew that was my primary motivation. Bruce was so humble and above reproach the whole time. I went to several of those Bible studies, and my impure motives went flying out the window and were replaced with a mission. A mission to make these Christians show their true colors and reject me. I wore the biggest earring possible, added more effeminate mannerisms, and made as many snide little remarks as I could.

When they passed the Bible around to read the Scriptures, I knew they would skip me…but they didn't. When they prayed, they prayed for all of our concerns. The husbands blessed and honored their wives and vice versa. They cared…they genuinely *cared*.

During one prayer, one of the women referred to God as "Abba." Not being raised in the church, I went up to her and said, "Why did you call God 'Abba'? The only Abba I know is the 70s disco group…you know, 'Dancin' Queen.'" And she just laughed. I praise God she laughed. She was honest and comfortable enough to laugh and with sweet eyes full of merriment she said to me "Oh my...I call God, our Father, Abba because it's a term of endearment. Abba is like saying daddy. God loves us like a daddy."

Right then her eyes turned from merriment to genuine compassion, and my heart was pierced through. I had never had a daddy. I credit this one event as being the tipping point for my coming to Christ three years later. That night I was given a drink of Living Water, and my soul couldn't ignore that my Abba was calling out to me.

Now check out the dynamics of this interchange. I had impure motives and the Christians didn't give me any special attention (even when I tried to manipulate it out of them). They included me in their prayer times and answered my questions with genuine confidence. But also look at what the Holy Spirit did. He moved on Bruce to think of me, empowered him to find me, empowered me to get to the group and witness His work in His people. The Spirit opened my ears to hear the word "Abba," which led to a new understanding of God that would tip my heart toward home.

You don't have to know all the ins and outs of what's going on inside the heart of your gay or lesbian neighbor. Be confident in your walk in the Lord to sustain you and for Him to do a work in his or her heart. It's this eternal, even mystical, if you will, symbiosis of witness that will reach your gay neighbor's heart.

More important than what *not* to do is what you *do* want to do— love the Lord your God with all your heart and your neighbor as yourself (Matthew 22:37-39).

Part 3
Reaching Further

Reaching homosexuals for Christ is in some ways no different than reaching any other sinners…and yet in other ways it's quite different.

The same is true within the homosexual community itself. In a very real way, reaching all homosexuals is basically the same: establish relationships, love them, and offer them shelter in Christ. But there are also wide differences among homosexuals, just as there are in nearly any community you can think of. For instance, there are some differences unique to lesbians as opposed to male homosexuals. Young homosexuals are at a far different place than, say, an older gay man or woman. Within the African-American community, there are still other differences. Reaching those with disabilities such as Matt Lieberman, a deaf young man, presents still other challenges (see Matt's story in chapter 12, p. 236).

A gay man in the last stages of AIDS will present yet other challenges than simply leading him to the Lord. For instance, are you willing to give him the practical ministry of meals and drive him to doctor visits?

In this section of *God's Grace and the Homosexual Next Door,* we'll take a look at some of these special circumstances. Scott Davis, who works as director of Exodus Youth, offers some practical advice about educating our young people about homosexuality. Melissa Fryrear works with gender issues with Focus on the Family and offers some great insights on the needs of lesbians.

Then, in a "24 Questions" format, we will answer some of the questions you may have that we didn't address in earlier chapters.

Finally, we want you to hear from six homosexuals who were without Christ and living the gay lifestyle. We think by hearing their stories of before and after someone reached out to them, you'll see how the Holy Spirit worked to draw them to Christ through someone who cared for them…someone like you and the people in your church.

9

What Do Our Youth Think About Homosexuality?

Scott Davis

—⁓⁓—

Homosexuality? Who cares? I have friends at school who are gay, and they're just like everyone else. I don't understand why it would be wrong for two people to love each other. Besides, *Will & Grace* is really funny!" This comment is typical of the changing attitude of youth toward homosexuality. Polls show that young people today increasingly approve of homosexuality as a valid life option for friends, family members, and classmates.

During the 1990s, the proportion of 13- to 19-year-olds who "don't have any problem" with homosexuality more than tripled, to 54 percent, according to a 1999 study commissioned by *Seventeen* magazine and the Kaiser Family Foundation. A nationwide poll of high school seniors in 2001 found that 61 percent disagreed with the statement "Gay lifestyles are morally wrong."[1]

This increasing acceptance of homosexuality among young people extends to politics as well. The same poll found that 66 percent of high school seniors back the legalization of same-sex marriage, compared to about 33 percent of adults.

No doubt part of the reason for these changing numbers is that American youth have been exposed to a consistent presentation of homosexual relationships as healthy, satisfying, and long-lasting by the media and in their schools.

In many cases, the media represents homosexual relationships in a far better light than corresponding representations of heterosexual marriage relationships. Many popular TV shows targeted to teens include a gay or lesbian teen character, who is almost always sympathetically portrayed. Any opposition to homosexual behavior is usually shown on the screen as coming from bigoted, close-minded, self-righteous, ignorant Christians.

So based on what they are hearing, it's no wonder so many youth approve of homosexuality!

Cultural revolutionaries have always been aware that the key to changing a culture is to capture the hearts of the youth. The 20-year effort to change the attitudes of youth toward homosexuality has been organized, constant, forceful...and highly effective. In that time frame, the movement has gone beyond seeking tolerance (equal rights, getting along) and acceptance (however you want to live) to promoting active approval and even a celebration of homosexuality.

In many schools, students who identify themselves with an alternative sexual identity are given special praise by teachers and classmates. A student who feels different or lonely can suddenly gain a spotlight of positive attention by proclaiming he or she is gay, bisexual, or any of a dozen other sexual classifications. Unsurprisingly, the incidence of same-gender sexual experimentation is on a rapid increase. Boys typically now have their first same-gender sexual experience at 13 years of age and girls at 15.[2] Boys and girls label themselves sexually as gay, lesbian, bisexual, or other by 16—down recently from 21.[3]

Clearly, and with no tolerance for a different opinion, children are being taught only one view of homosexuality...and that one view is leading many kids to conclude that embracing a gay identity and homosexual behavior is either *good* for them or, at worst, of no consequence. But Christians know that homosexual behavior does have lasting consequences—and that withholding the news that same-sex attraction *isn't* set in stone does a huge disservice to our youth.

> The reality of homosexuality isn't "out there." It's here, inside the church, in youth groups across the country.

What about Christian youth from conservative or Christian families? Are they immune to the cultural influences pushing them to approve of homosexuality? As leaders within Exodus International contact churches to help educate youth, they find many pastors who mistakenly believe this isn't a problem in their churches. "We don't have that problem here," is a frequent response.

Unfortunately, this response is naïve and almost always wrong. Exodus ministry directors from small midwestern towns to metropolitan cities are reporting a massive influx of youth and parents looking for help in dealing with same-sex attraction. These youth are primarily Christians, raised in the church, active in their youth groups, and deeply afraid of disclosing their struggle to anyone at church.

The reality of homosexuality isn't "out there" in hedonistic San Francisco. It's *here,* inside the church, in youth groups across the country.

Silence Is Deadly

Parents and church leaders can no longer afford to stay silent on this issue. Christian youth are caught in the middle of a difficult dilemma. On one hand, they're strongly influenced by the continuous parade of positive media representations of homosexuality. They can hardly watch a favorite show on television or catch a movie at the theater without being bombarded with messages that undermine biblical perspectives on sexuality. At school, many students are explicitly taught that Christian morality is antiquated and intolerant. "Tolerance" programs such as the yearly "Day of Silence" indoctrinate students with the myths that homosexuality is genetic and that opposing homosexuality is bigotry.

On the other hand, most parents and churches stay silent while their children are barraged. Or the message the students hear is one of judgment and rebuke, not redemption. And so in the absence of credible direction from positive moral authorities in their lives, students simply accept what the culture is teaching them. Even kids from Christian families, if they get no corresponding teaching about the options for those with same-sex attractions, wrongly assume there *are* no options to homosexuality. And if they are the ones who are dealing with attractions to their own sex, they'll likely be open to the voices that affirm the rightness of their feelings.

Christian students are caught in the middle. Do they hold to the instructions of Scripture, church, and parents—and risk being labeled bigots by school authorities and peers? Or do they reject their faith convictions as outdated and accept the new morality? Most decide it's simply not safe to have a contrary opinion in the hostile world of public school or the workplace, so they discard their Christian witness.

As mentioned, many churches that don't remain silent on homosexuality send the wrong message. Gays and lesbians are denounced from pulpits. Angry or militant anti-gay protesters line the streets at gay pride parades. Parents make it clear that homosexuality is not a valid choice for their children. But bare denunciations have little power against the careful arguments and vivid images used to promote the homosexual lifestyle. Students need more than anti-homosexual rhetoric. They desperately need to know *why* it is wrong and that there *are* options for those who are homosexually inclined. They need to hear a message about homosexuality that balances grace and truth, bringing the full gospel to bear.

Youth who are struggling with secret same-gender attractions need to hear that they don't have to be gay and that change is possible. Can you imagine how a young person feels when hearing angry denunciations of their secret shame from the pulpit or from their parents? Such condemnation pushes them away from the church when what they really need are welcoming arms to embrace them. They need the gospel message that God loves them despite their temptations, that He offers forgiveness for all sins, and that He promises to transform the very hearts of those who come to Him.

Students who do not struggle with this particular temptation need to hear that they can hold firmly to biblical sexuality without becoming hateful bigots. Both silence and angry denunciations only serve to stifle their confidence in sharing their faith with friends. They need to hear a positive gospel message about homosexuality so they can take a stand for what is true.

The Gospel on Homosexuality

- God designed sexuality as a beautiful part of His creation to powerfully unite husband and wife as they create new life together. Any use of sex outside this created order is harmful.

- As a result of our rebellion against God, we are each tempted to pursue our own ways, doing what seems most "natural" to us.

- Homosexuality—not being God's design for our sexuality—leads to sin, pain, and broken relationships, just like other sexual sins do.

- God loves people who struggle with homosexuality, just like He loves all other sinners.

- God offers His grace and forgiveness in Christ to any person who

will come to Him, regardless of his or her particular sins, including homosexuality.

- To those who come to faith, God promises that He will transform their very hearts to obey His law and desire what is right,
including proper use of their sexuality. This means that healing
and change are possible for people who struggle with homosexual temptations.

Speaking of Sex

Churches that plan to handle the topic of homosexuality proactively
and with clarity need to make some adjustments in how they present
the subject to their youth.

First, we need to acknowledge the mistake we've made in remov-
ing homosexuality from the list of sins we typically speak about with
our youth. Because it's an uncomfortable topic, we tend to either fail to
speak of it or speak of it in isolation from other sexual sins. Our youth
pick up on this discomfort and in turn view homosexuality as something different and in another category from every other sin. That can
lead to heterosexual students being more condemning toward homosexuals and homosexually attracted students feeling even more alienated from God than they otherwise would.

Many Christian youth who struggle with same-gender attractions
feel like their sin is the only one that cannot be discussed. Teenage boys
will say things like, "I wish my problem was that I kept having sex with
my girlfriend or looking at straight pornography or smoking pot. Then
I could talk about it with my youth pastor and friends. They would be
compassionate and try to help me. But I know that it's not safe for me to
talk about my struggle with homosexuality." If you work with a number
of youth, it's very likely that there's someone in your charge who feels
exactly like that. Are you the kind of leader this youth can approach
without fear about his homosexuality?

The first step to correcting this problem is to begin linking homosexuality to the general area of sex and dating. Speak to your youth about

homosexuality while talking about other sexual struggles. Don't divorce it from other sins or make it out to be the worst sin. *Any* sexual sin breaks God's design for our sexuality and leads to alienation from Him and harmful results in our lives. There is no need to speak of homosexuality as if it's completely different (and worse) than other sexual sins.

Second, we need to talk about gender and identity, not just sex. Homosexuality often plays out among youth as illicit sexual behavior. But the root of the problem isn't generally sexual in nature. Instead, it's a matter of identity and relationships.

In a culture like ours that has lost its understanding of gender, students are confused about how to live out their lives as men or women. Guys need consistent biblical training that clarifies how men are to relate to other men and to women. Girls likewise need consistent biblical training that clarifies how women are to relate to other women and to men. This training should go beyond simple stereotypes to plumb the depths of each gender as a unique reflection of the created image of God.

Third, we must begin to address the myths that our students are hearing from their culture. How can they hope to hold firm if parents and pastors refuse to address the lies that are bombarding our youth today?

Answering the Myths

Let's take a look at the myths your youth are being taught and how to refute them in simple language they can understand. In each of the myths discussed, I address my response as if I'm talking to the youth myself. Each response seeks not only to negate the myth, but to present a positive message that promotes biblical sexuality and redemptive themes from Scripture.

MYTH 1: *Homosexuality is hereditary; there is a "Gay Gene" that causes same-sex attraction*

Scientists have spent the past 20 years trying to prove that homosexuality is something a person is born with. Well guess what? They've failed. Study after study has failed to show anything like a gay gene.

For instance, scientists have studied identical twins, who share all of the same genes. But those experiments showed that when one twin is gay-identified, the other twin is often straight. Obviously if a gene forced someone to be gay, then identical twins would either be both straight or both gay. Other recent studies have also failed to confirm a "gay gene." There simply is no genetic link to homosexuality.

On the contrary, science suggests environmental factors, such as how your family treats you, sexual abuse, and experiences when you were a child, influence what sexual attractions you develop as you mature. This is exactly what Christian ministers who help people leave homo-sexuality have been saying for years! Homosexuality is not an inborn trait like race or gender. It's something that develops usually because of painful experiences when a child is young.

When we are really young, we each try to figure out where we fit in the world. When everything works like it should, little girls identify with their mothers and want to be like them, and little boys identify with their dads and want to be like them. But sometimes little girls are abused by men in their lives and decide it's not safe to be girls. And sometimes boys feel rejected by their dads, and decide that they must not be very good at being boys. These children will grow up feeling disconnected from their own gender as boys or girls, so instead of being attracted to the opposite sex, they develop attractions to the same sex. The problem isn't a gene; the problem is in their life experiences.

But you're not likely to hear that on TV or from programs at school because some adults are trying to sell you on the gay gene, even though science says there probably isn't one. Why? Because they believe if they can convince everyone that homosexuality is genetic, they can claim that homosexuality is no different from heterosexuality—no better, no worse. That means homosexual behavior can't be wrong.

Twenty years of research has failed to find a genetic cause for homo-sexuality. But what if they found one tomorrow? Would it really matter? According to the Bible, not one bit. God doesn't let us off the hook for our behavior just because we're tempted. In fact, the Bible says we'll each be tempted in all kinds of ways because of evil desires inside of us. Some people are tempted to have premarital sex. Some are tempted to cheat on their girlfriends or boyfriends. Science has shown that some people are tempted toward alcoholism because of certain genes. But that doesn't make alcoholism okay. It's still wrong, whether we're naturally tempted toward it or not.

Because humanity has rebelled against God, we are *all* tempted to do wrong. Some of us are tempted to shoplift, some of us are tempted in other ways. That doesn't mean we can go out and do whatever we want. That just means that it's hard for us to obey God. And when we fail, we all have to fall back on God's grace and mercy to restore us.

MYTH *2: Homosexuality is no different from heterosexuality*

Pro-gay leaders say that homosexuality is no different from heterosexuality, no better, no worse. But they're trying to indoctrinate you, to force you to believe that it's no different. Do you think I'm exaggerating?

Fifteen years ago almost everyone agreed there were many differences between homosexuality and heterosexuality. So two gay men wrote a book called *After the Ball* that described their plan to force America to accept homosexuality. They taught gay activists to knowingly lie to persuade the public that gays are victims of their genetics and to use the media to present a false picture of homosexuals as well-adjusted, happy people.

The authors describe how to purposefully represent homosexuals using non-gay actors and males in magazines and film in ways to suggest homosexuality in order to convince the public to accept homosexuality. They suggest advertising pictures of gay men "who not only don't look like his picture of a homosexual, but are carefully selected to look either like the bigot and his friends, or like any one of his other stereotypes of all-right guys....It makes no difference that the ads are lies."

Did anyone notice that both of the actors playing gay men in *Brokeback Mountain* are strong, handsome men who are straight in real life?

Fifteen years after the book *After the Ball* was published, gay activists are still using that dishonest tactic to indoctrinate you with their beliefs.

They want to call you a bully and a bigot and homophobic to force you to agree with them that homosexuality is perfectly acceptable. But is it true?

The truth is that God designed sex to be between a man and a woman in a lifetime marriage commitment. God invented sex. He came up with it! His first recorded words to man and woman in Scripture comes when He said, "Be fruitful and multiply, and fill the earth" (NASB). Now I may not be all that smart, but I know that the world is a big place, and it was going to take a whole lot of sex in order to fill it up!

God was in favor of sex. He designed man and woman's sexuality to be a powerful force that would unite them physically and spiritually in the creation of a new life. He created sex as such a powerful force that He knew it would be harmful to us outside of marriage. So He restricted sex to the special marriage relationship, where it could be safely used for good.

But we think we're smarter than God, that we can figure out how to live our lives better than our Creator planned. So we have premarital sex, and cheat on our spouses, and engage in homosexual sex. Each of these are outside of God's plan and harmful to us. They *injure* our precious souls.

Is homosexual behavior different from sex inside of marriage? Absolutely. Homosexuality is opposed to how God designed us. Temptations *feel* natural to us. But what's more true about us is that we were created by God, and He knows what's best for us.

I think that's probably why disease, depression, violence, and drug abuse are all way more prevalent in the gay community than most of the country. Ignoring what the Creator tells us we're made for hurts us! A sexual relationship with someone of the same gender might feel good for a time, but it can never heal the pain deep down inside in that place where we feel like we don't measure up as a man or woman. And a homosexual relationship can never fill the place that a relationship with the opposite gender is supposed to fill. It's just not how God made us.

MYTH 3: *Guys who are into art are gay*

Okay, let's move on to another myth: that guys who like art instead of sports are gay, or that girls who are into sports instead of dolls are lesbians. Is that true? No, it's not true. And I don't think any of you really believe it is.

No, the truth is that our gender, as male or female, is a gift from God that we all express differently. Our artistic and sports interests have nothing to do with sexuality, despite the stereotypes. Sure, many boys like sports. But that doesn't mean you are gay if you prefer music and art. Sure, many girls like dolls and dresses. But that doesn't mean you are a lesbian if you prefer jeans and like playing basketball. That's just a wonderful way you are growing into a unique man or woman!

Many students share with me that classmates assumed they were gay just because they were different. At first these students didn't accept the false labels. They were confused and not sure, but they were not ready to adopt a gay identity. But eventually they just said, "Well, if everyone else thinks I'm gay, maybe I am." So they gave up and accepted something that wasn't true about them because it was what other people said.

If you feel like you're different from your classmates—if you're a guy who likes art or a girl who doesn't like dresses—that's okay. Even if you feel confused about yourself, that doesn't mean you're gay.

MYTH 4: *Once gay, always gay*

What if someone does have homosexual attractions? Are they stuck with it forever? Is it true that once you're gay, you're always gay?

Here's the truth: Hundreds of thousands of men and women have left homosexuality, and those are just the ones we know about in the last 30 years through the ministry of Exodus International!

I'm going to be honest with you, though: Change isn't easy. Have you ever tried to get past a particular sin in your life? To stop doing something you know is wrong? It's not easy, but it's possible. And Exodus has helped hundreds of thousands of men and women leave homosexuality.

People leaving a gay lifestyle have a lot that changes. First, there's how they think about themselves. They stop thinking of themselves as gays or lesbians, and begin to think of themselves as men or women, creations of God and people He loves.

They also change their behaviors—stopping doing things that God says are wrong and learning to obey God and do what's right.

Then there's the matter of their wounded hearts. Remember I said that the causes of homosexuality usually have to do with pain in their lives as young children? That pain deep inside needs to be healed, and that takes the powerful work of God in hearts and time to work through the problems.

Finally there's the change of sexual attractions. This doesn't happen by just trying really hard to be attracted to the opposite sex. It doesn't happen by looking at straight pornography. And God usually doesn't choose to just take away the feelings immediately, though that sometimes happens. Instead, it is a *process* of changing how you view yourself, changing behaviors, changing the way you deal with emotions and relationships, finding healing for the painful places in your heart—and then the sexual attractions can change.

Once gay, always gay? *No!* The Good News of Jesus is that God loves us, accepts us, and promises to transform us if we let Him into our lives. It's not like God is demanding anything more of homosexually attracted people than everyone else—He wants the same thing: our love and obedience. And He promises to change us so we can love and obey Him. *All* Christians can experience deep changes in who they are through God's power. Paul wrote, "If anyone is in Christ, he is a new creation" (2 Corinthians 5:17), and that promise is for someone struggling with homosexuality just as much as for someone struggling with heterosexual pornography or any other sin.

MYTH 5: *It's mean to say homosexuality is wrong*

Okay, are you ready for another myth? Has a teacher or friend ever told you it's mean to say that homosexuality is wrong? That sounds like it might be true. Nobody wants to make someone feel bad about themselves, right?

But it *is* kind to help friends avoid bad decisions. If your friend told you he (or she) was going to jump off a bridge into oncoming traffic, would you say, "Hey, that's great, man. Whatever works for you"? If a friend told you she wanted to have a baby to force her boyfriend to stay with her, wouldn't you tell her it probably won't work and there will be huge consequences? Love means warning a friend if he (or she) is going to do something that will hurt in the long term as well as the short term.

Homosexuality is a lifestyle that is opposed to God's design. It ultimately can't meet our relational needs because we weren't designed for that kind of relationship. That's why the average gay man will have hundreds of sexual partners, according to the Department of Health and Human Services Center for Disease Control. He's always looking for the right guy to fill his emptiness and will never ever find it. That's why so many lesbian women will suffer emotional, verbal, and physical abuse from their partners. Women weren't made to be in sexual relationships with each other.

Sure, you can tell someone homosexuality is wrong and be mean about it. But you can also say it with deep compassion and real concern for your friends. Maybe if you tell them lovingly that God has something better for their lives, they won't try homosexuality in the first place. What if your boldness saves them from a lifetime of pain and regret?

MYTH 6: *If you think homosexuality is wrong, you're homophobic*

Homophobia is a label that's used to make fun of people who disagree with homosexuality. Maybe you have been accused of being homophobic for telling someone that homosexuality is wrong. But homophobia has nothing to do with your moral view on homosexuality. The word is a psychological term that means an irrational fear of homosexuals.

Unless you run screaming from the room, frothing at the mouth when you see someone who acts gay, afraid that they might touch you and make you gay, you are *not* homophobic!

In fact, when someone labels you as homophobic for disagreeing with them, that's bullying! They're bullying you. It's intolerant when someone refuses to hear your viewpoint and calls you names instead. "Homophobia" is almost always used as an embarrassing label to shut up people who refuse to be politically correct.

Don't let intolerance by people who label you as homophobic keep you from sharing the truth.

MYTH 7: *Tolerance means approving of however anyone lives*

What is tolerance? A popular myth is that tolerance means approving of however anyone lives. This view leads to people saying things like "Whatever works for you; it's all good." Or "that's not good for me, but that's good for him." That attitude means no one can say anything anyone else does is wrong. Everything is equally good. But God doesn't say everything is equally good. He has told us what is the best way to live and what is opposed to Him.

Besides, no one can really live consistently with this philosophy. If everything is equal, then working as a doctor is just as good as working as a drug pusher. If everything is equal, then bribing judges is just as good as giving money to care for poor children in Africa. People don't really approve of how everyone else lives; they just approve of different lifestyles.

But back to the myth. Tolerance doesn't mean approving of however anyone lives. Tolerance actually means respectfully disagreeing. You can be tolerant of someone while standing up for what you believe in. Tolerance doesn't mean you can't disagree with others.

The apostle Peter talks about this in the Bible in 1 Peter 3:15-16. He says, "If you are asked about your Christian hope, always be ready to explain it. But you must do this in a gentle and respectful way. Keep your conscience clear. Then if people speak evil against you, they will be ashamed when they see what a good life you live because you belong to Christ" (NLT). The key is gentleness and respect.

You don't have to force your opinions down other people's throats, even when they're doing that to you. But you can gently, respectfully, compassionately, share what you believe and why you believe it. Even in school you can do this. If others can't be tolerant in turn and hear you out, that's okay. Just let them know that you'd be happy to talk to them about it another time if they'd like.

If they're willing to listen and hear you out, you should listen and hear them out as well. You don't have to be afraid to hear what they believe because you know that God's Word is true. You don't have to be embarrassed about what the Bible says.

Disagreeing with someone doesn't make you a bully. The Bible tells about a woman who was caught cheating on her husband. Local leaders dragged her in front of Jesus and asked Jesus if He would join them in killing her for what she'd done. Jesus stepped in and protected the woman from the crowd. But then He said to her, "Go now and leave your life of sin."

Jesus was able to protect the weak against bullies, but still speak out against sin. I think that's how He wants you to treat your classmates. Don't be ashamed of the truth of Scripture. Talk about homosexuality with your classmates, but be respectful about it. And stand up against bullying when someone is being picked on. I think that's what Jesus would do.

Students Always Have Questions

If pastors and youth leaders and parents step out and educate youth with informative responses to the cultural myths about homosexuality, we can turn the tide on this issue. Silence simply will not cut it anymore.

As you share the truth about homosexuality, be sure to give your students time to ask questions. We have found that when given an opportunity, youth want to ask questions about their gay classmates and how to think about sexual issues. They will want to know how to lead a gay friend to Christ, how to stand up for God's truth in a way that doesn't get them labeled bigots, what to think about gay marriage, and how to deal with their gay teacher or relative or acquaintance.

Youth are probably more than ready to talk about this and want your input. The problem is that we as parents and leaders and mentors in their lives are often very uncomfortable talking about homosexuality. We need to get past our own fears and discomfort and trust God to guide our words as we speak to children and teens.

Kids, once educated, can be a force for truth in their schools. Many schools allow and even sponsor the "Day of Silence"—a yearly event where students refuse to speak for an entire day at school to protest mistreatment of gays and lesbians. In response, many Christian students have joined the new "Day of Truth," which aims to counter the promotion of homosexuality during the Day of Silence and to express a Christian perspective. (See www.dayoftruth.org.)

By participating in the Day of Truth, students learn to compassionately and graciously stand up for the truth. As a result, kids across the nation have the opportunity to hear that they have the option *not* to be gay. For those secretly struggling with same-sex attractions, the message is a lifeline of hope.

Day of Truth

The Day of Truth was established to counter the promotion of the homosexual agenda and express an opposing viewpoint from a Christian perspective.

In the past, students who have attempted to speak against the promotion of the homosexual agenda have been censored or, in some cases, punished for their beliefs. It is important that students stand up for their First Amendment right to hear and speak the truth about human sexuality in order to protect that freedom for future generations. The Day of Truth provides an opportunity to publicly exercise free speech rights.

Participating students are encouraged to wear T-shirts and pass out cards (not during class time) with the following messages:

I am speaking the Truth to break the silence.

Silence isn't freedom. It's a constraint.

Truth tolerates open discussion, because the Truth emerges when healthy discourse is allowed.

By proclaiming the Truth in love, hurts will be halted, hearts will be healed, and lives will be saved.

Notes

1. Hamilton College Gay Issues Poll, 2001, http://www.hamilton.edu/news/gayissuespoll.

2. G. Herdt and A. Boxer, *Children of Horizons,* 2nd ed. (Boston: Beach Press, 1996).

3. Ritch C. Savin-Williams, *The New Gay Teenager* (Cambridge, MA: Harvard University Press, 2005).

10

Ministry to Lesbian Women

Melissa Fryrear

———〰———

I've been a part of ministry to people affected by homosexuality since 1994. In that time I've had the opportunity to travel across the United States, as well as internationally, and I've met thousands of people affected by lesbianism and homosexuality. Regardless of whether I talk with someone from California or New York, or any state in between, I'm inevitably asked the question of how to reach out to a woman who is struggling with same-sex attraction.

Chris, a 32-year-old husband and father living in Seattle, asked how he should respond to his sister who has been living homosexually for almost a decade. Sherri, a 20-year-old college student from Virginia, shared about a young woman in her dorm who recently came out as a lesbian.

And perhaps the most heartbreaking of all, I've talked with hundreds of mothers and fathers desperate to know what they should do, or not do, now that they know their daughters are involved in lesbianism.

Given the complexity of this struggle, combined with the nuances of a woman's temperament, there are a number of important considerations to be aware of when reaching out to women who struggle with same-sex attraction.

First, it's important to understand *why* a woman would be emotionally, romantically, and/or sexually drawn to someone of the same sex. Understanding the "whys" is not only educational, it often elicits empathy from those who haven't experienced this particular struggle, and this empathy is essential to effective ministry.

When I teach on understanding the roots of female homosexuality, women and men alike often come up to me afterward and tell me that they've experienced many of the same things in their lives that a woman struggling with same-sex attraction has experienced. One woman once commented that I could take out the word "homosexuality" or "lesbianism" and everything I said would apply to her and her struggle with bulimia. The brokenness that sin brings may manifest differently in each of our lives, but often the contributing factors—or internal roots—are the same.

When people, sometimes Christians especially, learn that a woman is dealing with homosexuality, oftentimes they react inappropriately because they believe her struggle to be far removed from their own. Realizing, though, that our various struggles in life are often more similar than dissimilar fosters greater empathy and thus more compassion and grace for others.

Understanding the whys also provides a roadmap of how to respond to a woman struggling with homosexuality: what to say, what not to say, what to do, what not to do, as well as practical ways to help.

Two important truths have already been addressed in this book. Truth one: Homosexuality is *not* genetic. Truth two: Most people do not choose to be gay. Although more could be said concerning the studies that have attempted to prove female homosexuality, in particular, is genetic, no such study has ever proven a genetic link to homosexuality. (For a more complete examination of the topic of genetics and homosexuality, see *Homosexuality and the Politics of Truth* by Dr. Jeffrey Satinover and *Homosexuality: The Use of Scientific Research in the Church's Moral Debate* by Stanton Jones and Mark Yarhouse.) I can also say unequivocally that I have never met a woman who chose to be romantically or sexually attracted to another woman. These two truths aside, the question remains: Why would a woman be emotionally, romantically, and/or sexually drawn to someone of the same sex?

A number of factors can occur in a woman's life that might make her vulnerable, or susceptible, to same-sex attraction. It's these factors that lie beneath the surface, and like the roots of a tree, they feed the external fruit and give it sustenance. In the case of a woman broken sexually, that external fruit manifests as a homosexual attraction and a lesbian identity. Below is a list of the possible contributing factors to female homosexuality:

- Familial Dynamics: Mother/Daughter relationship and Father/Daughter relationship

- Personality Temperament

- Sexual Abuse

- Peer Pressures

- Spiritual Influences

- Cultural Affirmation

You may recognize that these contributing factors for women are similar to the contributing factors for men. This is true, but because the sexes are distinct—because women are different than men—the effects often manifest differently.

God created us as physical, emotional, and spiritual beings, and this is evident from the earliest part of our lives. While the events that may occur

in the first few years of life do not cause one to become lesbian or homosexual, they can set the stage for problems to develop later in life.[1]

Parents, of course, have a tremendous influence on the formation of
a child's self-perception. Not only must a child's physical needs be met—
food, shelter, and clothing—the emotional needs—affection, acceptance,
and approval—must also be met. These emotional needs are as critically
necessary as are the physical needs.[2]

Mother/Daughter Relationship

An infant girl's first two years of life are spent developing a deep and
secure bond with her primary caregiver—usually her mother. This leads
to a healthy sense of personal identity. Psychologist Erik Erikson calls
this the development of "basic trust,"[3] while author and teacher Leanne
Payne refers to the process as "coming into a sense of being."[4] With a
solid sense of identity and a confidence that her needs for love and care
will be met, a baby girl has a good foundation for future growth and
development.[5]

If this foundation isn't solidly laid or is disrupted at some point in
those critical first few years, a little girl may fail to come into this "sense
of being" and subsequently be vulnerable to an inner sense of emptiness
and longing. It's this inner sense of emptiness that can emerge later in
her life in the form of an overwhelming drive to connect with, and find
her identity in, another woman.[6]

As is true with male homosexuality, lesbianism at its core is also not
about acting out sexually with someone of the same gender. For women
it's about *connecting,* and because women are innately primarily relational,
it's about connecting *emotionally and relationally* with another woman.
This need to connect emotionally can later develop into a *sexual* expression. At its core, though, lesbianism is about emotional intimacy.

Because sexual identity seems to be more noticeably shaped by a lack
of bonding with the same-sex parent, a female baby is affected by her
lack of intimate attachment to Mom. And the same results occur, but

through the opposite relationship, for a male struggling with homosex-uality—he often feels detached and alienated from Dad.

If a child fails to connect with his or her same-sex parent and doesn't form a close relationship with him or her, some of the groundwork is laid for a possible future sexual identity struggle. In many ways it can be summed up this succinctly: A woman involved in an emotional or sexual relationship with another woman is ultimately seeking to satisfy that inner longing for a maternal presence, for attention, nurture, tender-ness, and love.[7]

Indicative of this lack of connection with Mom, are Ellie and Lisa. Ellie, a woman overcoming lesbianism said, "As I grew up, I remember spending much of my time observing my mother rather than connect-ing with her emotionally. I knew that I was meant to feel more for her, but because we seemed disconnected from one another, I did not."

Lisa said, "I always felt misunderstood by my mother and that I could never measure up to her expectations. There are no specific incidents I can point to, really. There was just this pervading sense of displeasure."

Father/Daughter Relationship

A healthy relationship between father and daughter is also neces-sary for a little girl's healthy identity development. Dads play a critical role in the lives of young children, and there are four things in particu-lar that a father needs to convey to his daughter for her developmental well being: protection, attention, adoration, and support.

When a father is able to meet these needs for his daughter, three important things happen. One, a little girl growing up with her father's protection and support develops a sense of worth as a person. Second, because the father is the opposite sex, the attention and adoration he shows her reflects back to his daughter her value specifically as a female. And third, because he represents the universal world of men and mascu-linity, he helps her learn how to interact in a healthy and appropriate way with the opposite sex.

If, however, the father isn't physically present or emotionally available to his daughter or she perceives he is unavailable to her, or if he's overtly abusive, the converse may occur: She will feel unworthy as a person; she won't feel valued as a female—and she will be inhibited from relating in a healthy way with the opposite sex.

Susan shared a story about the first time she went to a school dance. Although a pair of jeans and a T-shirt was her usual attire, she decided to wear a dress. Not owning any make-up herself, she borrowed her mother's. "The application process was difficult," she said. "How on earth do women manage to do this every day?" Persistence paid off, though. Timidly she proceeded down the stairs.

"Dad," she petitioned, "how do I look?" Her father glanced up from his evening newspaper, briefly examined her appearance, and then smirked, "Who hit you in the eyes?" Her dad may have been teasing, but his words sent her reeling—her budding femininity left in tatters. Running back to the bathroom, with tears streaming down her cheeks, she scrubbed her face raw and vowed, "I'll never do that again." Fifteen years later, when she told this story, she had still not worn any makeup since that night.

In understanding the significance of the mother–daughter and father–daughter relationships, I hope you can appreciate that these are legitimate needs—not merely whims—that need to be met, *God-given* needs in fact. A woman (as well as a man) involved in a same-sex relationship is seeking to meet a legitimate need in an illegitimate way. Surely all of us can identify with the need to be loved and the misdirected ways we attempt to meet that need for love.

Marriage

Another aspect of familial dynamics that may contribute to a woman falling into lesbianism is how a daughter perceives the relationship between her mother and father, as well as their roles as wife and husband. Many lesbian-identified women negatively judged their mother's representation of life as a woman, wife, and mother, and as such, had no desire to follow in her footsteps.

Whether because of real or perceived situations, Mom was not a female role model whom the daughter respected or wanted to emulate. Added to this may be the poor treatment of her mother by her father. If her father was belittling of her mother or minimized the significance of her roles as wife and mother, this may have caused the daughter to form negative attitudes about those roles. Again, the result was that she didn't aspire to be a wife and mother; and this may have further formulated negative attitudes about men in general, or more specifically their roles as husbands and fathers.

Anne Paulk, in interviews she conducted for her book *Restoring Sexual Identity: Hope for Women Who Struggle with Same-Sex Attraction*, was so struck by the repeated occurrence of this pattern she felt prompted to ask in her survey among ex-lesbian women: "Did you want to be like your mother when you were growing up?" More than 80 percent of the women responded with a resounding, "No!"[8]

Megan shared her perception of her parents' marriage, "I wanted to know the strength, joy, and beauty of my parents' love for one another but I never saw that. As such I did not desire marriage—I did not aspire to be a wife or a mother."

Personality Temperament

Inborn temperament also affects a girl's identity development. Often parents, and well-meaning family and friends, expect a young daughter to be a little princess—demure, sweet, and compliant—but some little girls are born with a tenacity for life and are ready to tackle the world! Sometimes a mother will struggle to accept a strong, assertive, and physically active daughter, especially if she envisioned raising the next Miss America.

A daughter may sense her mother's ambivalence or, in some cases, her overt disapproval. Feeling hurt and rejected, the girl unconsciously or consciously emotionally withdraws from her mother, thus cutting herself off from the primary source of love she needs to help her grow into her own female identity. This is what counselors label "Defensive Detachment" (DD).

DD is common among same-sex attracted women. Bob Davies and Lori Rentzel, in their book *Coming Out of Homosexuality,* define Defensive Detachment as "when we self-protectively close ourselves off from intimate relationships."[9] DD further exacerbates the increasing emotional distance and lack of connection between the daughter and her mother. The daughter is then left with what could be called a *same-sex love deficit.* If left ignored, this lack makes the young woman more vulnerable to future lesbian involvement.

Sexual Abuse

Another possible contributing factor to the development of lesbian attraction is sexual abuse. A disproportionate number of men struggling with homosexuality have been sexually abused, the majority of whom by someone of the same sex. A disproportionate number of women struggling with lesbianism have also been sexually abused, but by someone of the opposite sex. The effects of sexual abuse for men and women are often different even though the perpetrator for both was male. Some leaders in the ex-gay movement have said that while family dynamics, personality temperament, and peer pressures strongly shape a person's sexual identity, perhaps the single factor that most powerfully propels a girl toward a lesbian identity is sexual abuse, including incest, rape, or molestation.

Sexual abuse encompasses any kind of sexual interchange between a child and anyone bigger, stronger, or older. The spectrum of abusive behavior ranges from a lingering stare with or without verbal comments to inappropriate touching, kissing, oral sex, and anal or vaginal intercourse.

The incidence of sexual abuse among lesbians is incredibly high when compared to national estimates of sexual abuse against women in general. Commonly used statistics claim that 17[10] to 25[11] percent of the women in the United States will be sexually assaulted at some point during their lifetimes. But in Anne Paulk's survey of hundreds of women overcoming lesbianism, more than 60 percent of the women surveyed experienced *childhood* sexual abuse.[12]

According to Dr. Stanton Jones, provost of Wheaton College and author of *Homosexuality: The Use of Scientific Research in the Church's Moral Debate* and coauthor of *Modern Psychotherapies,* "Experience of sexual abuse as a child...more than tripled the likelihood of later reporting homosexual orientation."[13]

For a little girl sexually abused, this type of significant trauma and wounding can often seep underground and emerge later in her life in a variety of ways. With regard to same-sex issues, for example, it can emerge in a rejection of men and/or a turning exclusively to women for love and affirmation.

Being sexually violated also causes a number of women to reject their God-ordained gender as woman and the accompanying femininity. It's interesting to note that many lesbian women—not all, but many—lack any noticeable external feminine characteristics, even to the extreme of emulating typically masculine or mannish behaviors. Why is this? Michelle's experience is enlightening:

> Although I was not consciously aware of it during the many years that I lived as a lesbian, in retrospect I realized that I thought being a woman was a liability. Because I had been sexually abused by a man, I concluded that it was unsafe to be a woman. So, I reasoned, if I don't look like a woman, or in other words, if I am not thought attractive by men, I run less of a risk of being sexually abused again.

Karen, another lesbian-identified woman who had been sexually violated said, "Not looking like a woman, and looking like a man on top of that, was my suit of armor; it was my way of protecting me, of feeling safe."

Like Michelle and Karen, many women affected by sexual abuse who subsequently lived homosexually recognize they made numerous judgments and inner vows about themselves as women and about men. Jessica, a woman overcoming lesbianism, gave voice to her judgments: "I thought that being a woman was bad, that men could not be trusted, that I could only trust other women, and that men only want sex." Another woman overcoming lesbianism, Natalie, stated the inner vows she made. "I don't know that I vowed these consciously, but I know I vowed them in my heart: 'I will never trust men. I will never allow myself to be vulnerable to a man. I will only open myself up to women. I will never get married. I will never be sexual with a man.'"

The difficulty lies in that while such universal statements are not true, for these women what they believed was their truth—their perception became their reality.

Some women, though, have been sexually violated not by a male, but by an older female. But instead of being more of an aggressive act, these violations tend to be more seductive in nature. When this happens, the young girl may wonder if perhaps she is a lesbian because she experienced some degree of pleasure—first from the attention an older female gave her, and second, from the sexual activity itself.[14]

Some women haven't experienced abuse, whether sexual, physical, or emotional; however, they still have experienced the effects of abuse, having seen their mothers wounded at the hand of an abusive man. According to the survey Anne Paulk conducted, more than 60 percent witnessed some form of abuse against a family member.[15]

As a result of witnessing such grave suffering, some women made vows not to be like their mothers, whom they perceived to be weak and vulnerable, and so patterned themselves after males, rejecting their womanhood and female qualities.

Peer Pressure

In the grade-school years, while our home life and family still play a strong role in shaping our identities, peers also become increasingly influential. For some girls the grade-school years can often hold powerful events that contribute to later lesbian involvement.[16]

In the first few grades a tomboy isn't so likely to experience teasing and rejection from other girls. But our sexually oriented culture races children toward premature puberty. By second or third grade most little girls are concerned about being pretty, popular, having the right clothes, and giggling about boyfriends. The girl who does not share these interests, who truly prefers physical activity and/or being "buddies" with the boys versus romantic interests is starting to feel disconnected from other girls.[17]

Often when a girl with lesbian tendencies compares herself to peers of the same sex, she does not, in her own estimation, measure up. As other young women begin blossoming into womanhood, she feels trapped in a "third sex" mentality—she knows she isn't a man, but she doesn't feel like a woman either. As such, she may isolate and withdraw, which fuels her existing inner sense of rejection. This further alienates and separates her from the very ones with whom she has legitimate needs to spend her time—for healthy same-sex friendships as well as affirmation of her gender by members of the same sex.

Spiritual Influences

As Christians who believe in a biblical worldview, we know there is a spiritual component to our lives as well. The Bible speaks clearly about humankind's nature. "Surely I was sinful at birth, sinful from the time my mother conceived me," King David exclaims (Psalm 51:5). And regarding the nature of man and woman to go astray from God's design, the Bible teaches us, "We all, like sheep, have gone astray, each of us has turned to his own way; and the LORD has laid on him the iniquity of us all" (Isaiah 53:6). The analogy of the "roots" and "fruits" is pertinent again—the fruit of our sin nature may manifest differently in each of us, but we are each born with a universal propensity to sin.

Holding to a biblical worldview, we also know there are negative spiritual forces at work against us. Scripture teaches that the enemy of humankind—the devil—plans schemes against our lives (Ephesians 6:11). And regarding the enemy, God's Word teaches that there is no truth in him; he is the father of lies (John 8:44).

So clearly, another factor that can make a woman vulnerable to lesbianism is the various spiritual factors at work in, and against, her life.

Cultural Affirmation

At no other time in our history has lesbianism, homosexuality, and bisexuality been more accepted in American culture. In fact, in many circles it's been elevated beyond casual acceptance to a position of celebration. Within just a few minutes of tuning in to America's mainstream media, you'll see the extent to which homosexuality is glamorized.

There is not a network television station or cable channel exempt from promoting homosexuality. NBC, CBS, ABC, Fox, HBO, Showtime, Bravo, and FX all have either gay-identified characters or the show itself centers around the theme of homosexuality. Shows such as *ER* and *The L Word,* to name only two among dozens.

Following on the heels of—or some would say leading the way—are shows that glamorize bisexual behavior. For example, *Friends, The O.C.,* and reality dating shows like *ElimiDate.*

Some of today's hottest celebrities have come out of the proverbial closet to boldly proclaim their lesbian identity. Actresses Ellen Degeneres and Rosie O'Donnell, musical artists such as Melissa Ethridge, the Indigo Girls, and kd lang, and athletes such as tennis tycoon Martina Navratilova and most recently Sheryl Swoopes from the WNBA.

In addition, there are presently several magazines devoted to promoting the gay lifestyle, the most widely circulated probably being *The Advocate.* (Interesting choice of name for a gay-related magazine, isn't it?)

It's no surprise, then, that more and more women—especially younger women—are crossing gender and sexual boundaries and engaging in same-sex behaviors.

In the fall of 2005, *CBS News* cited a new study released by the Centers for Disease Control and Prevention's National Center for Health Statistics, that showed more American women—particularly those in their late teens and 20s—are experimenting with bisexuality or at least feel more comfortable reporting same-sex encounters.[18] Some experts, they said, who study sexuality say it's even more likely that many college students simply see experimentation as a rite of passage. The trend among college women has prompted some sexual behavior experts to lightheartedly refer to the term "LUG," or "Lesbian Until Graduation."

In the April 2005 edition of *Seventeen* magazine, 22-year-old Micol experimented with the idea of bisexuality because her brother is gay. "If my brother is gay, could I be gay too?" she asked. "I'd always been boy-crazy and dated a lot of guys in high school, but I started to wonder what it would be like to date a girl."

As we've seen, many possible influences are implicated in the development of same-sex attraction for women: familial dynamics, personality temperament, sexual abuse, peer pressures, spiritual influences, and cultural affirmation. Researchers from practically all viewpoints agree that a strong combination of multiple factors probably propel a woman or man toward same-sex attraction.

How Can You Minister to Lesbian Women?

Most people I meet who have not personally struggled with same-sex attraction feel they could be of no help to a woman dealing with lesbianism. This could not be further from the truth. Of course God often does use the experience of those who have walked a similar path to provide direction and encouragement to others, and this has certainly been true in my own life.

When I began my journey out of lesbianism, God sent many former lesbians and homosexuals to encourage me. But these aren't the only people who influenced me. Actually, those whom God used most significantly in my own healing were women and men who *never* struggled with homosexuality. This may come as a surprise to you. But actually I've heard this repeated so often by other former lesbians and gays that I've lost count. So if you are a woman or man who has never even had one same-sex thought in your entire life, please be encouraged that God can significantly use you to help a struggling woman.

And this should be no surprise to us really. As the apostle Paul writes in his second letter to the Corinthians: "Praise be to the God and Father of our Lord Jesus Christ, the Father of compassion and the God of all comfort, who comforts us in all our troubles, so that we can comfort those in any trouble with the comfort we ourselves have received from God" (2 Corinthians 1:3-4). Certainly this Scripture isn't specific to the homosexual struggle; it encompasses all of life's struggles. And Galatians 6:2 states, "Carry each other's burdens, and in this way you will fulfill the law of Christ."

If you've experienced hurt, rejection, or loss in your life; if you're someone who has felt unloved or that you didn't fit in with others; if you're someone who has wrestled with another type of life-dominating sin, then you're perfectly qualified to help a woman dealing with same-sex attraction.

Let's take a look at some specific and practical ways you can reach out and help. We know from studying Jesus' life that He responded to the needs of the individuals who came to Him. Joe Dallas, past Exodus board president, and founder of Genesis Counseling, in a resource booklet he wrote for Focus on the Family's Love Won Out Conference, said he believes one reason Christians have not been effective in ministering to homosexual men and women is because we have assumed that all of them are cut out of the same cloth—having the same need, needing the same response.[19] Joe believes there are essentially three types of homosexual women and men: Militant, Moderate, and Repentant. Because each of the three is different, each requires a different response.

Randy described these three types of homosexual in chapter 7. But let's review these three groups as they apply to lesbian women.

Joe explains that most militant homosexual women (and men) have a rigid agenda to normalize homosexuality combined with intolerance for opposing viewpoints. Given that I speak publicly on issues related to homosexuality, I have crossed the paths of many militant gays and lesbians.

What I've experienced is that no matter how respectful I am, no matter how gentle and sensitive I try to be, no matter how cordial my manner, the biblical truth I confess is offensive to those who do not agree with it. And when people are offended, oftentimes they react angrily. We can then be tempted to return the offense, *but we must not.* Retaliating is certainly not representative of the character of Christ. Joe explains that as Christians we are called to defend what we believe, and we must do that without attacking people.

The second group of women living homosexually include those we call "Moderate." This group is representative of most lesbian women. Most straight people have more in common with these women than they do differences. Much of our lives mirror one another—we pay our taxes every April 15, we dislike long lines of traffic, and we look forward to vacationing in the summer. We also share many of the same hopes and dreams—we want to enjoy what we do for a living, we hope to buy a nice home in a good neighborhood, and we long to find someone we can love and be loved by. Joe explains that to this group of women we must be ambassadors as Jesus was to the Samaritan woman. When Jesus approached the sexual sinner, He did not care to dialogue too extensively about her sex life. Instead, He led the conversation to the real point: Jesus wanted her to know who He is, and that He has something for her. "If you knew the gift of God and who it is that asks you for a drink, you would have asked him and he would have given you living water" (John 4:10).

More than their sexuality, God is most concerned about people's eternal position. Hopefully we all agree that heterosexuals can go to hell just as easily as gay women. The paramount issue is where do people *stand?* Are they dead in sin or alive in Christ? If they are dead in sin, it hardly matters what the sin is, they're dead and desperately need the new life offered through Jesus Christ! *The gospel—the good news of the crucifixion and the resurrection of Christ and redemption found in Him—must*

*be our priority for the woman living homosexually—just as it is for every-
one who is far off.*

The third group is "Repentant" lesbians. These are women who,
in abandoning lesbianism, are not just abandoning a sexual sin; often
they're giving up an entire network of support and identity—everything
and everyone they know.

Joe points out that having made the right decision, they come to
the church with virtually nothing. They are frightened, vulnerable,
and very, very alone. Regrettably, many in the church find it so hard
to relate to the particular sin of homosexuality that they fail to relate
to the individual. Lest Christians forget, Scripture teaches, "We all, like
sheep, have gone astray, each of us has turned to his own way..." (Isaiah
53:6). Joe states,

> As a counselor, I've seen people come from many back-
> grounds and many situations. Some of them have lovers. Some
> of them have been celibate. Some of them have just dealt with
> fantasies and the temptations....But one thing all of them have
> in common is that they wished to God that they could tell some-
> body in their church what they were going through.[20]

For the woman who has accepted Jesus Christ as her personal Savior,
who has repented of her sexual sin, and who is seeking to yield her life
to the Lordship of Christ, other believers must be willing to come alongside her, invite her into their homes, invite her into their families, invite
her into their lives, and help her fulfill her destiny in Christ.

Understanding whether a lesbian is a militant, moderate, or repentant will determine how you should respond to her and, especially in the
case of a woman who is repentant, specifically how you can help.

For women who are not yet repentant, again, we have a right to
defend our Christian worldview, but without attacking her as a person.
But beyond defending our biblical worldview, our greatest hope is that
we will have the opportunity to represent the person of Christ to her
and eventually share the gospel.

For women who do not yet personally profess Christ, your first effort can be to reach out to her with the hope of beginning a friendship. We do that in basically the same way we would with anyone, although there are a few particulars to keep in mind with regard to reaching out to someone who is lesbian-identified.

In your conversations, always mention lesbianism in a neutral context. Anita Worthen, author of the book *Someone I Love Is Gay*, points out that lesbians (and gays) are especially sensitive to the attitudes of those around them when it comes to issues related to homosexuality. Just one negative comment or casual joke can forever close the door to any possible friendship, much less the opportunity to share the gospel.

But this does not mean you shouldn't share what you believe if conversations gravitate toward issues related to homosexuality—in fact, you *should* share. That's what authentic friendship is all about—the sharing and exchanging of who we are and what we think and believe. When you state what you believe about homosexuality, though, you should do that within the larger scope of the biblical sexual ethic. Here is an example of how such a conversation might take place.

Kim: "So, Anne, exactly what to you think about homosexuality?"

Anne: "Well, Kim, the issue for me really isn't about homosexuality. You see, I hold to a biblical sexual ethic, and so I believe that *any* sexual behavior expressed outside the marital covenant between a man and a woman is not God's design for human sexuality, whether it's heterosexual or homosexual."

Responding in this way takes the focus off homosexuality and "neutralizes" it within the larger scope of biblical sexuality. You also run less of a risk of inadvertently offending someone like Kim because you're talking about homosexuality objectively and not about the person. Wording it in this way is also positive framing. It allows you to state what you're "for" versus what you're "against." You're not "against" homosexuality per se; rather, you're "for" God's design for human sexuality.

This response can also open the door to share other aspects of

Christian theology. For example, it's because God loves us that He has placed boundaries on sexual expression. He loved us so much that He sent His Son to die for us. Or, contrary to what many people believe today, gender—male and female—are not arbitrary. God specifically created humankind in the form of man and woman to reflect the Trinity. Or earthly marriage between a man and a woman is so significant to Christians because it is iconic of Jesus Christ, the bridegroom, ultimately marrying the church, His bride. These are opportunities we do not want to miss!

Another suggestion is for you to be open about your own struggles. Mike Haley, chairman of Exodus' Board of Directors and director of Focus on the Family's Gender Division, often remarks that vulnerability breeds vulnerability. Sexuality is an intimate area of life, and it takes a trusted friendship to discuss such personal matters. The woman to whom you're trying to reach out must know that you are a "safe" person and someone with whom she can allow herself to be open and honest. Candidly sharing about yourself and your own life will help to foster that type of environment.

Also, don't make lesbianism the primary point of your evangelistic conversations. Joe Dallas cautions that some Christians appear to be so obsessed with seeing people convert from homosexuality to heterosexuality that they forget the main issue. Remember, the most important concern is a person's salvation, not her sexuality.

And finally, you share the gospel with a lesbian-identified woman the same way you would share it with anyone else. We make a mistake when we imagine that the woman dealing with homosexuality needs to be approached with the claims of the gospel in some totally unique way. She doesn't.

How Women Can Help

Because a woman struggling with lesbianism is in need of attention and affirmation from same-sex peers, let's first address how another woman can best help her. Remember, one of the core issues is the need for same-sex approval and emotional bonding with other women. As such, women are in a unique and wonderful position to provide a godly example of nonsexual friendship.

Begin the friendship in the same way you would with any other woman—asking her general questions about herself and about her life. As the friendship develops and discussions gravitate to lesbianism in particular, a listening ear and an empathetic heart are invaluable.

> Take time just to enjoy life and one another's company. Have lunch together, catch a movie, or go shopping.

As she begins to open her heart, which is usually very scary for her to do, it's better to listen more and talk less. If there are areas she shares about her life that you can relate to, convey that with her. The more she realizes she's like every other woman versus being different from them, the more healing that will take place in her life.

One of the most healing aspects in my own journey was learning that many of the questions I had and frustrations I felt about being a woman were common to *many* women. This made me feel "normal" and more like "one of the girls."

As the discussions center on her involvement in lesbianism, you can take those opportunities to help her think through what the Bible says about human sexuality. Remember, the issue isn't homosexuality per se, but God's overarching plan that sexuality be expressed only within marriage between a man and a woman. You might also consider working through a relevant book together, such as *Restoring Sexual Identity* by Anne Paulk, *Out of Egypt* or *Into the Promised Land* both by Jeanette Howard, or *The Friendships of Women* by Dee Brestin. These books can be ordered through Exodus International, Focus on the Family, or a local Christian bookstore.

Don't use all the time you spend together working on her "issue." That will exhaust her as well as you. Take time just to enjoy life and one another's company. Have lunch together, catch a movie, or go shopping.

These are a few suggestions of what you can do to befriend an overcoming woman. Another excellent relationship between women is a mentoring relationship. Although a mentoring relationship entails some of the above suggestions, there are also dynamics unique to this type of relating that deserve specific attention. Anne Paulk outlines a number of suggestions for women who are mentoring a woman overcoming lesbianism:

> First, outline when and where you will meet. Set up specific times, including both starting and ending times. It is also best only to meet weekly or bi-weekly. For this type of relationship, it is also better to meet at a neutral location, for example a church office, rather than at the mentor's home. Doing these things will help avoid burnout for the mentor and help a woman not lean solely on one person for help.
>
> Second, communicate the purpose and direction of meeting together. For example, assign specific chapters of books to read, Scripture passages, or other related materials. Determine whether you will involve other activities such as journaling. Committing to these types of activities reminds the mentor that the weight of change is not on her shoulders and encourages the woman seeking help to "lift her eyes" to the One who provides the hope and healing, Jesus Christ.
>
> Third, minimize phone calls and one-on-one visits outside meeting times. Remember, the woman needing help should establish a broad base of support. Friends and other forms of support will help to meet these other needs in her life.[21]

Like a friend might do, a mentor can also help her to think through issues related to human sexuality from a biblical perspective. Working through relevant books, such as those mentioned previously, can also be a great tool.

Perhaps more than anything, a mentor acts as a coach. While the woman may depend on you primarily in the beginning, as time unfolds encourage her to involve other women in her life and model for her how to do that. For example, ask her to think of two or three women she would like to get to know better. Encourage her to ask each of them to lunch or to coffee.

Participating in a women's Bible study can also provide a great community of encouragement and support. I remember when the Lord first impressed on my heart that I begin attending a weekly women's Bible study at my church in Kentucky. I flatly refused! "Lord," I grumbled, "I don't know those women. I don't have anything in common with them. And I don't want to do it!" Needless to say, He remained resolute in His promptings.

In time—and because of God's grace—I did join that women's Bible study. Looking back, that season of my life became one of the most meaningful in my journey. The women and I never discussed my struggle with lesbianism, although I was okay with the fact that they knew. Just being around them, laughing with them, crying with them, and praying with them healed so many wounds in my heart. In essence my woman-hood and femininity began to blossom. Those women will never know this side of heaven how significantly they impacted my life. Ladies, thank you!

As you mentor an overcoming woman, be aware that your suggestions that she reach out to other women will seem overwhelming to her at first. Don't force her to do this, but do encourage her to set this as a goal. And once she begins to form friendships with other women, she will need a great deal of guidance and ongoing encouragement.

If those who are dealing with same-sex attraction embrace female friendships and find their place in the larger community of women—church, work, social interests—she will find greater commonality with other women and, as a result, feel more secure and content to be "just another woman." This alone resolves much of the same-sex attraction.

Special Cautions

While there are so many benefits to peer friendships and mentoring relationships between women, there are also pitfalls of which to be aware. Do not discount the danger of developing an overly emotional bond with a woman overcoming lesbianism. Some "ever straight" women fall into lesbian relationships, even though they have no previous history of lesbianism, because they are emotionally needy.[22] Anita Worthen, who has counseled hundreds of women affected by lesbianism, offers these insights:

> We cannot be naive in this regard. Same-sex attraction between women is based on a genuine God-given need for intimacy that has been twisted. We all have a need for love. God made us social beings, and it's common for women to find a deep satisfaction in forming significant friendships with other women. If these same-sex needs are currently unmet, even "straight" women can find themselves drawn into inappropriate relationships."[23]

As you walk alongside an overcoming woman, it's important that you maintain other close friendships as well. Encourage your friend also to pursue other friendships. In addition to time spent just between the two of you, spend time in groups. Invite others to lunch with the two of you. Get involved in church groups where you interact with others. These safeguards will help avoid the exclusivity that can lead to an emotional dependency.[24] (For further information on emotional enmeshment, see Lori Rentzel's booklet *Emotional Dependency*, available through Exodus International or Focus on the Family.)

At some point in the friendship you may have to draw specific boundaries. Many women involved in lesbianism often don't know proper boundaries when it comes to healthy relationships with other women. Drawing boundaries isn't a cruel thing to do; it is actually a caring and healthy thing to do.

For example, if you begin to feel that she's calling too often or at inappropriate times, gently mention this to her and offer specific windows of when it's convenient for her to call. You may unintentionally hurt her feelings, but you are not intentionally injuring her. This is an important distinction. We inevitably hurt other people's feelings. That is a fact of life. In the end, setting these specific boundaries will help her to benefit from the friendship or mentoring relationship without relying too heavily on you.

Keep in mind, too, that the Lord desires to bring to the surface those unresolved and unhealed issues in her life—and He may use you to do it! As such, you may find that something you say or do may unintentionally trigger a past hurt. If you commit a legitimate offense, even by accident, apologize; but if she has a strong emotional response, keep in mind that you may have touched something painful from her past. Explore this possibility with her and if so, pray and ask the Lord to heal any areas of wounding in her heart.

Also be aware that her struggle with lesbianism is often only one piece of her fractured puzzle. Many women overcoming homosexuality have other emotional problems as well, although there is interconnectedness among them all.

Of those who responded to Anne Paulk's survey, for example, 67 percent have dealt with some form of depression and one quarter have attempted suicide.[25]

Other related behaviors can include overeating, alcoholism, chemical dependency, and/or personal abuse such as cutting. Some women also suffer from borderline personality disorder or disassociate disorder. Given the seriousness of these types of emotional issues, professional help is often needed. To locate a qualified counselor in your area, contact Focus on the Family, Exodus, or NARTH (National Association for Research and Therapy of Homosexuality). Contact information for these organizations is listed in the appendix.

You will also want to be sensitive to, but not anxious about, the fact that she may develop an attraction toward you. This isn't uncommon because her attraction to another woman is usually her response to her own deep needs. Remember, she is starving for attention from women. When that legitimate need begins to be met, her emotions may revert to the only thing she has ever known—connecting with a woman in an illegitimate way, which is sexually.

If you sense this occurring, don't pull away totally, just ensure healthy boundaries exist in the relationship. Know, too, that as the friendship grows, the sexual attraction will often diminish as her legitimate needs are met in healthy ways. You are helping her immensely in providing a godly example of a *nonsexual* friendship.

It's helpful to mention that a woman overcoming same-sex broken-ness may relapse. One of my disciplers often commented, "Recovery is sometimes not without relapse." Certainly this isn't a license for her will-fully to sin. Rather it's an acknowledgment that her journey may involve successes as well as failures—three steps forward and one step back or five steps forward and two steps back. The Lord can work in the midst of it all though. As a friend or mentor, you mustn't take her failures person-ally. If she enters a sexual relationship with another woman, whether as a one-night stand or over a period of months, she is ultimately respon-sible only to one person for her life—the Lord Jesus Christ.

If she does make a mistake, don't reprimand or condemn her. Much more constructively help her learn from the situation. Help her recognize the "warning signs" as well as the different ways the Lord had provided a way out for her.

Also keep in mind the "fruits" versus the "roots." Acting out sexually isn't the critical issue, although it's certainly consequential. The critical issues are those areas in her heart not yet healed.

Many times the Lord can take such a painful and tragic situation and turn it around for her good. Finally, encourage her as she recom-mits to walking forward with the Lord and to becoming the complete and whole woman of God He intends her to be.

The most common mistake I see many Christians make is that they usurp the role of the Holy Spirit and attempt to passively manipulate or overtly force a woman to take steps she's not yet capable of taking or ones the Holy Spirit has not yet led her to take. Changing her is God's work, not any person's (Jeremiah 17:9,14). The road to changing sexual attraction and identity can be a long and difficult one. You, as a friend or mentor, are there for a specific season in her life. You are not her Savior.

Anne Paulk offers these perspectives of what to realistically expect of a woman who is pursuing overcoming lesbianism:

- She will grow personally, learn about the motivations of her same-sex longings, and gain ground in obeying God.
- She will experience greater power or authority over her own feelings.
- God will honor her obedience in a supernatural way, changing her inward perceptions and outward perspectives.
- Given hard work, obedience, faith, and perseverance, she will change over time.
- She will see herself as being just another woman among women of all types.[26]

How Men Can Help

Although the core need in the heart of a woman who is overcoming lesbianism is to bond correctly with other women, men can certainly be significantly helpful. Because many lesbian-identified women have been mistreated by men, some in horrific ways, and as such have a distorted view of men, the friendship of a godly man can be very healing.

Because a disproportionate number of gay women have been sexually abused, men need to be especially sensitive to how they interact with them. Often they have a real fear of, or intense hatred for men because of deep emotional wounding.

Give a lesbian-identified woman time to trust you as a person and the friendship as a whole. This may take a long time! It's also imperative that you respect her boundaries. She will probably recoil if you attempt to hug her, and more than likely she will even be uncomfortable shaking your hand or receiving a friendly pat on the shoulder.

As the friendship develops, though, she may be more open to godly physical affirmation, such as an arm squeeze around the shoulders—but always ask first! And if she hesitates or flatly declines, don't pressure or ridicule her.

Be aware, too, that she has a number of misperceptions about men. As such, most of what you say initially will be filtered through those misperceptions and may elicit a negative response. For example, you may make a sincere comment that you think a certain woman is attractive. Her first thought might be, "See, all that men care about is sex!" But as she gets to know you and your honorable character, you will help to dispel those misperceptions.

It will also be helpful to her if you avoid treating her like a "buddy." Lesbians are often comfortable relating to men in this fashion, but you can help by not feeding into past patterns. While she may not always appreciate it, you should respectfully treat her as a woman, which means a bit of extra courtesy is needed.[27]

If you're a single man and find that you feel romantically or sexually attracted to her, especially if she's just beginning her healing process, assume that she's not at all interested. Because you are a Christian and a "safe" friend, she may have her guard down. If you begin to pursue a premature romance, her healing process may be derailed and the friendship terminated. A woman overcoming lesbianism cannot enter into a successful heterosexual romance until she has resolved her lesbian issues.[28]

Ultimately, she needs to reconnect with the feminine side of herself, and this is done in relationships with both women *and* men because both sexes affirm gender identity in critically different ways. As you model godly masculinity—the good of man—and affirm her as a woman in nonsexual ways, you will be helping her to do this.

How Families Can Help

Many women mentors and counselors within Exodus ministries have observed that the best combination, and strongest support system, for female same-sex attracted women is pairing a same-sex attracted woman with a healthy married couple. Notice I didn't say *perfect,* but *healthy!*

Remember how important the healthy family is in the proper development of a young woman's sexual identity? Although these vital elements were missing in many women's lives who struggle with lesbianism, God can make up for these losses. One way He does is by exposing her to, and bringing her into, healthy families—again, not perfect, but healthy.

Psalm 68:5-6 shares what God's heart is to the needy: "A father to the fatherless, a defender of widows, is God in his holy dwelling. God sets the lonely in families, he leads forth the prisoners with singing...."

Hope and Tom, and their three beautiful children, are a family God used very significantly in my own life. They reached out to me in incredibly gracious and loving ways. I can't begin to add up all the dinners I had at their home. The meals were delicious, and the fellowship that followed even sweeter. Perhaps more influential than anything they ever said or did—although they said and did many wonderful things—was being able to observe each of them individually—Hope as a wife and mother, Tom as a husband and father, and all of them as a family unit. I saw the best of male and female, the beauty of complementarity, and the joy (and challenges!) of parenting. I became so close to this family that their children affectionately referred to me as Aunt Melissa, and I was privileged to be in the delivery room when Hope and Tom gave birth to their third child. They gave me so much more than their friendship; they embraced me into their family.

Mike Haley shares that he has never met a woman or man who left homosexuality who didn't do it without taking the outstretched hand of someone else. Because we're broken relationally, we're restored relationally. When a woman makes the decision to leave lesbianism for the joys of the Christian life, friends, mentors, a pastor, a counselor, and others who are willing to walk alongside her to listen, support, and encourage her can be valuable resources as she goes through a very painful and often difficult process of change.

A Powerful Help

I would be remiss if I did not stress how important prayer is on behalf of unrepentant, lesbian-identified women, moderates, and those who are seeking to overcome same-sex attraction. In reality, it is the most helpful and powerful thing we can do for them. The bondage is too great; the wounds too severe; the lies too deceptive; the counterfeit too seductive without the intervening power of the Holy Spirit and the matchless name of Jesus Christ. As a help, a personal friend of mine wrote a book of prayers specifically for individuals and families affected by homosexuality titled *The Healing Word: Praying Scriptual Promises for Those Who Struggle with Homosexuality*. To order this excellent resource, contact Exodus International.

Other Resources

There are a number of additional events and resources that can greatly help a woman overcome lesbianism. One is associating with an Exodus Member Ministry. For a complete list of Exodus ministries, access them on the web at www.exodus.to or call or write them. (Information about Exodus is provided at the close of this book.)

Also suggest she attend (and consider attending with her) educational conferences designed to help same-sex overcomers. Focus on the Family's one day Love Won Out conference is focused on "addressing, understanding, and preventing homosexuality" and is hosted in different cities around the United States and Canada at least six times a year. For information, you can call 800.A.Family [(800) 232-6459] and ask for details about Love Won Out, or you can visit their website at www.lovewonout.com.

Every summer Exodus hosts a powerful week-long conference for those overcoming lesbianism and homosexuality. The conference also includes a track of workshops specifically tailored for parents and family members as well as a track for pastors and other church leaders.

Given the severity of issues that often accompany a struggle with same-sex attraction, many women need the help provided by professional counselors or therapists who, of course, affirm an orthodox Christian view on homosexuality. To find a professional counselor in your area, contact Focus on the Family or Exodus. Or you can call NARTH (National Association for Research and Therapy of Homosexuality), a secular network of professionals who believe in the therapeutic process as a means to resolve same-sex attraction.

Given the complexity of female homosexuality and the severity of the inner wounds often associated with it, the overcoming process is just that, a *process!* For most women, becoming entangled in lesbianism occurs over a long period of time and thus untangling from lesbianism takes a long time as well, often many months or even years. The Bible calls this process sanctification. Sanctification can happen in both a moment (separation to God) and in a process (the course of life befitting those so separated).[29]

How long does transformation take? That can vary a great deal with each woman. Every woman is a unique creation. Each has unique weaknesses and strengths that can help or hinder God's work in her life. The depth and degree of involvement in same-sex attractions, behaviors, and identity also influences the change process. Women who have had long-term involvement in same-sex fantasies and relationships usually experience a longer process.

Overcoming same-sex attractions, behavior, and identity is a by-product of following Jesus. The change that God wants to bring about in a lesbian-identified woman is ultimately about adopting a new identity, acknowledging the truth about self, God, and others, and becoming the woman God designed her to be. This may or may not include marriage in her future and/or children. Marriage is not a measure of change. For some women who have overcome lesbianism, dealing with their same-sex attracted issues did result in an interest in the opposite sex and eventual marriage. (On a personal note, if you know of a tall, redheaded man in his forties who loves football and would look great in a Scottish kilt, let me know!) For other women, God has called them to, and graced them for, a life of singleness.

For the woman overcoming lesbianism, her journey must ultimately be her own. And in that regard, her central focus and primary motivation must always be about pursuing a relationship with Jesus Christ and not necessarily a change from homosexuality. The opposite of homosexuality is not heterosexuality—it is holiness.

But regardless of whether it takes a few months or several years, change *is* possible, and any woman who desires to overcome same-sex attraction, with God's enabling grace and help, can. No matter how broken or sinful her past may be, she can become more than she ever dreamed or imagined. With God all things are possible.

Notes

1. Bob Davies and Lori Rentzel, *Coming Out of Homosexuality: New Freedom for Men and Women* (Downers Grove, IL: InterVarsity Press, 1993), p. 44.

2. J. Michael Bailey and Kenneth J. Zucker, "Childhood Sex-Typed Behavior and Sexual Orientation: A Conceptual Analysis and Quantitative Review," *Developmental Psychology*, 31, 1995, p. 49.

3. Erik Erikson, *Childhood and Society* (New York: Norton, 1963), p. 249.

4. Leanne Payne, *The Broken Image* (Westchester, IL: Good News, Crossway Books, 1981), pp. 121-36.

5. Davies and Rentzel, *Coming Out*, p. 45.

6. Ibid.

7. This important subject is thoroughly explained in Elizabeth R. Moberly, *Homosexuality: A New Christian Ethic* (Cambridge, England: James Clarke & Co., 1983).

8. Anne Paulk, *Restoring Sexual Identity: Hope for Women Who Struggle with Same-Sex Attraction* (Eugene, OR: Harvest House Publishers, 2003), Appendix B.

9. Davies and Rentzel, *Coming Out*, p. 108.

10. National Institute of Justice and Centers for Disease Control and Prevention, *Prevalence, Incidence, and Consequences of Violence Against Women Survey*, 1998.

11. J. Frieldman and T. Crespi, "Child Sexual Abuse: Offenders, Disclosure, and School-Based Initiatives," *Adolescence*, vol. 37, no. 145: p. 151.

12. Paulk, *Restoring Sexual Identity*, p. 57.

13. Stanton Jones and Mark Yarhouse, *Homosexuality: The Use of Scientific Research in the Church's Moral Debate* (Downers Grove, IL: InterVarsity Press, 2000), p. 57.

14. Paulk, *Restoring Sexual Identity,* p. 59.

15. Paulk, Classification of Definitions of Abuse, *Restoring Sexual Identity,* Appendix B.

16. Davies and Rentzel, *Coming Out,* p. 47.

17. Ibid., p. 48.

18. *CBS News,* September 16, 2005, http://www.cbsnews.com/stories/2005/09/16/health/main851480.shtml; National Center for Health Statistics of the Centers for Disease Control and Prevention, http://www.cdc.gov/nchs/products/pubs/pubdad/361-370/ad362.

19. Joe Dallas, *How Should We Respond? An Exhortation to the Church on Loving the Homosexual* (Colorado Springs: Focus on the Family, 1999), p. 10.

20. Ibid., p. 13.

21. Paulk, *Restoring Sexual Identity,* p. 110.

22. Anita Worthen and Bob Davies, *Someone I Love Is Gay* (Downers Grove, IL: InterVarsity Press, 1996), p. 171.

23. Ibid.

24. Ibid., p. 172.

25. Paulk, *Restoring Sexual Identity,* p. 124.

26. Ibid., p. 119.

27. Worthen and Davies, *Someone I Love,* p. 176.

28. Ibid.

29. W. E. Vine, *Vine's Complete Expository Dictionary of Old and New Testament Words* (Nashville: Thomas Nelson Publishers, 1996), pp. 210, 545.

11

25 Questions and Answers About Gay Ministry

Alan Chambers

—⟪⟫—

1. How does Exodus partner with churches in reaching homosexuals?

In January of 2006, Exodus International launched the Exodus Church Network. This network consists of churches committed to the truth of Scripture and to walking alongside those impacted by homosexuality. These churches may not have special programs for those impacted by homosexuality, but they are safe places for people laying their sexuality at the foot of the Cross of Jesus Christ. Participation in the Exodus Church Network is simple, unburdensome, and guarantees churches regular resources and information on ministering to those impacted by homosexuality. Exodus hopes to ultimately have 10,000 churches nationwide participating!

2. If you could give the evangelical church a report card for how well it's ministered to the gay community in the past ten years, what grade would you give it and why?

Today I would say the church gets "Most Improved" for how they are reaching out via getting educated, seeking information, and begging to be equipped to minister in this vital area.

The church seemed slow to action ten years ago, but I believe that the many issues related to young people being bombarded with pro-gay theology and messages caused the church to realize a response was needed. Too, I believe that today's Christian men and women have a desire to balance the truth with grace. I believe that the church today is a place where people recognize their own fallibility—and that has caused Christians to have compassion for others.

Where I once was skeptical about the church's ability to reach out effectively, today I am most encouraged and very grateful.

3. You've mentioned your early struggle as a boy who was "pre-homosexual." Looking back, was there something your parents or someone in the church could have done to steer you clear of homo-sexuality? What advice would you give parents who may be seeing signs that their own young kids are struggling with homosexual feelings?

Absolutely. I look at books like *Bringing Up Boys* by Dr. James Dobson and *A Parent's Guide to Preventing Homosexuality* by Dr. Joseph Nico-losi that have brought great awareness to parents, teachers, and others in recognizing warning signs such as a boy's inability to identify with his own gender and to connect with other boys relationally and the similar warning signs for girls.

I was a classic pre-homosexual boy: emotionally isolated from my dad, afraid of sports and interacting with other boys, and overcompensating in my identification with mom and female peers. My relationships were primarily with little girls. I didn't perceive myself as being remotely similar to other boys. Looking back, my parents knew this and tried to steer me appropriately towards typically masculine activities such as sports, but they didn't understand the complexity or the depth of my gender identity struggles. Today, that information is more readily available and understandable for parents.

4. When it comes to homosexuality, pastors often feel they can't win no matter what they do. On the one hand, they don't want to dilute what the Bible says about homosexual sin. Yet on the other hand they don't want gay protesters at their door. And finally, they know they should be sensitive to those who are struggling with homosexuality. What encouragement can you give to pastors about this issue?

Pastors as well as all Christians must take the hand up/hand out approach. We must put our hand up against the advancement of agendas that are contrary to Christ. We must battle against bad legislation that seeks to legitimize sin. But at the same time, we must never put our hand up to an issue without reaching out a helping hand to those affected by that issue. We all know how to reach out with the same grace and compassion that reached out to us when we were lost in sin. Christ came for all of us or He came for none of us—and that is what we must remember when seeking to transform our congregations into ministries of redemption.

Additionally, I want to encourage pastors not to be intimidated by popular opinions, polls, or harsh criticisms. I'm reminded of the numerous churches that have hosted the Focus on the Family Love Won Out conferences since 1998. Those churches have been criticized in the public, attacked by the media, and vandalized by pro-gay activists. And yet they have not backed down from taking a stand. Nor have they reacted in anger. Just like Jesus, they have been full of grace and truth.

5. What does it take for homosexuals to change? And how can Christians help them transition out of the gay lifestyle?

Change takes making a conscious choice to do so and choosing to pursue obedience to Christ above all else. Lasting change takes honesty, accountability, and submission. It takes denying yourself and what *seems* natural.

Churches and Christians can help by surrounding the men and women seeking change. Usually those involved in homosexuality are leaving behind an entire way of life and a community that has supported them and been family to them.

Friends of mine like Mike Haley, who works at Focus on the Family, tell stories of church members inviting him to their houses on Friday nights to help him have healthy alternatives to going to gay bars. That's my story too. I needed something to fill my time while I was still very susceptible to temptation—church members and friends willingly met this need in my life.

Most of all I needed healthy male relationships with men who never struggled with homosexuality. After all, one of the causes of homosexuality is that deep-seated feeling of inadequacy and inability to relate to the same sex.

Don't place your time frame or your expectations on someone. Homosexuality took a long time to develop, and it will take time for it to be healed.

And dating someone of the opposite sex is a *benefit* of change, not a precursor to it.

6. What advice would you give to the pastor who wants to minister to a family in the church with a gay son or daughter? And how should pastors respond to homosexuals in their own families?

Start by releasing the parents from any shame or stigma that stems from the nature of the sin. Homosexuality is one sin among many. No parent should feel worse because his or her child is involved in homosexuality. And aside from recommending issue-specific materials and books and conferences, minister to them in the same manner you would if their child was involved in heterosexual sin.

Events like the Love Won Out or annual Exodus conferences are incredible tools for pastors as well as those with gay loved ones. And talking to other parents is a huge help. At Exodus we have an online forum filled with parents who can encourage, listen, and pray for one another. For more info on this group, see the appendix.

7. Talk to the pastor who may have been homophobic in the past and now wants to change his attitude toward homosexuals. What are some ways he can effectively reach out to the gay community?

Be open about your own story of brokenness and redemption. Those of us who counsel often say, "Never trust a pastor who doesn't walk with a limp." Pastors should be the first to share their vulnerabilities and model transparency. No one wants to be in relationship with someone who seems perfect. The largest churches today are often the ones that practice a lifestyle of openness, vulnerability, and transparency from the top down.

Share publicly that your church wants to welcome those who are searching for answers. Let it be known that your congregation is more than able to handle someone who might not be ready to leave homosexuality, but who is searching for truth. Emphasize how safe your church is.

Speak on homosexuality from a redemptive standpoint. Preaching against sin is common. I challenge pastors to spend more time talking about *what God is for* than they do about what He is against. We must remember there is more available then just stopping behaviors—real transformation and a full life is possible.

8. You say that homosexuality is a relational problem and that homosexuals are seeking an emotional connection when they act out sexually. How does that change when a person accepts Christ? Does He fill that emotional connection, does the need go away, or is the need

still there and the new believer must simply live without that emotional connection?

The emotional needs at the root of homosexuality are met by finding sufficiency in Christ and growing in true relationship with Him, but also by learning to relate in healthy ways with the same gender, and in building healthy, satisfying friendships with the opposite sex. Acting out sexually is a response to legitimate but unmet relational needs, and it does meet those legitimate needs in illegitimate ways. However, people who have walked away from homosexuality and who build healthy relationships with the same sex often report that the good relationships are much more satisfying than the illicit sexual relationships in which they used to indulge.

9. Is it harder to reach older or younger homosexuals? Are there any differences in reaching out to them?

This question is not easily answered. There are issues that make it easier and harder for both categories. Older homosexuals tend to be more fully entrenched in their own gay identities and in the gay community. That aspect makes it harder for them to break their ties with homosexuality.

At the same time, people who have lived homosexually for longer periods of time have a better grasp of the reality of the gay life, and as a result may be more open to discussion about something that might be "better." Young people may not have as much baggage, but the current climate in schools, media, and politics makes homosexuality seem legitimate and even cool. It can be difficult to convince young people that there is reason to change. Additionally, young people often carry attitudes of invincibility or think that things will somehow be different for them. As with anyone, people often have to make mistakes, face consequences, and realize the reality of their choices themselves.

As with any evangelical target, the key to reaching homosexuals is to meet them where they are and to understand their situation.

10. Are many gays addicted to pornography? Is that a separate issue or is it part of being homosexual? How can I help my gay friend overcome this addiction?

Many people—but not all—struggling with homosexuality also deal with issues surrounding the use of or addiction to pornography. However, pornography use and abuse is rampant within the church and culture at large, not just in the homosexual population. Overcoming a pornography addiction requires accountability and support. As with any addiction, the compulsion to look at pornography is strong, and when the compulsions are denied, the person can go through withdrawal-like symptoms. Give your friend a safe place to share the struggle. Be available for your friend during the difficult times and provide hard accountability.

11. Is it possible that a gay man or woman who accepts Christ will be tempted to form an emotional attachment to a mentor or a strong leader in the church? How can this be avoided?

Unfortunately, accepting Christ does not create instantly mature, healthy people. A gay or lesbian person who accepts Christ and desires to submit his or her homosexuality to Him is still emotionally broken and relationally immature. There are risks of emotional dependency or unhealthy relating with those attempting to help him or her.

The former homosexual has likely left all that he (or she) knows, and he will be lonely and insecure. The key is for the mentor to be sensitive to these issues and to realize that a big part of the healing process is *learning* how to relate to the same sex in healthy ways. The mentor should set solid boundaries in the relationship. The mentor should also be bold and gracious in discussing the dynamics of the relationship with the homosexual. This may be difficult on the person leaving homosexuality, but it is vital in his or her process of growing into a healthy, mature man or woman.

The risk of emotional attachment should never keep someone from reaching out to a struggling man or woman. It may not be an easy situation, but the blessings will outweigh the difficulties!

12. I've heard that some gays (particularly men) act out sexually due to loneliness. Is this true? How can I help my friend overcome loneliness without offering to be there every time he seems lonely?

Loneliness does indeed often work to make men and women more vulnerable to a sexual fall. The gay community, most of whom are single and very communal in the way they live and interact, is often a sharp contrast to the church community.

At the same time, it's important for the struggler to work through the issue of loneliness and learn to endure loneliness and to allow God to use seasons of loneliness to strengthen and mature him. In that regard, it's important for those wanting to help the struggler to *not* rush to fix their friend's loneliness every time he seems lonely.

However, there are ways to help alleviate the loneliness homosexuals feel that comes from being completely removed from their former support network. You can include them in your family activities. Have them over for Sunday lunch, or even better, on a Friday night for whatever your family has planned. Invite them to your kids' sporting events or to join you on father/son or father/daughter outings. Find out their birthdays and celebrate with them. Invite them to join you for church events. Call them on occasion just to see how they are. The key is to make sure they know that while they may have time alone, they are not alone. Let them know that someone cares about them and enjoys being with them.

13. I want to witness to the gay community in our large city, but I can't find anyone who has the same burden. Should I go it alone or is that dangerous in any way?

This all depends on whether or not you struggled personally with homosexuality. If you didn't, then I don't think evangelizing respectfully in this way is a problem. If you do have a past or present struggle with homosexuality, I encourage you to make sure you have a strong handle on your own issues, are accountable to one or more others, and that you never go it alone.

In fact, I recommend that you witness in non-gay settings. Don't go to known gay hangouts like bars, public parks, or other areas that might compromise your integrity. Also, I don't recommend that you witness in gay chat rooms or other areas on the internet that are typically for homosexuals only. These places only serve to trip you up.

If you are going to witness, do so with a friend who has never struggled with homosexuality and who is a strong Christian who understands the depths and complexities of your own struggle—someone who won't allow you to step over boundaries for the sake of reaching out.

Remember, nothing is worth compromising your own walk with the Lord. That would only serve as a stumbling block for those you are trying to reach.

My personal conviction is that there are plenty of others in the church who do not share my past struggle with homosexuality. They are far more equipped to go into areas where I have chosen never to go again because of the possibility of being tempted.

Whoever you are, regardless of your familiar sins, be prayed up. Be respectful of people. Be submitted to the Holy Spirit's leading, and stay accountable to others.

14. How do I begin reaching out to gays? Should I visit gay hangouts and try to strike up a conversation?

The first step should be reaching out to gays you know personally. It's very likely that someone in your world is gay. The key is to simply build a relationship with him or her in the same way you would build a relationship with anyone.

We don't recommend frequenting gay bars or gay pride events as a way of reaching out in most circumstances. However, if you are aware of an area of town with a large gay population or a coffee house or restaurant or store that has a large gay patronage, going to those places with the intention of making some friends would be a great idea. We believe the best way to win a homosexual to Christ is to become friends first, and through that friendship to "share the reason for the hope that you have."

Most gay people are not receptive to evangelism tracts or quotes from the Bible about homosexuality. If you come out with the gospel too early, you may sever the relationship prematurely. However, there is nothing wrong with that type of evangelism if you feel God prompting you to do that. Always commit all outreach to prayer and follow the leading of the Lord.

15. Does becoming a Christian affect the gay person's living arrangements? For instance, if a homosexual accepts Christ, but wants to continuing living with the same-sex partner to win the partner to Christ, but promises to refrain from any sexual contact, is that all right? What if both partners become Christians? Can they still live together in celibacy or must one of them move out?

If a new Christian (or a longtime Christian) realizes the need to walk away from homosexuality, he (or she) should be advised to remove himself from all situations likely to cause him to stumble, including changing living arrangements if that is a problem area. Continuing to live together makes it much more difficult to abstain from wrong behavior. However, as we have said many times, behavior is only part of homosexuality. Of greater concern would be the continuation of relationships based on unhealthy emotional or relational connections. It's important for people to do everything they can to extricate themselves from any and all emotionally enmeshed relationships. This being said, for the Christian ministering to a person in this situation, it's important to be patient and to let the Holy Spirit do His work. It may take time for the person leaving homosexuality to take each "next" step toward healing. Our job is not to force obedience, but to walk alongside the person and help him in whatever way God prompts us to help.

16. If a homosexual becomes a Christian, but his same-sex attractions are unknown to the church, should they be made public?

I don't think that anyone, regardless of their sin struggles, needs to have his personal business discussed publicly unless he chooses such a course of action. I believe that someone who is struggling with homosexuality needs to be in contact with a member of the pastoral staff or their designate to work through issues that relate to overcoming that struggle.

A wonderful option would be for that person to have a small group of fellow believers whom he can share with, be known by, and be in community with.

If a Christian continues in sin, there might need to be a confrontation, but that should be done according to Matthew 18:15-17.

17. Can a homosexual who has become a Christian work around children in the Sunday school or elsewhere?

First of all, becoming a Christian is not the issue. Practicing homosexuals, whether they are Christians or not, should not teach Sunday school to any age. However, the case may be different if someone has accepted Christ and surrendered his (or her) sexuality to God.

The majority of homosexuals are not pedophiles, and someone who has left homosexuality does not pose any specific risk to children as a result of his former homosexual practices.

Anyone, no matter his or her background, should be carefully screened before being entrusted with precious children. As with any childcare worker, criminal background checks should be done to ensure that the worker has no criminal history and especially no history of violence or abuse against children.

18. How does becoming a homosexual affect the nonsexual interests of the gay person? For instance, if a lesbian is extremely into sports, can she be expected to remain interested in what our society thinks of as more masculine activities or should her interests change? Likewise, if a gay man is interested in traditionally female interests (sewing, cooking, hairstyling, etc.), will those interests change?

I have always liked decorating. I love to shop. I like clothes. My favorite channels are HGTV, The Food Network, and any channel that has a good makeover show. I can tell you what designer made what suits just by looking at them. Do those things make me gay? Apparently not because I still like those things, and I am completely heterosexual. I am not a woman because I like the same things that women typically like. I am no less a man because I don't always care for the things that men typically care for. I may not be typical, but I am a man and no one can change that.

For the person coming out of homosexuality who, like me, enjoys fashion, decorating and the like, *enjoy!* God might have created you with a gift for these things. Unfortunately, the world you lived in as a child probably condemned you for it. Chances are you are more sensitive and that only caused you to internalize the teasing and condemnation you heard from others related to this.

There is something to be said for gender conformity. I think sports for boys are healthy and to some degree should be mandated, at least as something they have to learn. But I believe the same for girls. The truth is that sports promote security, and studies show that a child who is athletic is healthier emotionally and physically. For girls, studies indicate that girls who are athletic are far less likely to get into abusive relationships as adults.

At the same time, I think that a boy who wants to pursue other interests needs to be encouraged to do so and supported by his father. Even if the dad is completely out of his element, he needs to continue to support and be actively involved with his son in whatever interests he chooses.

The same holds true for girls. If you have an athletic daughter and she hates dolls and playing house, well then so be it. Don't force your likes and dislikes on her. My wife still has many of the dolls she was given as a child—they are in perfect condition...and not because she wanted to keep them that way. She hated dolls. She loved being active outside, and she became a nationally ranked competitive swimmer. She can play football and knows the rules of many other sports. But she never struggled with lesbianism. I think this was because she was raised by secure and supportive parents who nurtured her gifts and saw femininity as something far deeper than her interests and abilities, or lack thereof.

Masculinity and femininity is related to character and grounded in who God created us to be. I don't want to toot my own horn, but I am firmly grounded in my masculinity and in Christ, and many men involved in typically heterosexual, manly things but not grounded in Christ's character don't have anything on me. The standard is Christ, and we are measured against Him when it comes to true masculinity or femininity. I am thankful for the inner change that brought about the true masculine in my life.

19. Does the homosexual who becomes a Christian essentially give up any hope for a satisfying sex life?

A homosexual who decides to walk away from homosexuality absolutely does not give up hope for a satisfying sex life. The degree to which new attractions happen is different for every person. Rarely does God supply a raging lust for the opposite sex to replace a raging lust for the same sex. However, for those people who God sees fit to provide a spouse of the opposite sex, their marital sex life has great potential to be not only satisfying, but fulfilling and rich in a way that homosexual sex could never be.

20. Becoming a Christian involves repentance. How do homosexuals actually repent? Do they repent for their sexual acting out or their temptations? If being a homosexual is so much a part of a person's identity as is claimed, it seems like they'd be repenting for being the person they are, not for the sexual sins they've committed.

We are all born sinners in need of salvation. Salvation requires that we repent, i.e., acknowledge that our ways are wrong and that God's ways are right. I believe repentance is an event *and* a journey. The event is at salvation, when we choose Jesus for life. The journey is walking this out daily for the rest of our lives.

I believe that repentance for all of us is a sorrowing of who we are and committing to be who we were created to be. So, yes, repentance for the homosexual person and anyone else for that matter is repenting of who they are—behaviors, identity, and all.

This is why I believe that it is so important to clarify that just living a celibate gay life is just as sinful as living a sexually promiscuous one. The sin is in identifying with anything that is contrary to Christ, which homosexuality clearly is.

21. It seems like homosexuality is everywhere today. Is homosexuality on the rise?

Homosexuality in America is more noticeable today than ever before. We live in a society that seems more comfortable talking about difficult issues. Certainly we live in a culture that pushes the boundaries of sexuality more than ever. While I think that homosexuality might be on the rise to some degree, I think that a lot of the hype about it being on the rise is really that people are just seeing the prevalence of it for the first time because of our willingness to address it from every angle.

I don't have any current stats on it, but if homosexuality is on the rise, and again, I suspect it is, I believe we can attribute it to several things: the continued breakdown of the natural family, cultural acceptance of sin, and blatant attempts to dissolve the distinctions between genders.

More and more children are being born out of wedlock. Children are being raised intentionally without a male or a female parent. With gay adoption legal in so many states, kids are being purposely confused about the intrinsic need for one dad and one mom who are married and committed to one another for life.

And, unfortunately, our society is promoting gender nonconformity and a genderless society where all people are encouraged to choose sexual partners based on little more than whims and selfish desires rather than on what is moral, biblical, healthy, and best.

22. At what age should kids be taught about homosexuality and how

they should respond to peers at school who may be singled out and called names for being different?

Stay informed about what your local schools' curriculum contains. In some districts (especially in California), children are being taught that homosexuality is a valid lifestyle as early as kindergarten. While high schoolers are learning more graphic information, young children are being indoctrinated with a gentler message, like "men can love women *or* men or both." Even if your children don't attend a particular public school, they may hear this message repeated from their peers. Kids need to hear the truth *first* at home, rather than a counter-message made at school, on MTV, or from a peer.

Make sure you are addressing these questions on their level and not overloading them with information they're not ready for. For instance, teenagers can wrap their minds around the physical, psychological, social, and political aspects of this issue, but younger kids can't. Children should be taught from a young age about the love and relationships God has created us to have, and why their distinctions are important. This builds a firm foundation in their minds for God's truth concerning sexuality.

Kids need to know the devastating impact of teasing and bullying and how much it grieves the heart of God. It often takes a person many years to recover from the pain of isolation and harassment in school. Children should be encouraged to reach out to and include those who are "outcasts," never joining in on the name-calling. This is an intimidating task for children because sticking up for such a person usually invites the same teasing on them, and no one wants that. The most important remedy for this is to provide a safe place for them to run to where they are loved and their hurts and concerns matter to someone who is stronger than they are. Kids who enjoy this benefit of family have a security that makes them more likely to care for others.

23. How long after a gay-identified person becomes a Christian, can he or she be considered "normal"?

The inference is that only gay people are abnormal and that getting them saved ensures they will become normal. I think a far better question is, How long after *anyone* becomes a Christian can he or she be considered normal?

We are all fallen, and we all need Christ. And I have yet to meet anyone completely "normal," Christian or not.

Maybe this question refers to being normal as it relates to being sick. In that case, I want to confront the thought that being gay is a disease or a sickness any more than another sinful condition.

The truth is that coming to Christ is the beginning of a transformation process that can only continue when an individual chooses to allow it to do so. I accepted Christ at a young age, but there were many times that I was neither pursuing Christ nor growing in Christ. Only when I made the conscious choice to be obedient to Him, to follow His path, and commit to growing did I begin to see real, lasting, inner change occur. Then and only then did I show outward signs of inner change and healing.

I did become more socially acceptable in the church, but social acceptance wasn't my goal. Being reconciled to Christ and living the life He intended me to live was my intent.

Related to time, aren't we all on a lifelong process toward being perfected in Christ? I don't think I can put a time frame on that. However, when it comes to time frames for the sake of being involved in leadership, dating or the like, I say that someone needs a minimum of two years sobriety from emotional and physical immorality. Change takes time.

24. How does a straight Christian act toward a formerly gay-identified Christian? Can they really find mutual interests?

The straight Christian should treat the formerly gay-identified Christian simply like a straight Christian brother or sister. Sexuality is only a part of who we are. A formerly gay-identified person has many interests that have nothing to do with sexuality.

You may like the same sports, or the same kinds of movies, or the same music, or the same art. You may both enjoy cooking or gardening or traveling. And most of all, you share a Savior—and that's the only common interest needed for a fulfilling, godly relationship!

Remember, if you are scared of former gays, they are probably more scared than you are! Work to discover the common interests you surely have. Your desire to do so will bless them immensely!

25. What are the ramifications of the AIDS epidemic in reaching out to homosexuals? Can you refer me to any ministries that are already ministering to those with HIV? And how should this be handled in the church? If a gay man accepts Christ, but is infected with HIV, how will that affect his acceptance at our church? Should his condition be made public? How do I handle parishioners who feel uneasy sitting near a man with HIV?

The most effective way to reach anyone dealing with a serious health issue that will eventually take his life is to learn about the illness. Many doctors and nurses are Christian and will be able to share with you how they try to minister and serve their patients living with the HIV virus. They would probably be willing to prepare materials, identify resources, and possibly even teach about the virus and how it attacks a person's body.

Then, once informed, you can go to the person with HIV already having covered a lot of the learning curve and be able to pray, listen to, and serve. Pray for his (or her) relationship with the Lord and the welfare of his body. Pray for his family and loved ones. Pray for eyes to see and ears to hear what the Holy Spirit is saying. After praying and listening to what the Lord has to say, listen to this person's hopes, fears, and concerns. Listen for him to bring up points of conversation and only venture into the "open doors to the gospel" that the Lord opens for you. Listen to anything that he needs to get off his chest without judgment and with a true spirit of humility.

The HIV virus is devastating, and I have found that those who can genuinely weep with the sorrowful have credibility. After praying and listening, start serving. Many people today learn of their HIV status early, so you can serve them by helping them learn about how to prevent the virus from building up in their system and providing or participating in education on how to live a long time in spite of HIV. Once their bodies start adjusting to the medications and eventually deteriorating, you may be of some very valuable help to them by simply providing a ride to the doctor or running errands for them when they are too sick to do so. For the very advanced stages, many people are in and out of the hospital repeatedly. You could be that consistent friend who holds his or her hands in good times and bad.

> The HIV virus is the result of a
> fallen world, not God's curse.

Remember, this is the kind of thing you would do for anyone facing a long, mortal battle. Also remember the gospel is paramount. How they contracted AIDS is not the primary concern. The best way to serve one dealing with HIV is by staying with the practical and the helpful which, if done in genuine concern, will provide credibility to speak to the supernatural and/or potential healing of the soul type of issues. There is a great resource for those dealing with HIV from a Christian perspective: HIV Carelink can be found on the web at www.hivcare link.org/home.htm.

As for dealing with an HIV-infected person in church, most churches have elders or other leadership who decide what the criteria are for acceptance of membership at a church. I don't know of a single Scripture that would bar someone who has a physical ailment from becoming a church member. Indeed, the Scriptures talk of some men who ripped a hole in the roof to get one ailing friend in front of the Lord. Studies have shown that the virus is only spread through bodily fluids, so there is no reason, health-wise or scripturally, for someone with HIV to be barred from church attendance.

Of course practical measures should be applied in that any situation that might cause the infected person to bleed should be avoided.

Back in the 80s when AIDS was first named, many Christians unfortunately said that the HIV virus was a curse from God against homosexuals. My response? "That is a lie from the pit of hell." The HIV virus is a consequence of sinful actions for some but not a curse from God. Kind of like obesity and heart attacks can be the consequence of gluttony, HIV might be the consequence of IV drug use or sexual promiscuity (of all kinds). However, HIV also attacks the purely innocent. It is spread to babies, unsuspecting spouses, and blood transfusions (especially in the 80s.) The HIV virus is the result of a fallen world, not God's curse.

With regard to parishioners who feel uneasy, find and give them resources to educate them on the subject. Don't refer them to a source, give the information to them. Offer classes if it is a big concern within the congregation. I believe that once education is offered, most will come to see that they do not have to let HIV be a dividing point between themselves and the infected. In fact, it can be a compelling point to reach out to those who live with the virus.

In many ways the person living with HIV is the modern-day leper. The difference is that the person with HIV is not anywhere near as contagious. If Jesus reached out to the leper, I believe He expects us to do the same with those who have HIV/AIDS.

12

Five Stories of Transformation

—⟨⟨⟨⟩⟩⟩—

The fact that so many homosexuals have come to Christ and experienced changed lives is proof that God loves and responds to the prayers of homosexuals who seek Him. In this final chapter, we want to allow several Christians who were homosexually identified to tell how God reached them through the love and concern of Christians who reached out to them and walked them through the process of change.

_____ Story 1 _____

As mentioned several times in *God's Grace and the Homosexual Next Door,* the best evangelism with gay people—male, female, black, white, or whatever distinction—is done through friendship. Here is the testimony of an African-American young man who was won back to Christ through the prayers and friendship of those who loved him.

The Plans He Had

MARCUS MITCHELL

I was raised in a Christian home primarily by my mother. I had significant problems bonding with my father. My dad was a sportsaholic, and I wasn't very good at sports—but it wasn't for lack of trying. I played Little League baseball for three years and hated every minute of it.

I was, however, good at the arts and music. Unfortunately, my dad would not have any part of that. He never supported any of the activities I was involved in, yet he seemed to find time to go to my next-door neighbor's and my best friend's football games.

At school I was teased incessantly by all of the boys. I was called "sissy" and "fag" on a regular basis. Our neighborhood was predominately white, and most of my friends were also white. As the neighborhood became more integrated, the African-American kids also rejected me because they felt like I was a sellout. Not only did my peers ridicule me, but my father began telling my mother that I was a "punk."

Thank God that at the age of nine I accepted Jesus as my Lord and Savior! I loved the Lord, and at the age of ten I preached my first sermon in children's church. However, we began attending a new church that had started in the area. The pastor was single and was very interested in my mother, who was by then a single mom. It later came out that this pastor was really attempting to gain access to me. Eventually he did, and for a year and a half he molested me.

I was terrified and could not even think of telling my mother since she was interested in him. I prayed daily for God to rescue me from the abuse. Eventually God answered my prayers and the church folded. The pastor moved on to some other city, but the damage was done. I never spoke a word of this to anyone until I was 25 years old. I was tormented by this abuse throughout my childhood years.

By the time I was 16, I was deep into homosexual pornography and habitual masturbation. I was still trying to resist my feelings because I knew homosexuality was an abomination to God. I had my first voluntary sexual experience with a man at the age of 17. The fire was ignited, but I still tried to fight. At the age of 19, I gave up and chose to fully embrace the homosexual lifestyle. I felt so free! Finally men accepted me. Little did I know that these feelings of freedom would eventually turn into ones of bondage. I acted out in every way imaginable. Still, deep down inside, I believed that what I was doing was wrong.

I medicated my wounds and loneliness with alcohol, drugs, and sex, but I had a praying mother who never gave up on me. She desperately prayed I would change. I never thought change was possible because I believed I had committed the unforgivable sin of homosexuality.

In 1995, I finally hit rock bottom. I had everything: my own home, a great career, and a nice car. However, one thing still escaped me: a long-term relationship with a man. I know now that I was really craving an intimate relationship with Jesus Christ and the male affirmation I failed to receive from my father. I was miserable, so I figured there must be something wrong with me. I began seeing a non-Christian therapist. God used this therapist to speak these words to me: "You need to surrender." I was so outdone: here was this non-Christian therapist telling me to surrender.

Later that year God had a plan for me. God has a sense of humor! A friend of mine talked me into having a Tupperware party. The next thing I knew I was selling colored plastic bowls to women at parties. But through Tupperware, I met a true friend and a mighty woman of God.

Rita told me that the Lord said I was her "project." She knew I was homosexual, but she kept insisting that God loved me and wanted to forgive me. I told her that was impossible because I had committed the abomination of homosexuality, an unforgivable sin. She prayed with me. She set me straight, helping me know and understand that forgiveness and change were possible. She knew nothing about an ex-gay movement, but she knew Jesus and His power to heal and forgive. She told me that God showed her in a dream that I was married and had children of my own. This was impossible for me to see at this point, but I told her that I could at least have faith in her faith.

From there I got connected with a local church and began to renew and recultivate my relationship with the Lord. He, through His Word and prayer, walked me out of homosexuality. I knew nothing about Exodus or any other ex-gay ministry, but Jesus spoke to me and gently helped me mature in Him. I began to experience joy and peace like never before. I was so overjoyed to be in right relationship with Him! At that time I believed I was called to remain single. I was sold out and on fire for God…but He wasn't finished yet.

On April 12, 1997, I met a wonderful woman from my church at a friend's house. We all went to a Kirk Franklin concert together, and I got to spend some time with this beautiful princess named Sara. We exchanged numbers and began talking. For the first three weeks of our relationship, I didn't know she was interested in me in "that" way. When I found out through my friend, I was ready to run for the hills! I felt I had way too much baggage for this woman, but the Lord spoke quietly to me and said, "Stand still. I am trying to bless you. Don't move forward; don't run; just stand still."

Somehow I was able to stand still even though I was terrified and shaking in my boots. Our friendship blossomed into a beautiful, godly relationship. Everyone kept telling me, "This is your wife," but I just couldn't fathom this.

All my friends said I was totally different since I met Sara. I told them that if God meant for Sara to be my wife, I would have to hear it directly from God. I kept asking God, "But why? I never even asked You for this." God reminded me that this had always been His plan for me; I was the one who had veered off course. He gave me the Scripture Ephesians 3:20: "Now unto him that is able to do exceeding abundantly above all that we ask or think, according to the power that worketh in us" (KJV). Sara and I were engaged on April 12, 1998, one year from the day we met. We married on October 24, 1998. That day was one of the best days of my life. And I remember the joy on my mother's face.

Now Sara and I minister together at our church to those who are struggling with homosexuality. I could not imagine my life without her.

She is my best friend and number one support. She is truly my Ephesians 3:20.

I thank God for the faithful prayers of my mother, Othell Mitchell, who went home to be with the Lord in November of 2001. She never gave up on me and stayed on her face before the Lord for my salvation. She never rejected me. My relationship with my father has grown by leaps and bounds, and on my wedding day he told me how proud he was of me.

Parents please don't give up! *God* will answer your prayers and deliver your child as well!

Today I am a victorious overcomer because the Word says, "And they overcame him by the blood of the Lamb, and by the word of their testimony" (Revelation 12:11 KJV). Today I am a heterosexual man and a child of God who is married to a godly woman. My marriage is not a badge of healing but evidence of God's continued healing work in my life.

Marcus Mitchell resides in California with his wife, Sara, and their daughter, Victoria. They minister together in the Sacramento area and attend Bayside of South Sacramento.

_____ STORY 2 _____

Many men and women who come out of the gay lifestyle go through a period of feeling extremely alone…isolated. At that point, they are either severely tempted to turn back to the life they've known in the gay community…or will find an anchor with a Christian community that is welcoming to them.

The Isolation of Desire

KRISTIN JOHNSON

Seven years ago I found myself on my knees, praying: "Dear Jesus, I love You, but *I do not know what to do!*" At that time I was involved in an intimate relationship with a woman, and I had to decide whether I would continue this relationship.

I had been a Christian since I was five years old, the daughter and granddaughter of Presbyterian ministers, yet I struggled with same-sex attraction. I also had engaged in unhealthy relationships with men.

Although I dated in high school, I was ambivalent toward the boys I dated. I was very outgoing and participated in music, theater, cheerleading, and other activities. Yet, underneath all this activity and "normalcy" I was struggling with my sexuality and self-image.

In college, I had a nonphysical, emotionally dependent relationship with my roommate, which lasted more than four years. I was terrified of the romantic love I felt toward her, rationalizing the relationship as merely a deep friendship. Because of my attachment to her, I wasn't motivated to date men or desire marriage.

After college, however, I became physically involved with a man. While I was relieved to be in the arms of a man rather than a woman, the loss of my virginity, my increasing promiscuity, and my occasional abuse of alcohol began to take its toll. My relationship with this man ended when I had a miscarriage.

In my late twenties, I finally acted out my homosexual feelings and had an emotional and physical affair with a woman. Initially I felt euphoric, and yet at the same time I felt as if a war was raging inside of me. It was during this affair that I was forced to reconcile being a Christian and living in a homosexual relationship.

I wrestled with the Lord in prayer. I questioned Him, and I begged Him. I attempted to find peace by reading books that described Christians who had reconciled their faith and homosexuality, and I even tried attending a gay-friendly church. However, my anxiety only increased because God was making it clear as I read Scripture that His plan for my sexuality was staring at me in the book of Genesis and in the words of Jesus.

Even though I understood the intent of the Scriptures, my feelings and my need overruled what I knew to be true. For me to say no to this relationship was like someone telling me, "Kristin, you don't deserve to be loved like this. You'll never be loved as others are loved." These thoughts produced feelings of fear and anger. When I felt the Lord was making it clear to me that I needed to end the relationship with this woman, I would cry uncontrollably and shake my fists at Him for His apparent cruelty in depriving me of intimacy.

And yet despite my fear and resistance, I found myself on my knees, ending the prayer I had started: "Dear Jesus, I love You, and I do not know what to do...*but Lord, let Your will be done.*"

God answered my prayer, but it was a difficult answer. The relationship came to a sudden end, and as a result, I had to pull myself away from people and places I knew. I also had to address my anger at God and my circumstances. It was not an easy time.

I was alone. I was tempted. Difficulties still entered into my life. I struggled being single when I had prayed and hoped eventually to be married and have children. I felt alone at church and had a hard time staying committed to a church.

In this isolation and suffering, my worst fear of never again experiencing an intimate and passionate relationship was not realized. An amazing thing happened: *I discovered that Jesus was the best source of love I had ever known.* It was Christ's intense and demonstrative love for me that led me to obedience, and it was my obedience to Christ that led me to sexual healing and wholeness.

Although I had always believed in God and loved Him, what I failed to fully believe was how He longed to take care of me and provide for all my needs. I still have to stop daily and let the Lord remind me of this truth: that He is good, that He will provide, and that He loves me more than I can comprehend.

The world would have me believe that my identity is found in embracing lesbianism, or embracing a "healthy" sex life, or embracing Mr. Right and riding off into the sunset, but my identity and worth were (and are) found in embracing and obeying my Creator, my Lord and Savior. For I am a daughter and heir of the living God.

My greatest fear in confessing sin and turning from it was in thinking that God would have nothing waiting for me at the other end. How wrong I was. I am a living witness to the Scriptures that attest that God is able to do immeasurably more than all we can ask or imagine, according to His power at work in us. To Him be all glory in the church and in Christ Jesus throughout all generations.

Kristin Johnson is the executive director of OnebyOne, a renewal organization within the Presbyterian Church (USA) formed in 1995 to minister to the needs of those in conflict with their sexuality.

——————————— Story 3 ———————————
The prayers of loved ones in allowing the homosexual to come to the end of him- or herself and surrender to God are extremely important. Never stop praying for the homosexuals in your life!

A Song of Hope

DENNIS JERNIGAN

From my earliest memories, I felt different from other boys. I was gifted musically, and labeled "sissy" by other boys. By the time I was nine years old, I was playing regularly for the worship times at First Baptist Church in the small town we lived in.

I learned to play the piano from my grandmother. We lived far from any town with a piano teacher, so I learned to play "by ear"—by listening to melodies and mimicking them without seeing any music. Grandma was very patient with me as I practiced daily at her house, and I grew close to her.

I didn't feel as close to my parents. We were not an affectionate family, and I never remember receiving physical affection from my father. I found it hard to believe that he loved me. I felt worthless.

When I was nine years old, Jesus began calling me to Himself. On September 8, 1968, I asked my mother how to be saved. She explained that we were all sinners and that we deserved to perish in hell. But through the death of Jesus on the cross, we could come into a relationship with God. I asked Jesus into my life that afternoon and was baptized that evening.

But not perceiving love from my earthly father, I couldn't fully receive God's acceptance and forgiveness. So I tried to earn love by being "the best" at whatever I did. I made straight A's in school; my basketball team played in three state tournaments; I was valedictorian of my high school class. But what people thought was so good—my outward performance—only hid the deepest hurts of my heart. Rejection permeated every part of my life, including my sexuality. As a boy I needed a role model to show me the way to manhood. I began to yearn for intimacy with other men in perverse ways. Because of this wrong thinking, I came to believe that I was a homosexual.

At the same time, I knew God had something else for me. After I first became a Christian, I sensed Him telling me that someday I would have a large family of my own...with nine children! *That's crazy,* I thought. *How can I have children if I'm a homosexual?*

At church I heard people say, "All homosexuals should be shipped out of the country—they deserve to go to hell!" I felt condemned by their remarks, and I had no idea where to turn for help. So I hid my same-sex desires throughout high school. In college, I discovered other students who were also struggling with homosexual desires. We gravitated toward one another, and I became entrenched in the physical and emotional aspects of homosexuality. But the more I believed homosexuality was my "real" identity, the more miserable I became.

During my sophomore year, I met the woman who would one day become my wife. I thought Melinda was the most beautiful woman I had ever seen. Something drew me to her, something I had never felt before. But even though we dated on and off through college, I still had sexual encounters with other men on the side.

By my senior year, I was totally confused and frustrated. I decided that my life was not worth living. After all, I had begged God since childhood to remove these feelings, and it seemed like nothing had happened.

One night during my last semester of school, as I sat in my little apartment alone, I decided I would rather be dead than living "this life." After extinguishing the pilot light, I turned on the gas in my little heater, lay down, and waited to die.

After a few minutes, I grew very fearful and turned off the gas. *What does eternity hold?* I wondered. *Whatever it is, I'm not ready.*

Soon afterward I broke up with Melinda and told her I never wanted to see her again. That summer after graduation, I fully embraced my homosexuality and plunged into a three-month relationship with another man.

"This is who I am," I told myself. "I was born homosexual, and this kind of life is what God intended for me." But instead of finding happiness, I became more miserable.

I applied for seminary, thinking that more schooling might provide some answers. But three days before seminary began, a friend phoned me. "Dennis, God has brought you to mind a lot lately. In fact, I had a dream about you this week." In the dream, he explained, God was giving me all kinds of songs. I thought he was crazy, but was startled by his next remark: "What's more, my mother had the same dream this week!"

I abandoned plans for seminary and accepted this friend's invitation to live with his family in Oklahoma City. With my music degree, I had trouble finding a job. I finally became employed as a school-bus driver. Between my morning and afternoon routes, I had several free hours, which I used to cry out to God. I knew He was real, and that He was trying to say something to me.

At first I set my Bible on the piano and would sing the psalms of David back to God. I saw that David had an intimate and honest relationship with God—something I had desired my whole life. David exposed feelings and attitudes that I thought "good" people would hide. Yet God called him "a man after my own heart" (Acts 13:22). Soon I was singing my own thoughts and prayers, emptying my soul to Him as I exposed the hurts I had kept inside for so many years.

Then a well-known Christian group called "Second Chapter of Acts" came to our area, and I felt an inner prompting to attend. During their concert, I was captivated by their sincerity and love for God. Then, in the middle of one song, they suddenly stopped. "God has put something on my heart," one member said. "There is somebody here who is hiding something so hurtful, so terrible, that they would be devastated if anyone found out about it. But God wants you to know that He sees it and He loves you anyway." Then we were encouraged to lift our burdens up to the Lord as we raised our hands to Him.

This type of worship was new to me, but as I lifted my hands, God became more real to me than I had ever imagined! I realized that Jesus had lifted His hands for me—spreading them upon the Cross. I knew that He was right beside me, willing to walk with me. I could be honest with Him.

"Lord Jesus," I cried inside, "I can't change me or the mess I've gotten myself into—but You can." In that moment, I turned everything in my life over to Jesus: my thoughts, my emotions, my physical body...and my past.

For the first time, I realized that homosexuality was a sin that Jesus died for. I heard Him say in my heart, "Dennis, I'm making you somebody brand-new. My blood has paid your debt. You are free."

That night, many years ago, was the beginning of my incredible journey. For the first time I saw myself as forgiven and cleansed. The power of homosexuality in my life had been broken. From that moment, Jesus began to change my sexually perverse thoughts and desires to holy and pure thoughts about what sexual love was all about.

During this same time in my life, a close friend found out about my past. When he confronted me, I ran from the house, certain that I would be disgraced. I looked up into the darkness of the evening sky, pleading with God to speak to me. My eyes were drawn to a puffy white cloud floating above. It looked like an old man with outstretched arms. Nearby was a smaller cloud in the shape of a lamb. As I watched, the man engulfed the little lamb in his arms.

Immediately I knew that God was demonstrating what He wanted to do for me in this time of need. I returned to the house to face my friend, who reaffirmed his love for me. And God began to bring others into my life who were willing to love me unconditionally as I sought complete healing.

One year passed, and I sensed God's prompting to contact Melinda again. I loved her and knew I wanted to marry her. After several months I proposed and she accepted. I assumed that since I considered myself to be healed from homosexuality, there was no need to share my past with her.

In July 1988, I realized God wanted to take the greatest failures and weaknesses of my life and make them my greatest strengths. Not only this, but if I confessed my past freely, Satan would have no ammunition against me. No longer would I have to live in fear of others finding out about my homosexual background.

So I shared my past with Melinda. Although she had questions, she was grateful that I felt secure enough in her love to share my most intimate past sins. Then, three days later, I spoke in church about my past—and something beautiful took place. Afterward, people began to approach me who had deep wounds from their pasts, such as homosexuality, incest, rape, and abortion. As they confessed their sins and hurts, Jesus began healing them.

A year later, I realized in a new way God's calling upon my life. After leading worship at the community center in my hometown, one of my grandma's old prayer partners said to me, "Isn't it wonderful how your grandmother's prayers have been answered?"

"What prayers?" I asked.

"Didn't you know?" she answered. "Your grandmother told me she would stand behind you as you practiced the piano at her house each day, asking God to use you mightily in His kingdom to lead in music and worship!"

In the years since then, God has certainly answered those prayers. By His power and grace, God has enabled me to make over a dozen praise and worship recordings, with tens of thousands of copies distributed worldwide. I have had the privilege of sharing my story with audiences all over the world through live concerts, television interviews like *The*

700 Club, and in magazines such as *Charisma* and *Christian Life.* Today, my wife and I have nine children. He is bringing His perfect plan for my life to pass.

I have a heavenly Father who will never leave me or forsake me (Hebrews 13:5). I want to spend the rest of my life singing praise and worship to Him for all that He has done.

Dennis Jernigan is founder of Shepherd's Heart Music and a lead worshiper loved by audiences around the world. This testimony is adapted by permission from *Song of Hope: Freedom from Homosexuality,* available in audiocassette and booklet form. Used by permission. Visit Dennis's website at dennisjernigan.com

———————————————— Story 4 ————————————————

Homosexuality is a hard enough issue for a young person to deal with, but all the more so when accompanied by yet another distinctive that makes the already "different" person even *more* different than his peers. In Matt Lieberman's case, that extra difference was deafness.

Confused No More:
Freedom from Homosexuality as a Deaf Man

MATT LIEBERMAN

I will have a hard life, I thought when I first realized that I liked boys, not girls. It was just another year on the swim team in Kentucky in the summer of 1985, and I realized I had feelings for the boys on my team, though I didn't understand why. All I knew was that as I gazed at the boys in their swimsuits I was attracted to them. This realization caused me to fear what my life would be like in the future, so I kept those thoughts inside. I was too ashamed and scared to tell anyone how different I felt.

I was born deaf in 1975 in New Jersey, and two years later my family and I moved to Kentucky. I had a great active childhood with my family during our nine years there in Kentucky, although I didn't understand the communication taking place between my family members because of my deafness.

Dad was a busy, outgoing, successful businessman who traveled a lot. But he didn't know how to say, "I love you," or be emotionally close. He showed his love by taking me out and buying me things. My mom was a religiously dominant, compassionate mother who was in charge of the family. Due to a divorce, my grandmother joined the family. She always gave me coffee and chocolates, and she loved to laugh. My oldest brother was humble and had good manners. My second-born sister and I loved to play with hairstyles and wear fashions. My third-born brother, who is also deaf, loved sports and being "Mr. Cool." I'm the fourth-born, youngest son, who loved to climb trees and play.

Communicating with a deaf person takes time and patience. Few hearing people, especially males, are willing to do it. My relationships with my dad and older brothers were superficial, and that caused me to draw closer and become more comfortable with my grandmother, mom, sister, and other girls.

My deaf brother and I went to Louisville Deaf Oral School for speech therapy from 1978 to 1981. Then we were mainstreamed into schools for hearing students and began to be involved in sports activities. Unlike my deaf brother, I hated any sports that had a fast-moving ball. That scared me. So the only sport in which I felt safe and enjoyed participating in was swimming. It was during the summer of 1985 that I realized my attraction to boys was going to mean a hard future.

In 1986 my family moved to Missouri so my deaf brother and I could attend the St. Joseph Institute for the Deaf. This school also provided training in speech therapy and lip-reading, which we call oralism, or oral communication. I didn't want to move because I loved Kentucky, and I got angry at my father for the change. Already distant from him, I vowed never to be like him. I became even more comfortable with my grandmother, mother and sister, and other girls because I didn't have a male role model to look up to.

During my four years at the Institute, I hung around with girls all the time and began to develop my love for drama. At home, I would usually watch TV for hours, design art, and do landscaping. During this time I was inadvertently exposed to some X-rated videotapes and pornography, which stirred up more gay feelings. When my deaf brother and I got into a fight, he called me a fag and a sissy. All these things confused and hurt me. My mind was continually bombarded with negative thoughts: *What is wrong with me? Why can't I like girls?* My inner dialogue was constantly negative, and I put myself down all the time.

In 1990, I enrolled in a mainstream high school thinking I would do fine in the hearing environment with my oral communication training. But my year there was terrible because there were so many communication breakdowns and misunderstandings. I wanted to feel accepted, be recognized, and have friendships with other guys, instead I was left out, rejected, and isolated. I was experiencing significant "deaf phobia" and I got tired of the superficial friendships. I tried to get involved in the hearing drama department, but to no avail. Quickly, I went into severe depression. I thought about killing myself. I hated myself for being deaf in this hearing world. I got so fed up that I demanded a change in my life.

In the summer of 1991 I went to Gallaudet University (an all-deaf college) in Washington, D.C., for a deaf drama program called "Young Scholarship Program." I found many deaf friends, learned deaf culture (the way of life among deaf people), and felt genuinely accepted. Immediately, I quit my hearing school and moved to the District of Columbia to attend the Model Secondary School for the Deaf (MSSD). I learned American Sign Language (ASL), which is a vital language for interacting with others in deaf culture. While at this school I participated in many professional drama opportunities.

One of my dreams came true when I finally found a best guy friend at school. We trusted each other and did everything together. We felt safe to talk about our feelings and our friendship later turned into a secret gay relationship. I did feel a little guilty about this relationship, but it was the answer to my roller coaster feelings.

In the past, I had a few girlfriends, but none of the relationships were serious. It felt great to "come out of the closet" and be accepted. I could be myself! I gained a positive self-esteem and perspective in my gay and deaf identity.

When I visited St. Louis for my 1992 Christmas break, my father blurted out to me, "Get a girlfriend!" My parents had found out about my gay relationship and that I was busted for underage drinking at a gay bar in D.C. They tried to take me out of school, but I argued that they couldn't take away my deaf culture, community, friends, and my drama opportunities. I terrorized my parents in order to stay at the school. I feared losing my self-esteem and suffering again in a hearing school.

In January 1994, my parents forced me to go to "ex-gay therapy" and church. While at church with two lesbian friends, feeling bored, I decided to flip through the Bible. I was stunned to find that 1 Corinthians 6:9-11 said that homosexuality was wrong. I justified that being gay was okay with God. I never wanted to change, and I kept lying to my parents that I was getting "better" so they would leave me alone.

After graduating from the MSSD in June 1994, my boyfriend and I broke up for good because our gay relationship had become physically, verbally, and emotionally abusive. I entered Gallaudet University for my freshman year in the fall of 1994. A girl I knew there killed herself. This really shook me up and made me wonder what would happen to me after I died. I began zigzagging back and forth between homosexuality and God. I was so confused.

Feeling lonely in October 1994, I snuck off to a popular gay bar. While dancing drunk, I became uneasy because I felt God watching me. I couldn't ignore or hide from Him. I thought, *What am I doing?* I was still confused about homosexuality and God and life. So in December 1994, I left Gallaudet.

Back in St. Louis, I got two jobs to save money to move to Hollywood for my acting career. In the summer of 1996, I was accepted to the professional summer drama school at the National Theatre of the Deaf. It was a wonderful learning experience. I was trying to ignore my gay desires, but I didn't feel that I was a changed person. While I was confused and vulnerable, I met a gay actor and model from Hollywood. We started a relationship because I thought he was "Mr. Right." He and I planned for me to move with him to California so I could pursue my dream in acting.

My life changed on September 21, 1996, while attending a Deaf Christian retreat in Oklahoma. I saw an ASL drama about Jesus by "The Master's Hands" of Deaf Ministries Worldwide. God touched my heart deeply, and I cried and asked Him to forgive me. My confusion about homosexuality and God suddenly became clear—I knew homosexuality was a sin, I repented, received Jesus as my Savior and Lord, and felt a great sense of peace. This deaf Christian drama in ASL was the first time I had seen the message about Jesus presented so clearly.

I ended up not moving to Hollywood. Instead, God led me to a nondenominational evangelism training center, a deaf Bible School, at Deaf Ministries Worldwide in Oklahoma. By October 1998, I was thrilled to join their "Master's Hands" deaf Christian drama group, which traveled around the country. During this time, I didn't share much about my freedom from homosexuality.

My first Exodus Conference was in July 1999 in Chicago I was shocked to see more than 1,000 hearing people there, many who had left the gay and lesbian life for Jesus. I discovered the root causes of homosexuality. I met many new friends, and we talked about sexual issues openly. I was sad when I realized not many deaf people knew about Exodus resources.

I graduated from the deaf Bible school in May 2000, with a Deaf Culture Ministry Certificate. Then I was hired to work at Deaf Ministries Worldwide as an evangelist, public relations representative, assistant office manager, and an actor performing with "The Master's Hands." I also attended the Exodus-affiliated First Stone Ministries for support group sessions and was mentored by Stephen Black for nearly three years. It was a great experience working in these ministries.

In May 2003, I left Deaf Ministries Worldwide and First Stone Ministries because God wanted me to pursue other opportunities.

In September 2004, God paved the way for me to go to Portland Fellowship (PF) in Oregon. I was the first deaf person to go through this internship program. I stayed with PF for two years and learned how to facilitate a small men's group to talk about our struggles, teach about homosexual issues, conduct workshops, meet with leaders, and modify resources for use among the deaf.

There are more than 250 million deaf people worldwide, and not many know Jesus. Deaf gay people often feel more love and support in the gay community than in the church community. It's hard for hearing people to imagine what it's like being deaf. It is like living in a foreign land where you don't know the language. Everyone is talking to each other, but you are ignored or misunderstood or even ridiculed because of the communication barrier. You long to make a connection with someone, but it never happens because without the language there is little communication, and without communication there is no relationship, and without relationship, there is no identification. That is why many deaf people desire to be with other deaf people with whom they can talk and feel accepted. They have been rejected by hearing people who don't know sign language, and they have felt frustrated over communication barriers and breakdowns.

I want to see all Exodus ministry video resources made available with captions or interpreters for the deaf. I desire to see that any deaf person who wants to access Exodus can easily find help instead of having to find an interpreter or discover that the resources are not captioned.

Because deaf people have had so many negative experiences trying to adapt to a hearing world, they get very easily frustrated when they attempt to use resources that lack adaptation for use among the deaf. So they will often give up easily when they can't find usable resources right away.

For various reasons, leaving the homosexual lifestyle was extremely hard. Most of my deaf friends were gay, my struggles were so hard to deal with, and deaf Christians didn't know how to help me with my struggles. Plus, it seemed like I was the only deaf person I knew who was leaving homosexuality.

Also, in the deaf community, if a person proclaims that he or she is gay, almost everybody in the deaf world knows. The deaf world is so small that word travels fast and there is no way to hide. So when a gay deaf person becomes a Christian, everyone in the deaf world knows right away, making it harder for the person to gradually adjust to the new lifestyle.

Occasionally I get ridiculed and get a lot of fingers pointed at me: "That's ex-gay Matt there!" I get tired of the finger pointing, the spotlight, and the peer pressure, but God is helping me to deal with that. I know many other ex-gay deaf people who are so afraid to come out as Christians because the deaf community might put them in the spotlight. Ex-gay deaf people are scattered all over, and most don't have other ex-gay deaf friends to help and support them.

I am jealous of the more than 100 Exodus chapter ministries all over the USA where hearing people can easily walk in and get the help they need. But where does a deaf person go? I'm working to get Exodus Ministries to set up interpreting services for deaf people so seekers can get help right away and have access to resources that are designed for use by the deaf.

I want deaf people to understand that Exodus and similar ministries for the homosexual are alternatives for those who have accepted Jesus Christ and who choose to come out of homosexuality. I pray that deaf people who want freedom from homosexuality will seek help and resources from Exodus ministries. I also want to see deaf Christians respond and respect deaf gays and lesbians with God's love without attacking, condemning, or judging them.

I am aware of my homosexual triggers and how they can affect my feelings and attractions. Sometimes it's not easy, but God is helping me to not let these feelings and attractions control my life as they once did.

Remember a person who struggles with homosexual sin is no

different than any other Christian person who struggles with some other type of sin in their life.

God is helping me guard my heart and mind every day. I am experiencing healing and hope through a life of joy, peace, and true freedom by Jesus Christ. Philippians 4:13 says Christ gives us the strength to face anything. Before I was confused about Jesus and homosexuality, but now I am confused no more!

Matt Lieberman is now participating in a variety of deaf ministries including both drama and office support.

_____ Story 5 _____

Christians have been known to express anger to homosexuals instead of bearing witness to God's love. The former only hardens hearts; the latter can soften hearts.

Militant Lesbian Won Through Christian Kindness

YVETTE SCHNEIDER

I remember when I was 24 years old and a militant lesbian activist. One of my best friends was a politically active, flamboyant gay man named Jerry. We often talked about ways to make the world more accepting of homosexuality. We would go to book readings by gay and lesbian authors, and we would go to art exhibits by gay and lesbian artists. Our homosexuality was the foundation of our friendship.

Jerry was terrified of contracting AIDS, so he was in regular contact with volunteers from the AIDS hotline. He wanted to make sure that he wasn't engaging in any behavior that would put him at risk for contracting HIV. One summer Jerry went to Mexico for a few weeks. He got sick with what he assumed was an intestinal parasite. When he went to the doctor, the doctor told Jerry that he had full-blown AIDS and probably had about three months to live.

Jerry was shocked by the news. He had been practicing so-called safe sex, so something like this was not supposed to happen. I saw Jerry for the last time a few days before he died. He was angry and bitter at everyone and everything. I felt terrible that I didn't have anything to say to him that would encourage him or give him hope. I couldn't do anything more than say goodbye to my friend. It was an awful feeling. I looked at Jerry and saw his life as meaningless—and mine too. I couldn't offer Jerry any hope because I didn't have any hope.

I grew up in a family where there wasn't any hope that life was good. There was no confidence that our lives had meaning or that there was purpose for our being here on earth.

I was very distant from my parents when I was growing up. My dad spent all of his time sitting in a chair reading the newspaper and doing crossword puzzles. My mom was a rage-aholic. She screamed and yelled constantly about anything and everything. I was terrified of my mother, but at the same time I really wanted love and affirmation from her. I tried to win her approval by doing great at school and excelling as an athlete, but nothing I did seemed to make my mom like me.

My younger sister was the extroverted, cute daughter. It seemed like it was easier for my parents to love her and give her attention than it was for them to love and give me attention. As a result, I grew up feeling unlovable. When I was at home, I spent most of my time alone in my room. I thought, *Surely there has to be more to life than this.*

But when I was in high school, I found a best friend. We were together all the time. For the first time in my life I felt loved and appreciated for who I was. It was great. Suddenly my life was transformed. It was vibrant and exciting. My life finally had meaning. So when my mom sat me down and told me that she and my dad were getting a divorce, I just didn't care. Why should I? They had been fighting for as long as I could remember.

But I did care when my mom sat me down and asked me if my friend and I were having a homosexual relationship. I was devastated. How could my mom think that of me? I ran out of the room and locked myself in the bathroom. But later that night when I was crying in my room, I had to admit to myself that deep down inside I wished we *were* having a homosexual relationship—because then she would never leave me, and I would always feel the acceptance she gave me.

After high school, I went to the University of California at Irvine (UCI). I majored in English because I wanted to be a writer. I got good grades and was president of the pledge class of my sorority. I was editor-in-chief of the yearbook my freshman year, yet I still felt empty and unfulfilled.

I thought, *There's got to be more to life than this.* So I went to a therapist to find out what was wrong with me. After a few appointments, the therapist said, "Yvette, there's nothing wrong with you. You just expect too much from life. You have to learn to lower your expectations." I thought, *How on earth am I supposed to do that?* But my expectations were lowered for me when my mom told me that she wasn't going to pay for my college education.

Now I had to find a job so I could pay my way through college. I went to the job board at UCI and found a job working at a hotel in Laguna Beach. What I didn't know was that Laguna Beach had a large gay and lesbian population. About 70 percent of the clientele of the hotel I was working at was gay. This was my first contact with the gay community.

I became good friends with one of my coworkers, who was a gay man named Ed. By this time I had a new best friend whom I was spending my time with. Ed said about my new best friend and me, "You have an implicit homosexual relationship." I said, "Give me a break, Ed. Just because you're gay doesn't mean that everyone is gay." Still, I had to admit that I didn't have the same intense connection with the guys I had dated that I had with my best friend.

My dissatisfaction with life was starting to get to me. I needed a change, so I applied for the University of California's Education Abroad Program at the University of Delhi in India so I could study Hinduism and Buddhism for a year. I thought that maybe I could find some meaning to life.

While I was in India, I became good friends with my Hindi teacher.

After several months, at her initiation, the relationship became physical. The day after our encounter, I was horrified by what I had done. This couldn't be who I was.

I spent the day walking through the foothills of the Himalayas. From where I was, I could see the majestic snow-covered peaks up above and a tiny ribbon of water below that was the Jammu River. I felt so small and insignificant in comparison. But at the same time, I was consumed with inner turmoil. I didn't want to identify myself as a lesbian. But I was feeling loved and appreciated by this woman, and I couldn't walk away from that. Somehow I had to reconcile the fact that I thought homosexuality was wrong with the reality that I was having my emotional needs met through a homosexual relationship.

I finally decided that the only reason I thought homosexuality was wrong was because that was what my oppressive, controlling, Judeo-Christian culture had taught me. So I determined that once I got back to California, I would fight the oppressor. And in my mind, the oppressor was society.

When I got back to California, the first person I got in touch with was my old friend Ed. I said, "Guess what I learned about myself while I was in India. I'm lesbian." Ed said, "No, you're not. Whatever you do, don't go down that road. You'll regret it. And you'll go to hell."

I said, "First of all, I don't believe in hell. And second of all, *you're* gay! How can you tell me not to be? If you were really my friend, you would tell me where I can go to start meeting people."

And that's what I did. I started meeting people. I went to a lesbian bar in Long Beach, and met someone right away. We started spending all of our time together, as was my pattern. After awhile, my mom started getting suspicious. She said, "Are you having a lesbian relationship?" I told her I was. She said, "You need extensive psychological help." I said, "Oh really? That's not what the American Psychiatric Association says. They removed homosexuality from the Diagnostic and Statistical Manual back in 1973." My mom said, "Do what you want, but not in this house."

So I moved in with this woman. Everything was great for awhile. But it wasn't long before we became jealous, obsessive, and possessive. She knew exactly how far it was for me to go from our house to work and back, so she would check the odometer on my car to make sure I had come directly home. One day our relationship had become so dysfunctional that she became violent with me. She ended up ripping the phone out of the wall and throwing it at me, barely missing my head. I thought, *What have I gotten myself into?* But I couldn't leave. She was beautiful and popular, and I wasn't. I needed to be around someone like that.

As the relationship got worse, I became more militant in my gay activism. I was working for a law firm in downtown Los Angeles, and I insisted on wearing a pink triangle to work every day so everyone would know I was gay. I was out and I was proud. Closeted homosexuals would confess their fears to me, and I would say, "Every time you don't stand up for who you are, you oppress not only yourself but every other person involved in homosexuality."

I joined GLAAD, the Gay and Lesbian Alliance Against Defamation. I went to every Gay and Lesbian Pride Parade in Southern California, and I fought with the Christians who would carry their 1 Corinthians 6:9 signs saying how homosexuals would not inherit the kingdom of God. And every year I would try to pick a fight with them. I would go up to them and say, "If you don't like it, leave. No one invited you. And guess what? If you're going to be in heaven, I have no desire to go there." Every time I argued with those Christians, I could get at least one of them to yell at me. And when I did, I knew I had won.

But one Saturday, some friends and I were going out to a lesbian bar in Long Beach. From a distance, I could see a man and a woman handing out flyers. I thought maybe there was a new restaurant or shop opening. As I got closer, I could hear them talking, and I knew that they were Christians. I was instantly irritated and started walking straight toward them. My friends said, "Just ignore them. Who cares what they have to say?" But I went up to them and said, "Don't you have anything better to do on a Saturday night than to stand here and harass us?" The man said, "I am so sorry. I don't mean to offend you. You can take this tract and read it or you can throw it away. It's up to you. But I just came here to tell you how much Jesus loves you." When he said that, I felt about two inches tall. I thought, *What's wrong with me?* This guy isn't the mean one, I am. It didn't stop me from going into the bar that night. But it did begin to challenge my beliefs about Christians.

Around that time, I ended a three-year relationship and moved in with Ed and another gay man named Mike. Doors were opening for me in the publishing world, and I thought my ship had finally come in. I was going to be a writer. But even as things were looking up in terms of my career, many of my friends were sick and dying of AIDS. Ed and Mike both had full-blown AIDS. They were in and out of the hospital with things like cryptosporidium, Kaposi's Sarcoma, and pneumocystic pneumonia. There were times when I was functioning as their nurse-maid. I would help them change their IV bags. I would cook for them. Then eventually they would bounce back, and we would be back in the bars and partying again. I couldn't help but wonder, *Is this what life is all about? There's got to be more to life than this.*

Around this time, my boss at the law firm promoted me to a new position. It sounded great until I learned I would be leading a new department with a young man named Jeff who was a notorious Christian.

My friend Frank had worked with Jeff in a different department, and he told me that Jeff was always giving him Bible tracts to read and inviting him to lunch to talk about God. Frank said, "All I want to do in the morning is to come in and read the sports page. I'm sitting there reading, and Jeff comes in and says, 'Hey, Frank, did you read that tract I gave you?'" I laughed and said, "Better you than me." Now I was going to be working with Jeff, and I knew I didn't want to hear about Jesus.

On the first day we worked together, I walked in and Jeff had 3x5 index cards with Scriptures written on them posted all over his office space. I thought, *This can't be happening to me. This is a nightmare.*

Jeff said, "Hi, Yvette. What did you do this weekend?" I knew he was just trying to be friendly and strike up a conversation, but I wanted him to know that I didn't want to be his friend. I said, "I'm not telling you what I did this weekend. It's none of your business." I thought for sure that would shut him up. I was wrong. He said, "Well, a group of us went to the beach this weekend and invited people to our church." I said, "Really? You'll have to tell me what beach you went to, so I know never to go there."

I thought my responses to Jeff made it perfectly clear that I was *not* interested in hearing about Jesus. But Jeff talked about God constantly. He was always saying God this and God that, the Bible says this and the Bible says that. Jeff would even go so far as to tell me what God was doing in his life. Sometimes I found it interesting, and sometimes I would think, *I didn't know the Bible said practical things about how to live life.* But I never expressed any of those thoughts to Jeff.

Jeff and I would get into debates on things like premarital sex and abortion, but never homosexuality. And Jeff would always use the Bible to support his points. I said, "I don't believe the Bible, and I don't care what it says." Jeff said, "It doesn't matter if you believe the Bible or not, it's true." This exasperated me. Whatever Jeff believed he could back up by quoting the Bible. Whatever I believed, I couldn't back up at all. I would go home at night and look over my books on eastern mysticism. I was getting more and more involved in Native American mysticism and occult activities, but I couldn't give one practical answer for daily living…and Jeff could.

What's more, even though I was always mean to Jeff, every time he thought he had offended me, he would apologize. I never apologized to him, and I offended him all the time. I couldn't understand why he was nice to me and exhibited so much humility toward me. I hated it. It made me feel mean and nasty. I tried to find another job so I could get away from Jeff, but nothing worked out.

One day while Jeff was in Colorado for his father's funeral, I reported him to our boss for proselytizing at work. I was trying to get him fired. She said, "You need to tell Jeff that you appreciate his zeal, but that you don't share his beliefs and that you would appreciate it if he didn't talk to you about God anymore."

I intended to confront Jeff. I *wanted* to confront Jeff. But for some reason I couldn't bring myself to do it. Instead, I tried to ignore him. I wouldn't even talk to him about work-related issues. One morning Jeff came to work, put a cup down on my desk, and said, "Hey, Yvette, I stopped on my way to work and bought you a cappuccino." I couldn't believe it. Most people wouldn't get off the freeway in L.A. in the middle of rush hour traffic for a friend, let alone an enemy. I almost started crying out of frustration. I thought, *How can this guy continue to be nice to me when I am so mean to him?* Romans 2:4 says that the kindness of the Lord leads to repentance. There is no defense for genuine love and kindness with no strings attached.

I wanted to know more about Jesus, but I was afraid to express any interest to Jeff. I suspected that he would pressure me to go to church. Despite my fears, I ventured to ask Jeff a question about God. I said, "What's the deal with the Ten Commandments?" Jeff knew that Christians had bombarded me with unsolicited rantings about sin, so he said, "God loves us so much that He has given us the guidelines that will lead us to life." I believed, up until that point, that God was mean and oppressive. He gave us commandments in order to amplify His sovereign rule over us. The idea that God loved me and wanted what was best for me was a foreign concept.

I was starting to believe that Jesus might be the hope I was looking for, but I didn't want to go to church. I knew what Christians were like; I knew they would judge me and reject me. I didn't want to put myself in that situation. Jeff said, "You can't be a Christian on your own. The enemy will easily pick you off if you're separated from the flock."

So after working with Jeff eight hours a day, five days a week for two years, and hearing him talk about God every day, I finally went to church. When I stepped inside I could feel the presence of God so strongly that I couldn't even stand up during worship. I just sat there with my head in my hands.

After church the girl sitting next to me asked me what I was going to do about Jesus. I said, "What am I supposed to do?" She said, "Jesus took all of our sins upon Himself and paid the price of death so we can have everlasting life. You need to repent of your sins and accept Jesus as your Lord and Savior." I said, "Okay." And that's what I did. It was as if a huge weight was lifted off my shoulders. I experienced joy and peace for the first time in my life. But most of all I experienced the thrill of hope—the assurance that life did have meaning, that there was a purpose for my life.

Later Jeff told me that there were many times when he wanted to ignore me or to make a rude comment back to me, and he would sense the Holy Spirit saying to him, "Is that the way I treated you when you were lost?"

Once I became a Christian, other Christians from work began coming out of the woodwork. They were intimidated by me when I was a militant gay activist and didn't want to have anything to do with me. Jeff asked several of our female Christian coworkers to invite me to lunch. He thought I would relate better to a woman than I would to a man. None of them uttered a word to me.

My old friends wanted nothing to do with me now that I was a Christian. One of my friends said, "I knew you were malleable, but I didn't know you were *that* malleable."

My best friend said, "As a Jew you offend my spirit. There is no reason for us to ever get together again or even to talk over the phone." A lesbian couple who had been friends of mine for years wouldn't even let me in their house once they heard I had become a Christian.

As a new Christian, I found myself in the same position I had been in a few years before when I had nothing to say to my friend Jerry who was dying of AIDS. Now my friend Ed was very sick with AIDS and had about a year to live. But this time, instead of having nothing to say, I could offer Ed hope—the hope of everlasting life—that the end of his life could be the beginning of something great. I couldn't wait to see him.

Ed and I were going to meet for dinner in the gay part of West

Hollywood. I prayed for several days before we got together that Ed and everyone in West Hollywood would be able to see Jesus in me.

We ate dinner then went to a coffee house where we could talk. We went into a back room and I started telling Ed all the details about what had happened to me and how I came to know that Jesus was God. As I was talking, a homeless woman, who looked like she had been living on the streets for several years, made her way to the back room of the coffee house where Ed and I were sitting. She walked up to us, pointed at me and screamed, "I hate you! I hate you! I hate you!" for probably a full minute.

Finally the manager came and made her leave. Everyone was staring at us. Ed said, "What was that all about?" I said, "She probably saw Jesus in me." And I told him how I had been praying all week that Jesus would be visible in my life. That opened up a very deep and very fruitful conversation.

We talked about God a few more times after that, then Ed gave his life to Jesus. A year later, he died. But a few months before he died, he said, "I appreciate God's love and mercy so much. And soon I'l get to see Jesus face-to-face. There's nothing greater than that. But you get to stay here and see what it means to overcome and learn how to walk by faith. I'll never get to experience that."

Ed was right. I overcame lesbianism, and now I have a great husband and two wonderful daughters. I know what it means to walk by faith and trust the Lord with my life. But by far the greatest thing of all is to see people come to know the Lord and know that one day we will all be in heaven together. Because when all is said and done, the only thing we can take with us is other people.

So as someone who was difficult to reach out to and difficult to share the gospel with, I beg you not to grow weary in doing good and reaching out to the people around you. Because in due time you will reap, and the people you reach will be eternally grateful.

Yvette Schneider authors materials designed for athletic ministries, including *Bridging the Gap: Reaching Lesbian-Identified Women with the Love of Christ.* She and her husband, Paul, also homeschool their two daughters.

A Final Word
to the Church

Alan Chambers

—⟋⟍—

My heart breaks when I think of the men and women affected by homosexuality. It's become so easy for us to reduce them to activists fighting against tradition and biblical morality. Our hearts have hardened toward them to the point that we fail to see them as more than the issues they represent. I pray that this book has helped crack the shells of our hearts and enabled us to have Christ's heart toward homosexuals.

The truth is that God is absolutely in love with *all* of us—period. Gay men and women are not excluded or exempt from His love, grace, salvation, and healing. His passion should be our passion: that none should perish, but that all would have everlasting life (John 3:16).

As an extension of the church, I challenge you to pursue relationships with gay men and women in your life for the sake of getting to know them, learning to love them, and introducing them to Jesus Christ. By making Him Lord of their lives, homosexuals will find the freedom

He has been offering them all along. Pray that through the Holy Spirit these precious souls discover that change is possible and their eyes are open to the fullness of life that God offers all of us.

God has given this responsibility of outreach to all of us. You may be the only person who has the ability to make an eternal difference in the life of your homosexual neighbor—whether "neighbor" for you is a person in your subdivision, in your church, a coworker, or the lady in the checkout line in the supermarket.

Be ready and available to minister God's love and truth to the homosexual. If God can trust you to love gays, He will use you to win them.

I believe in and have every confidence in the church's ability, through Christ, to win the gay community to Christ. We are all in this work together through Him, fulfilling the Great Commission (Matthew 28:19-20). How great is our God that He allows us to be in on what He is doing on this earth!

In Luke 9, Jesus commissioned the 12 disciples and gave them the authority and power they needed to preach the news of God's kingdom and heal those who needed healing. Just as Isaiah proclaimed over himself in Isaiah 61:1, I proclaim over you:

> The Spirit of the Lord GOD is upon [you,] because the LORD has anointed [you] to bring good news to the afflicted; He has sent [you] to bind up the brokenhearted, to proclaim liberty [and freedom to *those held captive and imprisoned by the stronghold of homosexuality*] (NASB).

> *Dear Gracious Lord,*
> *Please open our eyes and hearts to those around us who need You. Haunt us with the realization that without us those You created might spend an eternity apart from You. Thank You for Your grace and truth in the form of Jesus. Lead us to and trust us with those who need You. Give us Your boldness to stand on the truth of Your Word as we minister through Your compassionate heart to those who are so empty and lost without You. Amen.*

Appendix

—⟋⟍—

Answers to "Test Your Knowledge About Homosexuality"

1. Most homosexuals first become aware of being "different" from their peers:
   a. as adults
   b. as teenagers
   c. **as children**
   d. they rarely express a feeling of being different.

   Most homosexuals recall distinct early feelings of being "different" from their peers.

2. Homosexuality is
   a. always a choice
   b. always genetic
   c. always related to childhood sexual abuse
   d. **none of the above**

   Acting upon one's homosexuality ("acting out") is a choice. However, same-sex attraction itself is not always a choice. Also, homosexuality has not been proven to be genetically caused, and while many homosexuals report some incidence of childhood sexual abuse, many do not.

3. Approximately what percentage of the population is homosexually oriented?
   a. 15 to 16%
   b. 10 to 12%
   c. 5 to 8%
   d. **2 to 3%**

   Although homosexual activists like to quote the 10 percent figure, that number is based in part on the imprecise surveys of the Kinsey Report conducted more than 50 years ago. The correct number is closer to 2-3 percent.

4. HIV can be transmitted by
   a. casual contact
   b. breathing the same air as an infected person
   c. **any exchange of bodily fluids with an infected person**
   d. only through sexual contact

   Casual contact such as shaking hands, hugging, or similar bodily contact *does not* transmit the AIDS virus. It is passed along through sexual contact. It can also be transmitted through blood transfusions from an infected person or other exchanges of body fluids.

5. A child raised in a strong Christian home
   a. will not develop homosexually
   b. may only choose homosexual feelings when older and if he or she doesn't stay close to God
   c. **can develop homosexually, just as a child from a non-Christian family**
   d. must reject God in order to develop homosexually

   Many men and women who struggle with same-sex attraction were raised in Christian homes. Others were raised in homes without any religious training. Although a Christian family that functions as God intended may have a lesser incidence of homosexuality, there is still the distinct possibility of a child developing same-sex attractions.

6. When a homosexual becomes a Christian, he or she will
   a. always become heterosexual at the point of conversion
   b. always become heterosexual somewhere down the line
   c. always have to deal with same-sex attractions
   d. **still likely deal with same-sex attractions for some time**

   Most homosexuals who become Christians do continue to struggle for some time. Many eventually completely overcome their attractions; others do not. It's very rare that a homosexual is instantly and permanently free set at the moment of conversion.

7. The ideal response to homosexuality is to
   a. "love the sinner, but hate the sin"
   b. always preach repentance
   c. **befriend them first, and allow God to bring up the matter of their homosexuality**
   d. ignore them. They're too much in the news anyway.

   Many well-meaning Christians assume that "loving the sinner but hating the sin" is a reasonable response. But it's not. To a homosexual, their attractions are so much a part of them that to tell them you hate their sin only, is meaningless. The far better approach is to *demonstrate* your love by being their friend and allowing God to direct your interaction with them.

8. Homosexuals are most often
   a. **normal people like those you meet every day**
   b. also pedophiles
   c. easily identifiable by their mannerisms
   d. actively engaged in promiscuous sexual activity

Most homosexuals are just like you are. They have jobs, they vote, they tend their gardens, make payments on their car loans, go to church, and so on. Unfortunately, it's the more militant homosexuals who seem to be most in the spotlight...and yet very few homosexuals are militant. Most are not pedophiles nor can you identify many of them by their mannerisms. Some are in long-term relationships and do not have promiscuous sex...although many do—as do many heterosexuals.

9. The only references to homosexuals in the Bible
   a. are full of condemnation
   b. offer acceptance of homosexuality
   c. are in the Old Testament
   d. **none of the above**

Although homosexual activity is condemned in both the Old and New Testaments, a very important positive reference is made in 1 Corinthians 6:9-11 to *former* homosexuals who had been washed, sanctified, and justified by their faith in Christ.

10. The leading pro-gay publication read by many homosexuals is
   a. ***The Advocate***
   b. *Gay Life Magazine*
   c. *Act Up*
   d. *Get Over It*

11. Homosexuality...

    a. **affects other aspects of a person's life than just sexual attractions**

    b. has to do with only a person's sexual attractions

    c. has nothing to do with a need for intimacy and affirmation

    d. is rooted in the need for a connection with the opposite-sex parent

Homosexuality is more than about sex. It really does affect the totality of a person's being. But when homosexuals come to Christ, they can find change from the inside out and will often find other aspects of their lives changing in addition to their sexual desires.

12. Which statement is the most true description of homosexuality?

    a. Homosexuality is an inability to relate properly to the opposite sex.

    b. **Homosexuality is an inability to relate properly to the same sex.**

    c. Homosexuality is an inability to perform sexually with an opposite-sex partner.

    d. Homosexuality is an inability to love others without sexual contact.

A developing homosexual has trouble relating to members of his or her own sex...often identifying instead with the opposite sex. That is, many pre-homosexual boys enjoy playing with girls more than boys. And pre-lesbian girls often find it hard to relate to other girls as being the same as they are. Instead, they identify with the boys they know and would prefer to be with them. This process continues into adulthood. And when a homosexual becomes a Christian and begins to accept his or her gender, there is a time of learning to be "one of the guys" or "one of the girls." Overcoming homosexuality, then, is in part learning to relate properly to one's own gender.

13. There is a gay-affirming Christian denomination called:
    a. Open Door Church of God in Christ
    b. Friends Affirming Fellowship
    c. Christian Community International
    d. **Metropolitan Community Church**

    The pro-gay Metropolitan Community Church—with churches in many cities around the world, was started by Reverend Troy Perry, a former Assembly of God pastor.

14. Often homosexuals will accept Christ and turn from their gay lifestyles for a while, only to return to it later. Which of the following reasons is the *least* likely cause for this?
    a. They miss the support they found in the gay community.
    b. They face a lack of support for their struggle in the church.
    c. They were promised instant heterosexuality and when it didn't happen, they lost hope for true change.
    d. **They missed the glitter and excitement of the gay culture.**

    In fact, many gays do *not* miss the gay culture to the degree that they're drawn back into it. Most failure is caused by the *support* they had found with like-minded friends, and, sadly, often the corresponding lack of support from a church that may not understand their temptations.

15. Why is the term "ex-gay" not really a proper way to refer to homosexuals who have become Christians?
    a. It's not really true. They remain gay throughout life...only they hide or sublimate their attractions.
    b. **It's a false identity because it defines them by their former attractions.**
    c. It's become too politically incorrect.
    d. There is nothing wrong with the term "ex-gay." It properly identifies those who have left the gay lifestyle.

As Mike noted in chapter 3; just as the term "gay" or "homosexual" indicates a false identity, so does the term "ex-gay." The desired change in identity should pull the focus from the sin or struggle with sin, and onto the true, fully righteous, fully holy identity bestowed on them via the Cross of Jesus Christ. This concept is *key* for the person leaving homosexuality because they begin to find freedom from untrue definitions of who they are, and to accept who God says they are.

Instead of the "ex-gay" tag, homosexuals must fully accept that their new identity is not based on their sexuality but on their having being born into God's family.

16. Which statement is most true about church leadership and homosexuality?

    a. **Pastors should know the basics of counseling homosexuals.**

    b. Pastors cannot grasp all that's involved in this issue and should have several places to which they can refer such people for professional help.

    c. Pastors should not attempt to counsel homosexuals until they're ready to accept Christ.

    d. Pastors should not attempt to counsel homosexuals without another person in the room.

As Randy noted in chapter 5, it's very important for a homosexual seeking help to have local pastoral support. Every pastor, as part of his ministry, should know the basics of counseling homosexuals. "The person dealing with homosexuality, like everyone seeking freedom from any besetting sin, needs wise counsel. If a person is denied counsel because the counselor is uncomfortable with homosexuality, the momentum for change may be hampered."

17. The word that best describes how most gays view the Christian church is:

    a. hate

    b. **distrust**

   c.   admiration

   d.   humor

Most gays distrust the Christian church. They've seen the "God Hates Fags" banners and have heard the harsh words that condemn them. Less often have they heard the "good news" of the gospel that Christ loves them and died for them. The most important message a gay man or woman can hear is being preached by a group that is distrusted by the gay community.

18. When talking to militant homosexuals, the most important thing to keep in mind is

   a.   scriptural support for your arguments

   b.   **having boundaries for your conversation**

   c.   not conceding an inch of ground as you talk

   d.   loving them as sinners, but hating their sin

As Randy said in chapter 7: The important thing to remember when dealing with militant homosexuals is to know your boundaries ahead of time and remember you can be completely human and not know everything (unless you are called to be an apologist or into debates). It's good to be humble enough to admit any potential mistakes and apologize if you feel the need to do so—operating out of compassion. See and listen to the person in front of you instead of arguing past them by reciting talking points. Just like with anyone, a militant homosexual is more complex than one issue, and more often than not will respect anyone who serves him or her in humility.

19. Which statement is most true regarding lesbianism:

   a.   Most homosexual women strongly desired to be like their mothers.

   b.   **Most homosexual women had a stronger attachment to their fathers than their mothers.**

   c.   The incidence of childhood sexual abuse among lesbian women is the same as among heterosexual women.

d. Heterosexual Christian women cannot be of much help to a woman struggling with same-sex attraction.

Most lesbians failed to connect in some important way with their mothers…and in fact, in surveys, they confirm that they did *not* have a desire to be like their mothers. The incidence of sexual abuse among lesbians is much higher than among women in general. Heterosexual Christian women can be an *immense* support to women coming out of lesbianism.

20. The statement "Homosexuality is worse than any other sin"
    a. is true scripturally
    b. isn't true scripturally, but is true practically speaking
    c. **shows a lack of understanding of one's own sin**
    d. means that it is harder to overcome than other sins

As Alan says in chapter 4: Why do people get so angry over this issue? Why do they feel so bitter toward those affected by homosexuality? Aside from the specifics of *their* particular sin, homosexuals are sinners just like everyone else. Have Christians forgotten so quickly what God saved *them* from?…Remember the depth of God's mercy for *all* who have sinned!

For More Help

Exodus International Resource List

—〰—

Exodus International boasts the largest referral network of ministries in the world. In North America we are comprised of 130 Member Ministries and Therapists. Additionally, we are in the early stages of building the Exodus Church Network, which we hope will include more than 10,000 churches desiring to reach out to those affected by homosexuality. For more information about the Exodus Member Ministry Network, the Exodus Therapist Network, and the Exodus Church Network please visit us on the web: www.exodus.to

Exodus International Departments

Exodus Youth

Exodus Youth exists to help youth and young adults who struggle with homosexuality—and the pastors, educators, and parents in their lives. The website contains resources for each of these groups: links to books, online support forums, videos, research, testimonies…and much more! www.exodusyouth.net

Campus Resources

Truth & Tolerance: Campus Faculty Guide by Exodus Youth
Truth & Tolerance: Student Leader Guide by Exodus Youth
Truth & Tolerance: Student Guide by Exodus Youth

Exodus *Groundswell* Conference

Groundswell is an initiative that will train and equip concerned youth pastors, campus ministers, and students to respond to homosexuality among our youth. Groundswell offers an array of events including youth worker training for leaders, youth rallies, and all-day conferences for youth leaders, educators, parents, and students. www.truthand tolerance.org

Exodus Freedom Conference

For over 30 years the Exodus *Freedom* Conference has been an annual event where those affected by unwanted homosexuality come to get educated, find support, and receive encouragement. More than 1,000 people attend the conference each year to hear from speakers like Dr. Erwin Lutzer, Dr. Kevin Leman, Drs. Les & Leslie Parrott, Bishop Joseph Garlington, Clay Crosse, Dr. Ken Hutcherson, and many more. This is a life-changing week for those who personally struggle and those who have loved ones who struggle with homosexuality. This is also a powerful week of training for those who are already ministering or wanting to minister in the area of homosexuality. To learn more about this must-attend event: www.exodusfreedom.org.

Exodus Books

Formerly Regeneration Books, this ministry was founded in 1989 and has served internationally as the leading book distributor for the numerous resources on the topic of overcoming homosexuality, transgender issues, pedophilia, sexual abuse, and other forms of sexual brokenness. To acquire a resource guide or to place an order: www.exodusbooks.org

Books

Here are some of the books we enjoy recommending. (All of the resources below can be ordered through Exodus Books, a division of Exodus International. For ordering information please log onto www .exodusbooks.org or call toll free 888-264-0877.)

For Men
Desires in Conflict by Joe Dallas
You Don't Have to be Gay by Jeff Konrad
Reparative Therapy for Male Homosexuality by Dr. Joseph Nicolosi
Growth into Manhood by Alan Medinger

For Women
Restoring Feminine Identity by Anne Paulk
Out of Egypt by Jeannette Howard
Into the Promised Land by Jeanette Howard
Friendships of Women by Dee Brestin

Apologetics
A Strong Delusion by Joe Dallas
101 Frequently Asked Questions About Homosexuality by Mike Haley
Homosexuality and the Politics of Truth by Jeffrey Satinover

Parents
Someone I Love Is Gay by Anita Worthen and Bob Davies
A Parent's Guide to Preventing Homosexuality by Dr. Joseph Nicolosi
When Homosexuality Hits Home by Joe Dallas

Youth Pastors
Truth & Tolerance: A Youth Leader's Resource for Addressing Homosexuality by Exodus Youth

Exodus Live-In Ministries

Love in Action (Memphis, TN)
John Smid, Executive Director
www.loveinaction.org
(901) 751-2468

Freedom at Last Ministries (Wichita, KS)
Mike Babb, Executive Director
www.freedomatlast.org
(316) 263-2350

Higher Ground Ministries (Billings, MT)
Carole Allison, Executive Director
(406) 690-1709

New Hope Ministries (San Francisco Bay area)
Frank Worthen, Executive Director
www.newhope123.org
(415) 453-6475

Exodus Specialty Ministries

Parents & Friends of Ex-Gays and Gays (PFOX) (Washington, D.C. Area)
Regina Griggs, Executive Director

Founded in 1998, PFOX is an organization providing outreach, education, and public awareness in support of the ex-gay community and families touched by homosexuality. To find a local chapter visit www. pfox.org or call (703) 360-2225.

Desert Stream (Kansas City, MO)
Andy Comiskey, Executive Director

Desert Stream Ministries has a number of programs and support groups designed to give hope and healing to those struggling with issues of sexual and relational brokenness. To find a group near you visit Desert Stream at www.desertstream.org
(816) 767-1730, ext. 102

Reality Resources (Lexington, KY)
Jerry Leach, Executive Director
    Reality Resources deals with many life-dominating behaviors, including those that deal with gender-identity disorder and transgender issues. www.realityresources.com
    (859) 388-9889

New Hope Outreach (Ontario, Canada)
Rev. Danny Blackwell, Executive Director
    New Hope Outreach's main focus is ministering to the homosexual and transgendered community. www.newhopeoutreachtoronto.org
(416) 763 9237

Exodus Online Forums

Exodus Online Parents Group
    Started in 1997 by Alan Chambers, the Exodus Online Parents Group is a popular resource. This group allows parents to share their burdens with one another, pray for their children, and receive encouragement. For more information on joining this group contact Exodus International at parents@exodus.to.

Living Hope Youth Forums
    Living Hope (a member ministry of Exodus) provides safe online support forums for youth and young adults ages 18 to 25 struggling with homosexual attractions. This is a terrific resource for those who do not have a local Exodus member ministry nearby. All forums are heavily moderated and participants only share first names. No contact information is exchanged. For more information, please log onto www.livehope.org

AIDS Ministries

He Intends Victory
    He Intends Victory is a Christian ministry to those affected by AIDS, to encourage a spiritual awakening within the HIV/AIDS community,

and to promote faith in Jesus Christ as a living and personal God. www
.heintendsvictory.com (800)HIV-HOPE

HIV Carelink

HIV Carelink provides spiritual counseling, in-home support, and
educational services for sufferers of HIV/AIDS and counseling for those
dealing with sexual addictions. www.hivcarelink.org (303) 382-1344

Denominational Ministries

One by One, a ministry of the Presbyterian Church (USA)
Kristin Johnson, Executive Director
kjohnson@fpco.org
www.oneby1.org

The Way Out, a task force of the Southern Baptist Convention
Bob Stith, Liaison
Bstith777@juno.com
(817) 488-6900

Transforming Congregations, a ministry of the United
Methodist Church
Rev. Karen Booth, Executive Director
www.transformingcong.org
(302) 945-9650

Grace & Truth, a ministry of the Charismatic Episcopal Church
Rev. Canon David Kyle Foster
(615) 507-4166

Harvest USA, a ministry of the Presbyterian Church (PCA)
John Freeman, Executive Director
www.harvestusa.org
(215) 342-7114

Courage, a ministry of the Catholic Church
Rev. John Harvey, Executive Director
www.couragerc.net
(212) 268-1010

The Zacchaeus Fellowship, a ministry of the Anglican Communion of Canada
Rev. Dawn MacDonald, Executive Director
http://www.zacchaeus.ca

Jews Offering New Alternatives to Homosexuality (JONAH)
Arthur Goldberg & Elaine Silodor Berk, Co-Directors
www.jonahweb.org
201-433-3444

Scientific/Research/Mental Health

National Association for Research & Therapy of Homosexuality (NARTH)
Dr. Joseph Nicolosi, Ph.D., President
www.narth.com
(818) 789-4440

Conferences on Homosexuality

Exodus Freedom & Groundswell Conferences
(See Campus Resources)

Love Won Out
A one-day conference hosted by Focus on the Family addressing, understanding, and preventing homosexuality.
www.lovewonout.com
1-800-A-Family

NARTH Conference
Kim Niquette, Conference Director
narth3@earthlink.net

Public Policy Ministries

Focus on the Family
Dr. James Dobson, President
www.family.org
(800)A-Family

Family Research Council
Tony Perkins, President
www.frc.org
(202) 393-2100

Legal Ministries

Alliance Defense Fund
Alan Sears, President
www.alliancedefensefund.org
(800) TELL-ADF

Liberty Counsel
Mat Staver, President and General Counsel
www.lc.org
(800) 671-1776

Medical Resources

Christian Medical & Dental Associations
David Stevens, M.D., Executive Director
www.cmdahome.org
(423) 844-1000

About Exodus International

—✑—

What Is Exodus?

Exodus is a nonprofit, interdenominational Christian organization promoting the message of *"Freedom from homosexuality through the power of Jesus Christ."*

Since 1976, Exodus has grown to include more than 120 local ministries in the USA and Canada. We are also linked with other Exodus world regions outside of North America, totaling more than 150 ministries in 17 countries.

Within both the Christian and secular communities, Exodus has challenged those who respond to homosexuals with ignorance and fear and those who uphold homosexuality as a valid orientation. These extremes fail to convey the fullness of redemption found in Jesus Christ, a gift that is available to all who commit their lives and their sexuality to Him.

What Does Exodus Do?

Exodus is the *largest Christian referral and information network dealing with homosexual issues* in the world. Most of our members are "lay" (nonprofessional) ministries, while some are professional counseling centers and some are churches' ministries. Each provides unique services and resources. Our member ministries provide support for individuals who want to recover from homosexuality, as well as provide support for their families (parents, spouses, children, relatives) and friends.

Monthly Newsletter

In order to keep interested Christians informed of the national and worldwide ministry to homosexuals, we offer a free monthly newsletter, *Exodus Update.* Each issue includes a testimony of healing, current events in the national "ex-gay" movement, new book and video reviews, prayer requests for the month, and news of upcoming local, regional, and national events. If you would like to receive *Exodus Update,* write to us at the address below or visit our website. You will be placed on our *confidential* mailing list. (We do not loan or sell our mailing list to any organizations or individuals for any purposes whatsoever.)

Annual Exodus Freedom Conference

Each year more than 1,000 men, women, youth, pastors, therapists, spouses, parents, and other interested persons come together for a unique gathering of instruction and celebration. Besides powerful worship and inspirational messages, dozens of workshops are presented on counseling, relationships, sexual struggles, societal issues, support for family and friends, ministry development, and various other topics. This five-day event is held annually in late July in different cities throughout North America.

Speaking Engagements

Exodus leaders are available for media interviews and speaking engagements at church events. Representatives from Exodus have been interviewed by such major media as *60 Minutes, Good Morning America, 20/20, Time, Newsweek, The Washington Post, Christianity Today, CBN News*, and countless radio and television talk shows.

Contact Exodus at:

Exodus International
PO Box 540119
Orlando, FL 32854
407-599-6872
http://www.exodus-international.org/

Acknowledgments

—✺—

From Alan Chambers...

Thank You, Jesus, for loving me before I ever loved You. Thank You for saving me and then giving me more than I could ever ask for or deserve.

Thank you, Leslie, for loving me, marrying me, and choosing me every day since then. I treasure and love you dearly. Isaac and Molly, you guys can't read this, but you absolutely know that your dad is crazy about you. Your mom and I will live every day of our lives in such a way that ensures you have every opportunity to be all that God created you to be.

Mom and Dad, thank you for encouraging me to dream big and for showing me that marriage can last more than 50 years. Thank you both for being my biggest fans and supporters and for laying a solid Christian foundation in my life.

Bob and Sue, thanks for raising such an amazingly godly daughter, for allowing me to marry her, and for telling me that I am your favorite son-in-law (sorry Kelly).

I want to thank my personal rescue team, the people who made up Discovery Church during my years there—especially Kirk Bane, whose example made me want to be a real man. I wouldn't be here today if it hadn't been for all of you.

And to my friend and pastor over the last decade, Clark Whitten. Thank you for introducing me to grace and for not only believing in me and this ministry but for hiring me as a pastor when few others would take such a chance.

Finally, I wish to thank the people of Exodus, especially those heroes with whom I work daily—you know who you are. I love you guys with all of my heart. Thanks for making me look so good.

From Randy Thomas...

I would like to acknowledge my Lord Jesus who explained this whole issue to me in a way that I had never heard. I not only revere Him, I am deeply in love with Him.

I want to thank my first mentor and founder of Living Hope Ministries in Arlington, Texas, Scott Musick.

I want to say thank you to Living Hope leadership, past and present, for being a great place to not only learn how to fly but to soar.

Thanks Eddie Traughber and Paul Webster for being dear brothers in the Lord. Mike Haley, Mike Goeke, Tim Sneed, and Scott Davis...I love you guys and enjoy you as coworkers and friends. Melissa Fryrear and other beautiful sisters, thank you for reflecting our Lord so wonderfully.

Alan Chambers, you are a great leader and dear friend. Thanks for the encouragement and yes even the sharpening. You *rock!*

Last and not least, thanks to Exodus past and present. The Lord's favor is with you so stand strong. Let us move forward in this confidence...for freedom, for His glory.

From Mike Goeke...

I would like to thank my Savior, Jesus Christ, first and foremost. It was the revelation of His powerful love for me that began my journey out of homosexuality.

I am ever grateful to my wife, Stephanie, and for the amazing way she submitted first to God, and then to me, as she vulnerably allowed the Lord to heal our wounded marriage. Her commitment and love for me defies words and understanding, and she is precious and of immeasurable value to me.

The Lord provided me the perfect counselor in Skip Hedgpeth, a no-nonsense man whose eyes sparkled when he talked about the Lord and who did more than any man to show me how God saw me and what it meant to be a man in Christ. I was surrounded during this time by my family and by a small cadre of loyal friends (you all know who you are) who loved me when I was at my most unlovable and who will never know their impact in my life.

I would like to thank my good friend and former pastor Patrick Payton. Patrick boldly put me on the stage to tell my story, which was the beginning of the fulfillment of my destiny.

Finally, I would like to thank the men of Stonegate Fellowship in Midland, Texas, who taught me about being a husband, a dad, the rules of various sports, and how to hunt. In so many unique ways, these men ushered me fully into the world of men, the world that eluded me for so long.

From Scott Davis...

My first thanks must go to my parents, Wendy and Randy Davis, who taught me through their own example about deep Christian faith, strong godly masculinity, and the beauty of godly femininity. I find my own courage and conviction to be rooted in the faith they taught me, and I'm steeled by their confidence in me.

Second, thanks to my college pastors, JR Woodward and Jim Pace. Their example of personal sacrifice and commitment to God's calling challenged me to give up small dreams and live in the wild freedom of service to God.

Finally, special thanks to my wife, Caryn, whose unwavering love provides the confidence to move forward boldly in the face of fear and danger.

From Melissa Fryrear...

When one commits to a writing project, especially on a subject so personally relevant, the names and faces of many people come to mind as you recount your life. This book is written primarily for those who have never struggled with same-sex attraction but who have a burden and a love for those who do. As such, there are several very special women and men I would like to thank who came alongside me in my own journey and who helped me to yield, commit, and dedicate my life to Jesus Christ.

Bill Martinez: Thank you for living your life for your Lord so honestly and transparently that it instilled within me a hunger and a desire to know Jesus Christ personally.

Doris and L.J. Crain: Thank you for meeting me where I was, accepting me with such grace, and praying for me fervently.

Hope and Tom Connolly and your beautiful children Nina, Leah, and David:

Thank you for embracing me into your family and for modeling the beauty and strength of biblical femininity and masculinity.

My best friend since first grade, Lesley Dineen: Thank you for never judging me and for having always offered your friendship. You are a true F.B.P.

My brother, Bill: Thank you for being a perfect big brother...which meant watching over me as your little sister as well as scaring me with a dead garden snake. (No, I have not forgotten!)

My parents, Bill and Jean Fryrear: Thank you for the depth and enormity of your love lavished on me throughout my life. I will forever thank God for giving me to you and you to me. I love you with all my heart.

And to my beautiful Savior and Lord Jesus Christ, thank You for sacrificing Your life for me that I might live with You eternally and for allowing me the privilege to proclaim Your forgiving love and transforming grace on this earth. Along with Your Father and Your Holy Spirit, You are my everything.

More excellent Harvest House books on homosexuality

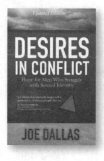

Desires in Conflict: Hope for Men Who Struggle with Sexual Identity

Joe Dallas

For more than a decade, *Desires in Conflict* has been the definitive "must–read" for those who wonder "Can a homosexual change?" This new edition with updated information offers more compelling reasons why the answer is "yes!"

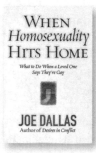

When Homosexuality Hits Home: What to Do When a Loved One Says They're Gay

Joe Dallas

The heart-wrenching declaration that a loved one is a homosexual is increasingly being heard in Christian households across America. How can this be? What went wrong? Is there a cure?

In this straightforward book, Joe Dallas offers practical counsel, step by step, on how to deal with the many conflicts and emotions parents, grandparents, brothers and sisters, or any family member will experience when learning of a loved one's homosexuality.

Drawing from his own experience and from his many years of helping families work through this perplexing and unexpected situation, Joe offers scriptural and compassionate advice to both struggling gays and those who love them.

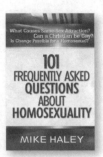

101 Frequently Asked Questions About Homosexuality

Mike Haley

Almost daily we hear news reports that confirm the acceptance of homosexuality in our culture. Homosexuals are adopting children, appearing as characters on television programs, taking vacations catering to an exclusively gay clientele, and even seeking the right to "marry" their partners. But is this acceptance healthy for society?

Few topics can raise questions so quickly. And for many readers, those questions hit close to home as they learn of the homosexuality of a loved one or close friend.

Here are the answers to the most often asked questions about homosexuality, fielded by an expert on the subject...and a former homosexual himself.

Restoring Sexual Identity: Hope for Women Who Struggle with Same-Sex Attraction

Anne Paulk

Restoring Sexual Identity offers answers to the most commonly asked questions from both homosexuals desiring change and friends and relatives of women struggling with same–sex attraction.

Is lesbianism an inherited predisposition, or is it developed in childhood? Does becoming a Christian eliminate all desire for members of the same sex? What support is available for women who struggle with lesbianism? Can a woman be a lesbian and a Christian at the same time? How does childhood sexual abuse relate to the development of lesbianism?

These and other important questions are answered as the author draws from her own experience and that of many other former lesbians who participated in an extensive survey on same-sex attraction.